AFRO-AMERICAN LITERATURE

An Introduction

AFRO-AMERICAN LITERATURE
An Introduction

Robert Hayden
University of Michigan

David J. Burrows
Douglass College at Rutgers University

Frederick R. Lapides
University of Bridgeport

Harcourt Brace Jovanovich, Inc.

New York / Chicago / San Francisco / Atlanta

COVER PHOTO BY GERI DAVIS

Prepared in consultation with David Levin, Stanford University

ISBN: 0-15-502075-7

Library of Congress Catalog Card Number: 79-151066

PRINTED IN THE UNITED STATES OF AMERICA

Preface

The purpose of this book is to introduce students to modern Afro-American writing. It is hoped that the materials presented will afford insight into the role of this writing in the struggle of black Americans and will broaden appreciation of the writing as literature. Arranged by genres, the selections have been made with a view to indicating range and variety. A brief introduction to each genre provides both background information and critical commentary.

Of modest proportions, this anthology is clearly not to be thought of as comprehensive. Our aim has been simply to offer a generous sampling of work by twentieth-century black authors, most of them well known and a few still in the process of earning their reputations. The book can be used as a reader in undergraduate courses in composition or literature, serving to acquaint students with an area of American literature too often ignored in the past. The volume will also be found useful in contemporary black literature courses as a basic text easily supplemented by paperback editions of complete works. The accompanying questions and topics for papers are offered as aids to analysis and as a means of stimulating further reading and independent research.

For helpful suggestions we wish to thank Professors Arna Bontemps of Yale University and Helen Armstead Johnson of York College of the City University of New York, who reviewed early drafts of the manuscript.

Robert Hayden
David J. Burrows
Frederick R. Lapides

Contents

part 3   DRAMA

part 4   AUTOBIOGRAPHY

part 5   CRITICAL ESSAYS

AFRO-AMERICAN LITERATURE

An Introduction

Introduction

Afro-American writers, with few exceptions, have been from almost the very beginning *engagés*. Most of them have felt it their inescapable task to denounce racial injustice and plead the cause of Negro freedom. They have produced, in J. Saunders Redding's phrase, a "literature of necessity," a literature preoccupied with the urgent realities of the racial situation. It is this concern that accounts for the literature's distinctive traits and, in the view of critics black and white, for its limitations.

A great deal of Afro-American writing today is a literature of anger and crisis, a cry of revolt. It continues a long-established protest tradition that can be traced back to folk sources—to the spirituals, work songs, tales, and legends originating in the era of slavery. That some of this writing is more journalistic than belletristic, more polemical than aesthetic, is undeniable. The work of the best Afro-American authors, however, transcends insularity and achieves a unity of social vision and significant literary form.

Despite some insistence that Afro-American writing bears little or no organic relationship to American writing in general, the contours of this literature cannot be seen in true perspective without reference to literary trends in the United States. Phillis Wheatley, the first poet of African descent to gain some recognition here and abroad, wrote in the neo-classic style cultivated by English poets during the eighteenth century and imitated in the Colonies. The plantation lyrics of James Weldon Johnson and Paul Laurence Dunbar in the late nineteenth century were in the dialect genre made popular by Thomas Nelson Page and Irwin Russell, among others. Richard Wright's *Native Son* is a novel in the naturalistic mode pioneered by Frank Norris and Theodore Dreiser. Certain motifs in contemporary literature—alienation, the quest for identity, the search for a spiritual father, to name a few—recur in the work of both Afro-American and other writers. Iconoclasm in style and attitude are salient features of Afro-American and white avant-garde writing alike.

When we consider Afro-American authors in relation to other American writers, we are tempted to raise possibly disturbing and certainly controversial questions: Is there really an "Afro-American" or "black" or "Negro" literature in this country? Are we not using these terms as convenient and ultimately imprecise labels that designate racial identity rather than literature *qua* literature? Do they have any fundamental significance beyond this? In the past, the rubric "Negro literature" was often used pejoratively to indicate inferior performance, "overspecialized" content. At present, writers of the Black Revolution are attempting to create what they consider an authentic *black* literature. They eschew the "white aesthetic" and scorn existing artistic standards as decadent and racist. As writers primarily, if not exclusively, concerned with "black experience," "black pride," "black consciousness," they have no desire to enter the mainstream of American letters, preferring instead membership in a separate school of black writing. The questions remain.

There are Afro-American writers today, as there have been in the past, who feel burdened by an attitude, a reaction, that can best be described, perhaps, as the "sociological fallacy." By this is meant the unwillingness or failure of readers and especially critics to evaluate the work of the black author in any but strictly racial (or sociological) terms. This kind of criticism allows impact as social statement to supersede considerations of literary quality. Countee Cullen, whose reputation was established during the Harlem Renaissance in the nineteen-twenties, objected strongly to this biased critical approach. He insisted that his poetry should be judged as *poetry*, not as something considered "racial utterance," and that it should be judged by the same criteria applied to the work of other American poets.

Afro-American literature encompasses aspects of the human condition in general and of the Negro condition in particular not otherwise articulated in American writing. Literature, like other forms of art, is always a clue to the spirit, the ethos, of a people. There is much to be learned about "the souls of black folk," as W. E. B. DuBois put it, from Afro-American authors. And there is much to be learned from them about man as man.

part 1

Fiction

The following short stories could be cited as evidence of the futility of try-ing to generalize about Afro-American authors beyond the obvious fact that they have written imaginatively about Negro life. Each of the writers repre-sented in this section has his own characteristic style and point of view. Jean Toomer's vision of life, for instance, seems pessimistic, if not tragic. The characters of "Blood-Burning Moon" move in a landscape of passion and violence at once real and dreamlike. Atmosphere, mood, sensuous im-agery, nuance, give Toomer's stories a haunting, poetic quality. Langston Hughes wrote with less subtlety, achieving effects of immediacy and spon-taneity. He had a good ear for the urban Negro folk-idiom, as shown by "Soul Food" from his Jesse B. Simple series, and he knew how to treat bas-ically serious matters with engaging satiric humor.

Richard Wright's "The Man Who Lived Underground" is a rather harrow-ing story whose significance is not restricted to the ethnic, although the racial identity of the protagonist is of central importance. It is a story that raises questions about psychic freedom, the illusory values of materialism, and the dehumanization of the individual. That these questions grow out of the plight of a victimized black intensifies the meaning of the story. In both Wright and Ellison, realism is heightened by symbolism and irony. Ralph Ellison's "King of the Bingo Game" derives much of its force as nar-rative and as moral statement from archetypal symbols and concepts—for-tune's wheel, fate, hubris, and so forth.

James Baldwin in "Sonny's Blues" has written a story that synchronizes some of his major themes—the quest of the artist, alienation, inner conflict. Sonny, although he is less the protagonist than the focal character, is in many ways typical of Baldwin's heroes. He is a victim of the ghetto, his struggle toward fulfillment exacerbated by his lot as a black man, and he is at the same time a victim of his own weakness. Such dramatic tension as this story contains is generated more by the observations and responses of the first-person narrator (Baldwin's mask) than by Sonny's actions; for he, not Sonny, is the real protagonist.

James Alan McPherson, whose recent collection of short stories, Hue and

Cry, *has been highly praised, shows some kinship to Baldwin and Ellison in that he portrays his black characters in all their human complexity. He has a feeling for the subtleties of human relationships, as demonstrated by "On Trains"; neither are his heroes necessarily black nor his villains necessarily white. In his stories he often works with an interracial cast. "As a matter of fact," he has said, "certain of the people happen to be black, and certain of them happen to be white; but I have tried to keep the color part of most of them far in the background, where these things should rightly be kept."*

Blood-Burning Moon

Jean Toomer

1

Up from the skeleton stone walls, up from the rotting floor boards and the solid hand-hewn beams of oak of the pre-war cotton factory, dusk came. Up from the dusk the full moon came. Glowing like a fired pine-knot, it illumined the great door and soft showered the Negro shanties aligned along the single street of factory town. The full moon in the great door was an omen. Negro women improvised songs against its spell.

Louisa sang as she came over the crest of the hill from the white folks' kitchen. Her skin was the color of oak leaves on young trees in fall. Her breasts, firm and up-pointed like ripe acorns. And her singing had the low murmur of winds in fig trees. Bob Stone, younger son of the people she worked for, loved her. By the way the world reckons things, he had won her. By measure of that warm glow which came into her mind at thought of him, he had won her. Tom Burwell, whom the whole town called Big Boy, also loved her. But working in the fields all day, and far away from her, gave him no chance to show it. Though often enough of evenings he had tried to. Somehow, he never got along. Strong as he was with hands upon the ax or plow, he found it difficult to hold her. Or so he thought. But the fact was that he held her to factory town more firmly than he thought for. His black balanced, and pulled against, the white of Stone, when she thought of them. And her mind was vaguely upon them as she came over the crest of the hill, coming from the white folks' kitchen. As she sang softly at the evil face of the full moon.

A strange stir was in her. Indolently, she tried to fix upon Bob or Tom as the cause of it. To meet Bob in the canebrake, as she was going to do an hour or so later, was nothing new. And Tom's proposal which she felt on its way to her could be indefinitely put off. Separately, there was no unusual significance to either one. But for some reason, they jumbled when her eyes gazed vacantly at the rising moon. And from the

---

jumble came the stir that was strangely within her. Her lips trembled. The slow rhythm of her song grew agitant and restless. Rusty black and tan spotted hounds, lying in the dark corners of porches or prowling around back yards, put their noses in the air and caught its tremor. They began plaintively to yelp and howl. Chickens woke up and cackled. Intermittently, all over the countryside dogs barked and roosters crowed as if heralding a weird dawn or some ungodly awakening. The women sang lustily. Their songs were cotton-wads to stop their ears. Louisa came down into factory town and sank wearily upon the step before her home. The moon was rising towards a thick cloud-bank which soon would hide it.

> Red nigger moon. Sinner!
> Blood-burning moon. Sinner!
> Come out that fact'ry door.

2

Up from the deep dusk of a cleared spot on the edge of the forest a mellow glow arose and spread fan-wise into the low-hanging heavens. And all around the air was heavy with the scent of boiling cane. A large pile of cane-stalks lay like ribboned shadows upon the ground. A mule, harnessed to a pole, trudged lazily round and round the pivot of the grinder. Beneath a swaying oil lamp, a Negro alternately whipped out at the mule, and fed cane-stalks to the grinder. A fat boy waddled pails of fresh ground juice between the grinder and the boiling stove. Steam came from the copper boiling pan. The scent of cane came from the copper pan and drenched the forest and the hill that sloped to factory town, beneath its fragrance. It drenched the men in circle seated around the stove. Some of them chewed at the white pulp of stalks, but there was no need for them to, if all they wanted was to taste the cane. One tasted it in factory town. And from factory town one could see the soft haze thrown by the glowing stove upon the low-hanging heavens.

Old David Georgia stirred the thickening syrup with a long ladle, and ever so often drew it off. Old David Georgia tended his stove and told tales about the white folks, about moonshining and cotton picking, and about sweet nigger gals, to the men who sat there about his stove to listen to him. Tom Burwell chewed cane-stalk and laughed with the others till someone mentioned Louisa. Till someone said something about Louisa and Bob Stone, about the silk stockings she must have gotten from him. Blood ran up Tom's neck hotter than the glow that flooded from the stove. He sprang up. Glared at the men and said, "She's my gal." Will Manning laughed. Tom strode over to him. Yanked him up and knocked him to the ground. Several of Manning's friends got up to fight for him. Tom whipped out a long knife and would have cut them to shreds if they hadnt ducked into the woods. Tom had had enough. He nodded to Old David Georgia and swung down the path to factory town. Just then, the dogs started barking and the roosters began to crow. Tom felt funny. Away from the fight, away from the stove, chill got to him. He shivered. He shuddered when he saw the full moon rising towards the cloud-bank. He who didnt give a godam for the fears of old women. He forced his mind to fasten on Louisa. Bob Stone. Better not be. He turned into the street and saw Louisa sitting before her home. He went towards her, ambling, touched the brim of a marvelously shaped, spotted, felt hat, said he wanted to say something to her, and then found that he didnt know what he had to say, or if he did, that he couldnt say it. He shoved his big fists in his overalls, grinned, and started to move off.

"Youall want me, Tom?"

"Thats what us wants, sho, Louisa."

"Well, here I am—"

"An here I is, but that aint ahelpin none, all th same."

"You wanted to say something? . . ."

"I did that, sho. But words is like th spots on dice: no matter how y fumbles em, there's times when they jes wont come. I dunno why. Seems like th love I feels fo yo done stole m tongue. I got it now. Whee! Louisa, honey, I oughtnt tell y, I feel I oughtnt cause yo is young an goes t church an I has had other gals, but Louisa I sho do love y. Lil gal, Ise watched y from them first days when youall sat right here befo yo door befo th well an sang sometimes in a way that like t broke m heart. Ise carried y with me into th fields, day after day, an after that, an I sho can plow when yo is there, an I can pick cotton. Yassur! Come near beatin Barlo yesterday. I sho did. Yassur! An next year if ole Stone'll trust me, I'll have a farm. My own. My bales will buy yo what y gets from white folks now. Silk stockings an purple dresses—course I dont believe what some folks been whisperin as t how y gets them things now. White folks always did do for niggers what they likes. An they jes cant help alikin yo, Louisa. Bob Stone likes y. Course he does. But not th way folks is awhisperin. Does he, hon?"

"I dont know what you mean, Tom."

"Course y dont. Ise already cut two niggers. Had t hon, t tell em so. Niggers always tryin t make somethin out a nothin. An then besides, white folks aint up t them tricks so much nowadays. Godam better not be. Leastawise not with yo. Cause I wouldnt stand f it. Nassur."

"What would you do, Tom?"

"Cut him jes like I cut a nigger."

"No, Tom—"

"I said I would an there aint no mo to it. But that aint th talk f now. Sing, honey Louisa, an while I'm listenin t y I'll be makin love."

Tom took her hand in his. Against the tough thickness of his own, hers felt soft and small. His huge body slipped down to the step beside her. The full moon sank upward into the deep purple of the cloud-bank. An old woman brought a lighted lamp and hung it on the common well whose bulky shadow squatted in the middle of the road, opposite Tom and Louisa. The old woman lifted the well-lid, took hold the chain, and began drawing up the heavy bucket. As she did so, she sang. Figures shifted, restlesslike, between lamp and window in the front rooms of the shanties. Shadows of the figures fought each other on the gray dust of the road. Figures raised the windows and joined the old woman in song. Louisa and Tom, the whole street, singing:

> Red nigger moon. Sinner!
> Blood-burning moon. Sinner!
> Come out that fact'ry door.

3

Bob Stone sauntered from his veranda out into the gloom of fir trees and magnolias. The clear white of his skin paled, and the flush of his cheeks turned purple. As if to balance this outer change, his mind became consciously a white man's. He passed the house with its huge open hearth which, in the days of slavery, was the plantation cookery. He saw Louisa bent over that hearth. He went in as a master should and took her. Direct, honest, bold. None of this sneaking that he had to go through now. The contrast was repulsive to him. His family had lost ground. Hell no, his family still owned the niggers, practically. Damned if they did, or he wouldnt have to duck around so. What would they think if they knew? His mother? His sister? He shouldnt mention them, shouldnt think of them in this connection. There in the dusk he blushed at doing so. Fellows about town were all right, but how about his friends up North? He could see them incredible, repulsed. They didnt know. The thought first made him laugh. Then, with their eyes still upon him, he began to feel embarrassed. He felt the need of explaining things to them. Explain hell. They wouldnt understand, and moreover, who ever heard of a Southerner getting on his knees to any Yankee, or anyone. No sir. He was going to see Louisa to-night, and love her. She was lovely—in her way. Nigger way. What way was that? Damned if he knew. Must know. He'd known her long enough to know. Was there something about niggers that you couldnt know? Listening to them at church didnt tell you anything. Looking at them didnt tell you anything. Talking to them didnt tell you anything—unless it was gossip, unless they wanted to talk. Of course, about farming, and licker, and craps—but those werent nigger. Nigger was something more. How much more? Something to be afraid of, more? Hell no. Who ever heard of being afraid of a nigger? Tom Burwell. Cartwell had told him that Tom went with Louisa after she reached home. No sir. No nigger had ever been with his girl. He'd like to see one try. Some position for him to be in. Him, Bob Stone, of the old Stone family, in a scrap with a nigger over a nigger girl. In the good old days . . . Ha! Those were the days. His family had lost ground. Not so much, though. Enough for him to have to cut through old Lemon's canefield by way of the woods, that he might meet her. She was worth it. Beautiful nigger gal. Why nigger? Why not, just gal? No, it was because she was nigger that he went to her. Sweet . . . The scent of boiling cane came to him. Then he saw the rich glow of the stove. He heard the voices of the men circled around it. He was about to skirt the clearing when he heard his own name mentioned. He stopped. Quivering. Leaning against a tree, he listened.

"Bad nigger. Yassur, he sho is one bad nigger when he gets started."

"Tom Burwell's been on th gang three times fo cutting men."

"What y think he's agwine t do t Bob Stone?"

"Dunno yet. He aint found out. When he does— Baby!"

"Aint no tellin."

"Young Stone aint no quitter an I ken tell y that. Blood of th old uns in his veins."

"Thats right. He'll scrap, sho."

"Be gettin too hot f niggers round this away."

"Shut up, nigger. Y dont know what y talkin bout."

Bob Stone's ears burned as though he had been holding them over the stove. Sizzling heat welled up within him. His feet felt as if they rested on red-hot coals. They stung him to quick movement. He circled the fringe of the glowing. Not a twig cracked beneath his feet. He reached the path that led to factory town. Plunged furiously down it. Halfway along, a blindness within him veered him aside. He crashed into the bordering canebrake. Cane leaves cut his face and lips. He tasted blood. He threw himself down and dug his fingers in the ground. The earth was cool. Cane-roots took the fever from his hands. After a long while, or so it seemed to him, the thought came to him that it must be time to see Louisa. He got to his feet and walked calmly to their meeting place. No Louisa. Tom Burwell had her. Veins in his forehead bulged and distended. Saliva moistened the dried blood on his lips. He bit down on his lips. He tasted blood. Not his own blood; Tom Burwell's blood. Bob drove through the cane and out again upon the road. A hound swung down the path before him towards factory town. Bob couldnt see it. The dog loped aside to let him pass. Bob's blind rushing made him stumble over it. He fell with a thud that dazed him. The hound yelped. Answering yelps came from all over the countryside. Chickens cackled. Roosters crowed, heralding the bloodshot eyes of southern awakening. Singers in the town were silenced. They shut their windows down. Palpitant between the rooster crows, a chill hush settled upon the huddled forms of Tom and Louisa. A figure rushed from the shadow and stood before them. Tom popped to his feet.

"Whats y want?"

"I'm Bob Stone."

"Yassur—an I'm Tom Burwell. Whats y want?"

Bob lunged at him. Tom side-stepped, caught him by the shoulder, and flung him to the ground. Straddled him.

"Let me up."

"Yassur—but watch yo doins, Bob Stone."

A few dark figures, drawn by the sound of scuffle, stood about them. Bob sprang to his feet.

"Fight like a man, Tom Burwell, an I'll lick y."

Again he lunged. Tom side-stepped and flung him to the ground. Straddled him.

"Get off me, you godam nigger you."

"Yo sho has started somethin now. Get up."

Tom yanked him up and began hammering at him. Each blow sounded as if it smashed into a precious, irreplaceable soft something. Beneath them, Bob staggered back. He reached in his pocket and whipped out a knife.

"Thats my game, sho."

Blue flash, a steel blade slashed across Bob Stone's throat. He had a sweetish sick feeling. Blood began to flow. Then he felt a sharp twitch of pain. He let his knife drop. He slapped one hand against his neck. He pressed the other on top of his head as if to hold it down. He groaned. He turned, and staggered towards the crest of the hill in the direction of white town. Negroes who had seen the fight slunk into their homes and blew the lamps out. Louisa, dazed, hysterical, refused to go indoors. She slipped, crumbled, her body loosely propped against the woodwork of the well. Tom Burwell leaned against it. He seemed rooted there.

Bob reached Broad Street. White men rushed up to him. He collapsed in their arms.

"Tom Burwell . . . ."

White men like ants upon a forage rushed about. Except for the taut hum of their moving, all was silent. Shotguns, revolvers, rope, kerosene, torches. Two high-powered cars with glaring search-lights. They came together. The taut hum rose to a low roar. Then nothing could be heard but the flop of their feet in the thick dust of the road. The moving body of their silence preceded them over the crest of the hill into factory town. It flattened the Negroes beneath it. It rolled to the wall of the factory, where it stopped. Tom knew that they were coming. He couldnt move. And then he saw the search-lights of the two cars glaring down on him. A quick shock went through him. He stiffened. He started to run. A yell went up from the mob. Tom wheeled about and faced them. They poured down on him. They swarmed. A large man with dead-white face and flabby cheeks came to him and almost jabbed a gun-barrel through his guts.

Tom's wrists were bound. The big man shoved him to the well. Burn him over it, and when the woodwork caved in, his body would drop to the bottom. Two deaths for a godam nigger. Louisa was driven back. The mob pushed in. Its pressure, its momentum was too great. Drag him to the factory. Wood and stakes already there. Tom moved in the direction indicated. But they had to drag him. They reached the great door. Too many to get in there. The mob divided and flowed around the walls to either side. The big man shoved him through the door. The mob pressed in from the sides. Taut humming. No words. A stake was sunk into the ground. Rotting floor boards piled around it. Kerosene poured on the rotting floor boards. Tom bound to the stake. His breast was bare. Nails scratches let little lines of blood trickle down and mat into the hair. His face, his eyes were set and stony. Except for irregular breathing, one would have thought him already dead. Torches were flung onto the pile. A great flare muffled in black smoke shot upward. The mob yelled. The mob was silent. Now Tom could be seen within the flames. Only his head, erect, lean, like a blackened stone. Stench of burning flesh soaked the air. Tom's eyes popped. His head settled downward. The mob yelled. Its yell echoed against the skeleton stone walls and sounded like a hundred yells. Like a hundred mobs yelling. Its yell thudded against the thick front wall and fell back. Ghost of a yell slipped through the flames and out the great door of the factory. It fluttered like a dying thing down the single street of factory town. Louisa, upon the step before her home, did not hear it, but her eyes opened slowly. They saw the full moon glowing in the great door. The full moon, an evil thing, an omen, soft showering the homes of folks she knew. Where were they, these people? She'd sing, and perhaps they'd come out and join her. Perhaps Tom Burwell would come. At any rate, the full moon in the great door was an omen which she must sing to:

> Red nigger moon. Sinner!
> Blood-burning moon. Sinner!
> Come out that fact'ry door.

QUESTIONS

1. "Blood-Burning Moon" is the final story in the first section of Jean Toomer's *Cane* (1923), a collection of sketches, stories, and poems. (The first section deals with the world of blacks in Georgia, the second section with the black community in Washington, D.C., and

the final section—a quasi-drama, "Kabnis"—returns to rural Georgia.) In discussing this book Arna Bontemps has said that it is the sensual power of the work that most critics and readers note and remember. Discuss this statement in relation to "Blood-Burning Moon." Do you agree that this is the most significant or memorable aspect of the story?

2. Examine Toomer's use of simile, metaphor, and color in this story. What do these images contribute to the mood and theme of the story?

3. Toomer's expressed creed was that "a symbol is as useful to the spirit as a tool is to the hand." How does he use the full moon and the cane as symbols in this story?

4. The same refrain is used at the end of each of the three sections of the story. Is the meaning or implication of the refrain the same each time? What function does it serve?

5. Study other uses of repetition throughout the story. What effects are achieved through the use of this device?

6. Bob Stone, on his way to meet Louisa, contrasts his present situation, "in a scrap with a nigger over a nigger girl," with the "good old days." Do you think he is longing for the past? How, in general, would you characterize his attitude toward Louisa?

7. What is Toomer's attitude toward his characters and the situation? For example, is he condemning Louisa's affair with Stone? Or is he simply telling a story without wishing to make moral judgments?

Soul Food

Langston Hughes

"Where is that pretty cousin of yours, Lynn Clarisse, these days?" I asked.

"She has moved to the Village," said Simple.

"Deserted Harlem? Gone looking for integration?"

"She wants to see if art is what it's painted," said Simple. "All the artists lives in Greenwich Village, white and colored, and the jazz peoples and the writers. Nobody but us lives in Harlem. If it wasn't for the Antheny Annie Arts Club, Joyce says Harlem would be a cultural desert."

"You mean the Anthenian Arts Club," I said.

"I do," said Simple. "But Joyce tells me that thirty years ago Harlem was blooming. Then Duke Ellington and everybody lived here. Books was writ all over the place, pictures painted, lindy hoppers hopping, jitterbugs jumping, a dance hall called the Savoy with fine big bands playing. No more! The only things Harlem is famous for now is Adam Powell, who seldom comes home, and the last riots. So Lynn Clarisse has moved to the Village. But we can always get on the subway and go down and fetch her."

"Or join her," I said.

"Or let her re-join me," said Simple. "Although I am not worried about Lynn Clarisse. She is colleged, like you, and smart, and can take care of herself in the Village—just like my Cousin Minnie can take care of herself in Harlem. Every fish to his own water, I say, and the devil take them that cannot swim. Lynn Clarisse can swim, and Minnie dead sure can float, whereas some folks can only dog-paddle. Now me, my specialty is to walk on water. I been treading on the sea of life all my life, and have not sunk yet. I refuses to sink. In spite of womens, white folks, landlords, landladies, cold waves, and riots, I am still here. Corns, bunions, and bad feet in general do not get me down. I intends to walk the water until dry land is in sight."

"What land?"

"The Promised Land," said Simple, "the land in which I, black as I am without one plea in my country 'tis of thee, can be *me*. American the beautiful come to itself again, where you can see by the dawn's early light what so proudly we hailed as civil rights."

"The very thought makes you wax poetic, heh?"

"It do," said Simple. "But Joyce thinks Lynn Clarisse should have moved to Park West Village, halfway between Harlem and downtown. Joyce thinks Greenwich Village is a fast place where colored are likely to forget race and marry white. My wife is opposed to intermarriage on the grounds of pride. Joyce says she is so proud of her African heritage she don't want nobody to touch it. But do you know what Lynn Clarisse says? She says, 'There is no color line in art.'

"My cousin and my wife was kind of cool to each one another on the surface that day Lynn Clarisse moved out of Harlem. But you know how easy womens get miffed over little things. I don't pay them no mind myself. The only thing that makes me mad is Cousin Minnie wanting to borrow five dollars, which is always once too often. Lynn Clarisse do not borrow. She came to New York with her own money."

"Are her parents well off?"

"Her daddy, my first cousin on my half-brother's side, owns one of the biggest undertaking parlors in Virginia. He makes his money putting Negroes in segregated coffins in segregated graveyards. He sent Lynn Clarisse to college, and now has give her money for 'a cultural visit' to the North. Young Negroes used to have to struggle to get anything or go anywhere. Nowadays some of them have parents who have already struggled for them, so can help them get through college, and get up North, and get more cultured and live in Greenwich Village where rents is higher than they is in Harlem. Thank God, my cousin's daddy is an undertaker."

"Morticians and barbers are almost the only Negro businessmen whose incomes have not yet been affected by integration," I said. "Certainly, restaurants and hotels in Harlem have suffered. Banquets that once were held at the Theresa are now held at the Hilton and the Americana or the New Yorker. And the Urban League's annual Beaux Arts Ball is at the Waldorf. Negro society has taken almost all its functions downtown."

"But as long as white undertakers refuse to bury black bodies, and white barbers will not cut Negro hair, colored folks still have the burying and barbering business in the bag."

"Except that here in New York, I suppose you know, some wealthy Negroes are now being buried from fashionable downtown funeral homes."

"Where the mourners dare not holler out loud like they do at funerals in Harlem," said Simple. "It is not polite to scream and carry on over coffins in front of white folks."

"Integration has its drawbacks," I said.

"It do," confirmed Simple. "You heard, didn't you, about that old colored lady in Washington who went downtown one day to a fine white restaurant to test out integration? Well, this old lady decided to see for herself if what she heard was true about these restaurants, and if white folks were really ready for democracy. So down on Pennsylvania Avenue she went and picked herself out this nice-looking used-to-be-all-white restaurant to go in and order herself a meal."

"Good for her," I said.

"But dig what happened when she set down," said Simple. "No trouble, everybody nice. When the white waiter come up to her table to take her order, the colored old lady says, 'Son, I'll have collard greens and ham hocks, if you please.'

" 'Sorry,' says the waiter. 'We don't have that on the menu.'

" 'Then how about black-eyed peas and pig tails?' says the old lady.

" 'That we don't have on the menu either,' says the white waiter.

" 'Then chitterlings,' says the old lady, 'just plain chitterlings.'

"The waiter said, 'Madam, I never heard of chitterlings.'

" 'Son,' said the old lady, 'ain't you got no kind of soul food at all?'

" 'Soul food? What is that?' asked the puzzled waiter.

" 'I knowed you-all wasn't ready for integration,' sighed the old lady sadly as she rose and headed toward the door. 'I just knowed you white folks wasn't ready.' "

"Most ethnic groups have their own special dishes," I said. "If you want French food, you go to a French restaurant. For Hungarian, you go to Hungarian places, and so on."

"But this was an American place," said Simple, "and they did not have soul food."

"The term 'soul food' is still not generally used in the white world," I said, "and the dishes that fall within its category are seldom found yet in any but colored restaurants, you know that. There's a place where jazzmen eat across from the Metropole that has it, and one or two places down in the Village, but those are the only ones I know in Manhattan outside of Harlem."

"It is too bad white folks deny themselves that pleasure," said Simple, "because there is nothing better than good old-fashioned, down-home, Southern Negro cooking. And there is not too many restaurants in Harlem that has it, or if they do, they spoil everything with steam tables, cooking up their whole menu early in the morning, then letting it steam till it gets soggy all day. But when a Negro fries a pork chop *fresh*, or a chicken *fresh*, or a fish *fresh*, I am telling you, it sure is good. There is a fish joint on Lenox Avenue with two women in it that can sure cook fish. But they is so evil about selling it to you. How come some of these Harlem eating places hire such evil-acting people to wait on customers? Them two ladies in this fish place stand behind the counter and look at you like they dare you to 'boo' or ask for anything. They both look mad no sooner than you enter."

"I'll bet they are two sisters who own the place," I said. "Usually by the time Negroes get enough money to own anything, they are so old they are evil. Those women are probably just mad because at their age they have to wait on anybody."

"Then they should not be in business," said Simple.

"I agree," I said. "But on the other hand, suppose they or their husbands have been skimping and saving for years. At last, at the age of forty or fifty they get a little business. What do you want them to do? Give it up just because they have got to the crabby age and should be retiring, before they have anything to retire on?"

"Then please don't take out their age on me when I come in to order a piece of fish," said Simple. "Why them two ladies never ask you what you want politely. They don't, in fact, hardly ask you at all. Them womens looks at customers like they want to say, 'Get out of here!' Then maybe one of them will come up to you and stand and look over the counter.

"You say, 'Have you got any catfish?' She will say, 'No!' And will not say what other kind she has or has not got.

"So you say, 'How about buffalo?' She will say, 'We had that yesterday.'

"Then you will say, 'Well, what have you got today?'

"She will say, 'What do you want?' I have already said twice what I wanted that they did not have. So now I say, 'How about butterfish?'

"She says, 'Sandwich or dinner?'

"I say, 'Dinner.'

"She says, 'We don't sell dinners after ten P.M.'

" 'Then why did you ask me if I wanted a dinner?' says I.

"She says, 'I was paying no attention to the time.'

"I said, 'You was paying no attention to me neither, lady, and I'm a customer. Gimme two sandwiches.'

" 'I am not here to be bawled out by you,' she says. 'If it's sandwiches you want, just say so, and no side remarks.'

" 'Could I please have a cup of coffee?'

" 'We got Pepsis and Cokes.'

" 'A Pepsi.'

"She rummages in the cooler. 'The Pepsis is out.'

" 'A Coke.'

"She comes up with a bottle that is not cold. Meanwhile the fish is frying, and it smells good, but it takes a while to wait, so I say, 'Gimme a quarter to play the juke box.' Three records for a quarter.

"Don't you know that woman tells me, 'We is all out of quarters tonight.'

"So I say, trying to be friendly, 'I'll put in a dime and play just one then. What is your favorite record?'

"Old hussy says, 'There's nothing on there do I like, so just play for yourself.'

"'Excuse me,' says I, 'I will play "Move to the Outskirts of Town," which is where I think you ought to be.'

"'I wish my husband was here to hear your sass,' she says. 'Is your fish to eat here, or to go?'

"'To go,' I says, 'because I am going before you bite my head off. What do I owe?'

"'How much is two sandwiches to go?' she calls back to the other woman in the kitchen.

"'Prices is gone up,' says the other hussy, 'so charge him eighty cents.'

"'Eighty cents,' she says, 'and fifteen for the Pepsi.'

"'I had a Coke,' I says.

"'The same. You get a nickel change.'

"'From a five-dollar bill?' I says.

"'Oh, I did not notice you give me a five. Claybelle, have you got any change back there?'

"'None.'

"'Neither is I. Mister, you ought to have something smaller.'

"'I do not carry small change around on payday,' says I. 'And what kind of restaurant is this, that can't even bust a five-dollar bill, neither change small change into a quarter for the record player? Don't you-all have nothing in the cash register? If you don't, no wonder, the way you treat a customer! Just gimme my five back and keep your fish.'

"'Lemme look down in my stocking and see what I got there,' she says. And do you know, that woman went down in her stocking and pulled out enough money to buy Harry Belafonte. But she did not have a nickel change.

"So I said, 'Girl, you just keep that nickel for a tip.'

"If that woman owns the place, she ought to sell it. If she just works there, she ought to be fired. If she is the owner's girl friend, was she mine I would beat her behind, else feed her fish until a bone got stuck in her throat. I wonder how come some Harlem places have such evil help, especially in restaurants. Hateful help can spoil even soul food. Dear God, I pray, please change the hearts of hateful help!"

QUESTIONS

1. What usual conventions of the short-story form are missing from "Soul Food"?

2. What is the function of the character Simple in this story?

3. How is the discussion of Lynn Clarisse's move to the Village related to the rest of the story?

4. How would you describe Hughes's comic invention?

5. Despite the light, playful nature of this story, Hughes is discussing serious problems. What, specifically, are these problems? Do you feel that this discussion is helped or hindered because it is woven into a humorous story?

The Man Who Lived Underground

Richard Wright

I've got to hide, he told himself. His chest heaved as he waited, crouching in a dark corner of the vestibule. He was tired of running and dodging. Either he had to find a place to hide, or he had to surrender. A police car swished by through the rain, its siren rising sharply. They're looking for me all over . . . He crept to the door and squinted through the fogged plate glass. He stiffened as the siren rose and died in the distance. Yes, he had to hide, but where? He gritted his teeth. Then a sudden movement in the street caught his attention. A throng of tiny columns of water snaked into the air from the perforations of a manhole cover. The columns stopped abruptly, as though the perforations had become clogged; a gray spout of sewer water jutted up from underground and lifted the circular metal cover, juggled it for a moment, then let it fall with a clang.

He hatched a tentative plan: he would wait until the siren sounded far off, then he would go out. He smoked and waited, tense. At last the siren gave him his signal; it wailed, dying, going away from him. He stepped to the sidewalk, then paused and looked curiously at the open manhole, half expecting the cover to leap up again. He went to the center of the street and stooped and peered into the hole, but could see nothing. Water rustled in the black depths.

He started with terror; the siren sounded so near that he had the idea that he had been dreaming and had awakened to find the car upon him. He dropped instinctively to his knees and his hands grasped the rim of the manhole. The siren seemed to hoot directly above him and with a wild gasp of exertion he snatched the cover far enough off to admit his body. He swung his legs over the opening and lowered himself into watery darkness. He hung for an eternal moment to the rim by his finger tips, then he felt rough metal prongs and at once he knew that sewer workmen used these ridges to lower themselves into manholes. Fist over fist, he let his body sink until he could feel no more prongs. He swayed in dank space; the siren seemed to howl at the very rim of the manhole. He dropped and was washed violently into an ocean of warm, leaping water. His head was battered against a wall and he wondered if this were death. Frenziedly his fingers clawed and sank into a crevice. He steadied himself and measured the strength of the current with his own muscular tension. He stood slowly in water that dashed past his knees with fearful velocity.

He heard a prolonged scream of brakes and the siren broke off. Oh, God! They had found him! Looming above his head in the rain a white face hovered over the hole. "How did this damn thing get off?" he heard a policeman ask. He saw the steel cover move slowly until the hole looked like a quarter moon turned black. "Give me a hand here," someone called. The cover clanged into place, muffling the sights and sounds of the upper world. Knee-deep in the pulsing current, he breathed with aching chest, filling his lungs with the hot stench of yeasty rot.

From the perforations of the manhole cover, delicate lances of hazy violet sifted down and wove a mottled pattern upon the surface of the streaking current. His lips parted as a car swept past along the wet pavement overhead, its heavy rumble soon dying out, like the hum of a plane speeding through a dense cloud. He had never thought that cars could sound like that; everything seemed strange and unreal under here. He stood in darkness for a long time, knee-deep in rustling water, musing.

The odor of rot had become so general that he no longer smelled it. He got his cigarettes, but discovered that his matches were wet. He searched and found a dry folder in the pocket of his shirt and managed to strike one; it flared weirdly in the wet gloom, glowing greenishly, turning red, orange, then yellow. He lit a crumpled cigarette; then, by the flickering light of the match, he looked for support so that he would not have to keep his muscles flexed against the pouring water. His pupils narrowed and he saw to either side of him two steaming walls that rose and curved inward some six feet above his head to form a dripping, mouse-colored dome. The bottom of the sewer was a sloping V-trough. To the left, the sewer vanished in ashen fog. To the right was a steep down-curve into which water plunged.

He saw now that had he not regained his feet in time, he would have been swept to death, or had he entered any other manhole he would have probably drowned. Above the rush of the current he heard sharper juttings of water; tiny streams were spewing into the sewer from smaller conduits. The match died; he struck another and saw a mass of debris sweep past him and clog the throat of the down-curve. At once the water began rising rapidly. Could he climb out before he drowned? A long hiss sounded and the debris was sucked from sight; the current lowered. He understood now what had made the water toss the manhole cover; the down-curve had become temporarily obstructed and the perforations had become clogged.

He was in danger; he might slide into a down-curve; he might wander with a lighted match into a pocket of gas and blow himself up; or he might contract some horrible disease . . . Though he wanted to leave, an irrational impulse held him rooted. To the left, the convex ceiling swooped to a height of less than five feet. With cigarette slanting from pursed lips, he waded with taut muscles, his feet sloshing over the slimy bottom, his shoes sinking into spongy slop, the slate-colored water cracking in creamy foam against his knees. Pressing his flat left palm against the lowered ceiling, he struck another match and saw a metal pole nestling in a niche of the wall. Yes, some sewer workman had left it. He reached for it, then jerked his head away as a whisper of scurrying life whisked past and was still. He held the match close and saw a huge rat, wet with slime, blinking beady eyes and baring tiny fangs. The light blinded the rat and the frizzled head moved aimlessly. He grabbed the pole and let it fly against the rat's soft body; there was shrill piping and the grizzly body splashed into the dun-colored water and was snatched out of sight, spinning in the scuttling stream.

He swallowed and pushed on, following the curve of the misty cavern, sounding the water with the pole. By the faint light of another manhole cover he saw, amid loose wet brick, a hole with walls of damp earth leading into blackness. Gingerly he poked the pole into it; it was hollow and went beyond the length of the pole. He shoved the pole before him, hoisted himself upward, got to his hands and knees, and crawled. After a few yards he paused, struck to wonderment by the silence; it seemed that he had traveled a million miles away from the world. As he inched forward again he could sense the bottom of the dirt tunnel becoming dry and lowering slightly. Slowly he rose and to his astonishment he stood erect. He could not hear the rustling of the water now and he felt confoundingly alone, yet lured by the darkness and silence.

He crept a long way, then stopped, curious, afraid. He put his right foot forward and it dangled in space; he drew back in fear. He thrust the pole outward and it swung in emptiness. He trembled, imagining the earth crumbling and burying him alive. He scratched a match and saw that the dirt floor sheered away steeply and widened into a sort of cave some five feet below him. An old sewer, he muttered. He cocked his head, hearing a feathery cadence which he could not identify. The match ceased to burn.

Using the pole as a kind of ladder, he slid down and stood in darkness. The air was a little fresher and he could still hear vague noises. Where was he? He felt suddenly that someone was standing near him and he turned sharply, but there was only darkness. He poked cautiously and felt a brick wall; he followed it and the strange sounds grew louder. He ought to get out of here. This was crazy. He could not remain here for any length of time; there was no food and no place to sleep. But the faint sounds tantalized him; they were strange but familiar. Was it a motor? A baby crying? Music? A siren? He groped on, and the sounds came so clearly that he could feel the pitch and timbre of human voices. Yes, singing! That was it! He listened with open mouth. It was a church service. Enchanted, he groped toward the waves of melody.

> *Jesus, take me to your home above*
> *And fold me in the bosom of Thy love.* . . . . .

The singing was on the other side of a brick wall. Excited, he wanted to watch the service without being seen. Whose church was it? He knew most of the churches in this area above ground, but the singing sounded too strange and detached for him to guess. He looked to the left, to the right, down to the black dirt, then upward and was startled to see a bright sliver of light slicing the darkness like the blade of a razor. He struck one of his two remaining matches and saw rusty pipes running along an old concrete ceiling. Photographically he located the exact position of the pipes in his mind. The match flame sank and he sprang upward; his hands clutched a pipe. He swung his legs and tossed his body onto the bed of pipes and they creaked, swaying up and down; he thought that the tier was about to crash, but nothing happened. He edged to the crevice and saw a segment of black men and women, dressed in white robes, singing, holding tattered songbooks in their black palms. His first impulse was to laugh, but he checked himself.

What was he doing? He was crushed with a sense of guilt. Would God strike him dead for that? The singing swept on and he shook his head, disagreeing in spite of himself. They oughtn't to do that, he thought. But he could think of no reason *why* they should not do it. Just singing with the air of the sewer blowing in on them . . . He felt that he was gazing upon something abysmally obscene, yet he could not bring himself to leave.

After a long time he grew numb and dropped to the dirt. Pain throbbed in his legs and a deeper pain, induced by the sight of those black people groveling and begging for something they could never get, churned in him. A vague conviction made him feel that those people should stand unrepentant and yield no quarter in singing and praying, yet *he* had run away from the police, had pleaded with them to believe in *his* innocence. He shook his head, bewildered.

How long had he been down here? He did not know. This was a new kind of living for him; the intensity of feelings he had experienced when looking at the church people sing made him certain that he had been down here a long time, but his mind told him that the time must have been short. In this darkness the only notion he had of time was when a match flared and measured time by its fleeting light. He groped back through the hole toward the sewer and the waves of song subsided and finally he could not hear them at all. He came to where the earth hole ended and he heard the noise of the current and time lived again for him, measuring the moments by the wash of water.

The rain must have slackened, for the flow of water had lessened and came only to his ankles. Ought he to go up into the streets and take his chances on hiding somewhere else? But they would surely catch him. The mere thought of dodging and running again from the police made him tense. No, he would stay and plot how to elude them. But what could he do down here? He walked forward into the sewer and came to another manhole cover; he stood beneath it, debating. Fine pencils of gold spilled suddenly from the little circles in the manhole cover and trembled on the surface of the current. Yes, street lamps . . . It must be night . . .

He went forward for about a quarter of an hour, wading aimlessly, poking the pole carefully before him. Then he stopped, his eyes fixed and intent. What's that? A strangely familiar image attracted and re-pelled him. Lit by the yellow stems from another manhole cover was a tiny nude body of a baby snagged by debris and half-submerged in water. Thinking that the baby was alive, he moved impulsively to save it, but his roused feelings told him that it was dead, cold, nothing, the same nothingness he had felt while watching the men and women singing in the church. Water blossomed about the tiny legs, the tiny arms, the tiny head, and rushed onward. The eyes were closed, as though in sleep; the fists were clenched, as though in protest; and the mouth gaped black in a soundless cry.

He straightened and drew in his breath, feeling that he had been staring for all eternity at the ripples of veined water skimming imper-sonally over the shriveled limbs. He felt as condemned as when the policemen had accused him. Involuntarily he lifted his hand to brush the vision away, but his arm fell listlessly to his side. Then he acted; he closed his eyes and reached forward slowly with the soggy shoe of his right foot and shoved the dead baby from where it had been lodged. He kept his eyes closed, seeing the little body twisting in the current as it floated from sight. He opened his eyes, shivered, placed his knuckles in the sockets, hearing the water speed in the somber shadows.

He tramped on, sensing at times a sudden quickening in the current as he passed some conduit whose waters were swelling the stream that slid by his feet. A few minutes later he was standing under another man-hole cover, listening to the faint rumble of noises above ground. Street-cars and trucks, he mused. He looked down and saw a stagnant pool of gray-green sludge; at intervals a balloon pocket rose from the scum, glistening a bluish-purple, and burst. Then another. He turned, shook his head, and tramped back to the dirt cave by the church, his lips quivering.

Back in the cave, he sat and leaned his back against a dirt wall. His body was trembling slightly. Finally his senses quieted and he slept.

When he awakened he felt stiff and cold. He had to leave this foul place, but leaving meant facing those policemen who had wrongly accused him. No, he could not go back aboveground. He remembered the beating they had given him and how he had signed his name to a confession, a confession which he had not even read. He had been too tired when they had shouted at him, demanding that he sign his name; he had signed it to end his pain.

He stood and groped about in the darkness. The church singing had stopped. How long had he slept? He did not know. But he felt refreshed and hungry. He doubled his fist nervously, realizing that he could not make a decision. As he walked about he stumbled over an old rusty iron pipe. He picked it up and felt a jagged edge. Yes, there was a brick wall and he could dig into it. What would he find? Smiling, he groped to the brick wall, sat, and began digging idly into damp cement. I can't make any noise, he cautioned himself. As time passed he grew thirsty, but there was no water. He had to kill time or go aboveground. The cement came out of the wall easily; he extracted four bricks and felt a soft draft blowing into his face. He stopped, afraid. What was beyond? He waited a long time and nothing happened; then he began digging again, soundlessly, slowly; he enlarged the hole and crawled through into a dark room and collided with another well. He felt his way to the right; the wall ended and his fingers toyed in space, like the antennae of an insect.

He fumbled on and his feet struck something hollow, like wood. What's this? He felt with his fingers. Steps . . . He stooped and pulled off his shoes and mounted the stairs and saw a yellow chink of light shining and heard a low voice speaking. He placed his eye to a keyhole and saw the nude waxen figure of a man stretched out upon a white table. The voice, low-pitched and vibrant, mumbled indistinguishable words, neither rising nor falling. He craned his neck and squinted to see the man who was talking, but he could not locate him. Above the naked figure was suspended a huge glass container filled with a blood-red liquid from which a white rubber tube dangled. He crouched closer to the door and saw the tip end of a black object lined with pink satin. A coffin, he breathed. This is an undertaker's establishment . . . A fine-spun lace of ice covered his body and he shuddered. A throaty chuckle sounded in the depths of the yellow room.

He turned to leave. Three steps down it occurred to him that a light switch should be nearby; he felt along the wall, found an electric button, pressed it, and a blinding glare smote his pupils so hard that he was sightless, defenseless. His pupils contracted and he wrinkled his nostrils at a peculiar odor. At once he knew that he had been dimly aware of this odor in the darkness, but the light had brought it sharply to his attention. Some kind of stuff they use to embalm, he thought. He went down the steps and saw piles of lumber, coffins, and a long workbench. In one corner was a tool chest. Yes, he could use tools, could tunnel through walls with them. He lifted the lid of the chest and saw nails, a hammer, a crowbar, a screwdriver, a light bulb, a long length of electric wire. Good! He would lug these back to his cave.

He was about to hoist the chest to his shoulders when he discovered a door behind the furnace. Where did it lead? He tried to open it and found it securely bolted. Using the crowbar so as to make no sound, he pried the door open; it swung on creaking hinges, outward. Fresh air came to his face and he caught the faint roar of faraway sound. Easy now, he told himself. He widened the door and a lump of coal rattled toward him. A coalbin . . . Evidently the door led into another basement. The roaring noise was louder now, but he could not identify it. Where was he? He groped slowly over the coal pile, then ranged in darkness over a gritty floor. The roaring noise seemed to come from above him, then below. His fingers followed a wall until he touched a wooden ridge. A door, he breathed.

The noise died to a low pitch; he felt his skin prickle. It seemed that he was playing a game with an unseen person whose intelligence outstripped his. He put his ear to the flat surface of the door. Yes, voices . . . Was this a prize fight stadium? The sound of the voices came near and sharp, but he could not tell if they were joyous or despairing. He twisted the knob until he heard a soft click and felt the springy weight of the door swinging toward him. He was afraid to open it, yet captured by curiosity and wonder. He jerked the door wide and saw on the far side of the basement a furnace glowing red. Ten feet away was still another door, half ajar. He crossed and peered through the door into an empty, high-ceilinged corridor that terminated in a dark complex of shadow. The belling voices rolled about him and his eagerness mounted. He stepped into the corridor and the voices swelled louder. He crept on and came to a narrow stairway leading circularly upward; there was no question but what he was going to ascend those stairs.

Mounting the spiraled staircase, he heard the voices roll in a steady wave, then leap to crescendo, only to die away, but always remaining audible. Ahead of him glowed red letters: E—X—I—T. At the top of the steps he paused in front of a black curtain that fluttered uncertainly. He parted the folds and looked into a convex depth that gleamed with clusters of shimmering lights. Sprawling below him was a stretch of human faces, tilted upward, chanting, whistling, screaming, laughing. Dangling before the faces, high upon a screen of silver, were jerking shadows. A movie, he said with slow laughter breaking from his lips.

He stood in a box in the reserved section of a movie house and the impulse he had had to tell the people in the church to stop their singing seized him. These people were laughing at their lives, he thought with amazement. They were shouting and yelling at the animated shadows of themselves. His compassion fired his imagination and he stepped out of the box, walked out upon thin air, walked on down to the audience; and, hovering in the air just above them, he stretched out his hand to touch them . . . His tension snapped and he found himself back in the box, looking down into the sea of faces. No; it could not be done; he could not awaken them. He sighed. Yes, these people were children, sleeping in their living, awake in their dying.

He turned away, parted the black curtain, and looked out. He saw no one. He started down the white stone steps and when he reached the bottom he saw a man in trim blue uniform coming toward him. So used had he become to being underground that he thought that he could walk past the man, as though he were a ghost. But the man stopped. And he stopped.

"Looking for the men's room, sir?" the man asked, and, without waiting for an answer, he turned and pointed. "This way, sir. The first door to your right."

He watched the man turn and walk up the steps and go out of sight. Then he laughed. What a funny fellow! He went back to the basement and stood in the red darkness, watching the glowing embers in the furnace. He went to the sink and turned the faucet and the water flowed in a smooth silent stream that looked like a spout of blood. He brushed the mad image from his mind and began to wash his hands leisurely, looking about for the usual bar of soap. He found one and rubbed it in his palms until a rich lather bloomed in his cupped fingers, like a scarlet sponge. He scrubbed and rinsed his hands meticulously, then hunted for a towel; there was none. He shut off the water, pulled off his shirt, dried his hands on it; when he put it on again he was grateful for the cool dampness that came to his skin.

Yes, he was thirsty; he turned on the faucet again, bowled his fingers and when the water bubbled over the brim of his cupped palms, he drank in long, slow swallows. His bladder grew tight; he shut off the water, faced the wall, bent his head, and watched a red stream strike the floor. His nostrils wrinkled against acrid wisps of vapor; though he had tramped in the waters of the sewer, he stepped back from the wall so that his shoes, wet with sewer slime, would not touch his urine.

He heard footsteps and crawled quickly into the coalbin. Lumps rattled noisily. The footsteps came into the basement and stopped. Who was it? Had someone heard him and come down to investigate? He waited, crouching, sweating. For a long time there was silence, then he heard the clang of metal and a brighter glow lit the room. Somebody's tending the furnace, he thought. Footsteps came closer and he stiffened. Looming before him was a white face lined with coal dust, the face of an old man with watery blue eyes. Highlights spotted his gaunt cheekbones, and he held a huge shovel. There was a screechy scrape of metal against stone, and the old man lifted a shovelful of coal and went from sight.

The room dimmed momentarily, then a yellow glare came as coal flared at the furnace door. Six times the old man came to the bin and went to the furnace with shovels of coal, but not once did he lift his eyes. Finally he dropped the shovel, mopped his face with a dirty hand-kerchief, and sighed: "Wheeew!" He turned slowly and trudged out of the basement, his footsteps dying away.

He stood, and lumps of coal clattered down the pile. He stepped from the bin and was startled to see the shadowy outline of an electric bulb hanging above his head. Why had not the old man turned it on? Oh, yes . . . He understood. The old man had worked here for so long that he had no need for light; he had learned a way of seeing in his dark world, like those sightless worms that inch along underground by a sense of touch.

His eyes fell upon a lunch pail and he was afraid to hope that it was full. He picked it up; it was heavy. He opened it. *Sandwiches!* He looked guiltily around; he was alone. He searched farther and found a folder of matches and a half-empty tin of tobacco; he put them eagerly into his pocket and clicked off the light. With the lunch pail under his arm, he went through the door, groped over the pile of coal, and stood again in the lighted basement of the undertaking establishment. I've got to get those tools, he told himself. And turn off that light. He tiptoed back up the steps and switched off the light; the invisible voice still droned on behind the door. He crept down and, seeing with his fingers, opened the lunch pail and tore off a piece of paper bag and brought out the tin and spilled grains of tobacco into the makeshift concave. He rolled it and wet it with spittle, then inserted one end into his mouth and lit it: he sucked smoke that bit his lungs. The nicotine reached his brain, went out along his arms to his finger tips, down to his stomach, and over all the tired nerves of his body.

He carted the tools to the hole he had made in the wall. Would the noise of the falling chest betray him? But he would have to take a chance; he had to have those tools. He lifted the chest and shoved it; it hit the dirt on the other side of the wall with a loud clatter. He waited, listening; nothing happened. Head first, he slithered through and stood in the cave. He grinned, filled with a cunning idea. Yes, he would now go back into the basement of the undertaking establishment and crouch behind the coal pile and dig another hole. Sure! Fumbling, he opened the tool chest and extracted a crowbar, a screwdriver, and a hammer; he fastened them securely about his person.

With another lumpish cigarette in his flexed lips, he crawled back through the hole and over the coal pile and sat, facing the brick wall. He jabbed with the crowbar and the cement sheered away; quicker than he thought, a brick came loose. He worked an hour; the other bricks did not come easily. He sighed, weak from effort. I ought to rest a little, he thought. I'm hungry. He felt his way back to the cave and stumbled along the wall till he came to the tool chest. He sat upon it, opened the lunch pail, and took out two thick sandwiches. He smelled them. Pork chops . . . His mouth watered. He closed his eyes and devoured a sandwich, savoring the smooth rye bread and juicy meat. He ate rapidly, gulping down lumpy mouthfuls that made him long for water. He ate the other sandwich and found an apple and gobbled that up too, sucking the core till the last trace of flavor was drained from it. Then, like a dog, he ground the meat bones with his teeth, enjoying the salty, tangy marrow. He finished and stretched out full length on the ground and went to sleep. . . .

. . . His body was washed by cold water that gradually turned warm and he was buoyed upon a stream and swept out to sea where waves rolled gently and suddenly he found himself walking upon the water how strange and delightful to walk upon the water and he came upon a nude woman holding a nude baby in her arms and the woman was sinking into the water holding the baby above her head and screaming *help* and he ran over the water to the woman and he reached her just before she went down and he took the baby from her hands and stood watching the breaking bubbles where the woman sank and he called *lady* and still no answer yes dive down there and rescue that woman but he could not take this baby with him and he stooped and laid the baby tenderly upon the surface of the water expecting it to sink but it floated and he leaped into the water and held his breath and strained his eyes to see through the gloomy volume of water but there was no woman and he opened his mouth and called *lady* and the water bubbled and his chest ached and his arms were tired but he could not see the woman and he called again *lady lady* and his feet touched sand at the bottom of the sea and his chest felt as though it would burst and he bent his knees and propelled himself upward and water rushed past him and his head bobbed out and he breathed deeply and looked around where was the baby the baby was gone and he rushed over the water looking for the baby calling *where is it* and the empty sky and sea threw back his voice *where is it* and he began to doubt that he could stand upon the water and then he was sinking and as he struggled the water rushed him downward spinning dizzily and he opened his mouth to call for help and water surged into his lungs and he choked . . .

He groaned and leaped erect in the dark, his eyes wide. The images of terror that thronged his brain would not let him sleep. He rose, made sure that the tools were hitched to his belt, and groped his way to the coal pile and found the rectangular gap from which he had taken the bricks. He took out the crowbar and hacked. Then dread paralyzed him. How long had he slept? Was it day or night now? He had to be careful. Someone might hear him if it were day. He hewed softly for hours at the cement, working silently. Faintly quivering in the air above him was the dim sound of yelling voices. Crazy people, he muttered. They're still there in that movie . . .

Having rested, he found the digging much easier. He soon had a dozen bricks out. His spirits rose. He took out another brick and his fingers fluttered in space. Good! What lay ahead of him? Another basement? He made the hole larger, climbed through, walked over an uneven floor and felt a metal surface. He lighted a match and saw that he was standing behind a furnace in a basement; before him, on the far side of the room, was a door. He crossed and opened it; it was full of odds and ends. Daylight spilled from a window above his head.

Then he was aware of a soft, continuous tapping. What was it? A clock? No, it was louder than a clock and more irregular. He placed an old empty box beneath the window, stood upon it, and looked into an areaway. He eased the window up and crawled through; the sound of the tapping came clearly now. He glanced about; he was alone. Then he looked upward at a series of window ledges. The tapping identified itself. That's a typewriter, he said to himself. It seemed to be coming from just above. He grasped the ridges of a rain pipe and lifted himself upward; through a half-inch opening of window he saw a doorknob about three feet away. No, it was not a doorknob; it was a small circular disk made of stainless steel with many fine markings upon it. He held his breath: an eerie white hand, seemingly detached from its arm, touched the metal knob and whirled it, first to the left, then to the right. It's a safe! . . . Suddenly he could see the dial no more; a huge metal door swung slowly toward him and he was looking into a safe filled with green wads of paper money, rows of coins wrapped in brown paper, and glass jars and boxes of various sizes. His heart quickened. Good Lord! The white hand went in and out of the safe, taking wads of bills and cylinders of coins. The hand vanished and he heard the muffled click of the big door as it closed. Only the steel dial was visible now. The typewriter still tapped in his ears, but he could not see it. He blinked, wondering if what he had seen was real. There was more money in that safe than he had seen in all his life.

As he clung to the rain pipe, a daring idea came to him and he pulled the screwdriver from his belt. If the white hand twirled that dial again, he would be able to see how far to the left and right it spun and he would have the combination! His blood tingled. I can scratch the numbers right here, he thought. Holding the pipe with one hand, he made the sharp edge of the screwdriver bite into the brick wall. Yes, he could do it. Now, he was set. Now, he had a reason for staying here in the underground. He waited for a long time, but the white hand did not return. Goddamn! Had he been more alert, he would have counted the twirls and he would have had the combination. He got down and stood in the areaway, sunk in reflection.

How could he get into that room? He climbed back into the basement and saw wooden steps leading upward. Was that the room where the safe stood? Fearing that the dial was now being twirled, he clambered through the window, hoisted himself up the rain pipe, and peered; he saw only the naked gleam of the steel dial. He got down and doubled his fists. Well, he would explore the basement. He returned to the basement room and mounted the steps to the door and squinted through the keyhole; all was dark, but the tapping was still somewhere near, still faint and directionless. He pushed the door in; along one wall of a room was a table piled with radios and electrical equipment. A radio shop, he muttered.

Well, he could rig up a radio in his cave. He found a sack, slid the radio into it, and slung it across his back. Closing the door, he went down the steps and stood again in the basement, disappointed. He had not solved the problem of the steel dial and he was irked. He set the radio on the floor and again hoisted himself through the window and up the rain pipe and squinted; the metal door was swinging shut. Goddamn! He's worked the combination again. If I had been patient, I'd have had it! How could he get into that room? He *had* to get into it. He could jimmy the window, but it would be much better if he could get in without any traces. To the right of him, he calculated, should be the basement of the building that held the safe; therefore, if he dug a hole right *here*, he ought to reach his goal.

He began a quiet scraping; it was hard work, for the bricks were not damp. He eventually got one out and lowered it softly to the floor. He had to be careful; perhaps people were beyond this wall. He extracted a second layer of brick and found still another. He gritted his teeth, ready to quit. I'll dig one more, he resolved. When the next brick came out he felt air blowing into his face. He waited to be challenged, but nothing happened.

He enlarged the hole and pulled himself through and stood in quiet darkness. He scratched a match to flame and saw steps; he mounted and peered through a keyhole: Darkness . . . He strained to hear the typewriter, but there was only silence. Maybe the office had closed? He twisted the knob and swung the door in; a frigid blast made him shiver. In the shadows before him were halves and quarters of hogs and lambs and steers hanging from metal hooks on the low ceiling, red meat encased in folds of cold white fat. Fronting him was frost-coated glass from behind which came indistinguishable sounds. The odor of fresh raw meat sickened him and he backed away. A meat market, he whispered.

He ducked his head, suddenly blinded by light. He narrowed his eyes; the red-white rows of meat were drenched in yellow glare. A man wearing a crimson-spotted jacket came in and took down a bloody meat cleaver. He eased the door to, holding it ajar just enough to watch the man, hoping that the darkness in which he stood would keep him from being seen. The man took down a hunk of steer and placed it upon a bloody wooden block and bent forward and whacked with the cleaver. The man's face was hard, square, grim; a jet of mustache smudged his upper lip and a glistening cowlick of hair fell over his left eye. Each time he lifted the cleaver and brought it down upon the meat, he let out a short, deep-chested grunt. After he had cut the meat, he wiped blood off the wooden block with a sticky wad of gunny sack and hung the cleaver upon a hook. His face was proud as he placed the chunk of meat in the crook of his elbow and left.

The door slammed and the light went off; once more he stood in shadow. His tension ebbed. From behind the frosted glass he heard the man's voice: "Forty-eight cents a pound, ma'am." He shuddered, feeling that there was something he had to do. But what? He stared fixedly at the cleaver, then he sneezed and was terrified for fear that the man had heard him. But the door did not open. He took down the cleaver and examined the sharp edge smeared with cold blood. Behind the ice-coated glass a cash register rang with a vibrating, musical tinkle.

Absent-mindedly holding the meat cleaver, he rubbed the glass with his thumb and cleared a spot that enabled him to see into the front of the store. The shop was empty, save for the man who was now putting on his hat and coat. Beyond the front window a wan sun shone in the streets; people passed and now and then a fragment of laughter or the whir of a speeding auto came to him. He peered closer and saw on the right counter of the shop a mosquito netting covering pears, grapes, lemons, oranges, bananas, peaches, and plums. His stomach contracted.

The man clicked out the light and he gritted his teeth, muttering, Don't lock the icebox door . . . The man went through the door of the shop and locked it from the outside. Thank God! Now, he would eat some more! He waited, trembling. The sun died and its rays lingered on in the sky, turning the streets to dusk. He opened the door and stepped inside the shop. In reverse letters across the front window was: NICK'S FRUITS AND MEATS. He laughed, picked up a soft ripe yellow pear and bit into it; juice squirted; his mouth ached as his saliva glands reacted to the acid of the fruit. He ate three pears, gobbled six bananas, and made away with several oranges, taking a bite out of their tops and holding them to his lips and squeezing them as he hungrily sucked the juice.

He found a faucet, turned it on, laid the cleaver aside, pursed his lips under the stream until his stomach felt about to burst. He straightened and belched, feeling satisfied for the first time since he had been underground. He sat upon the floor, rolled and lit a cigarette, his bloodshot eyes squinting against the film of drifting smoke. He watched a patch of sky turn red, then purple; night fell and he lit another cigarette, brooding. Some part of him was trying to remember the world he had left, and another part of him did not want to remember it. Sprawling before him in his mind was his wife, Mrs. Wooten for whom he worked, the three policemen who had picked him up . . . He possessed them now more completely than he had ever possessed them when he had lived aboveground. How this had come about he could not say, but he had no desire to go back to them. He laughed, crushed the cigarette, and stood up.

He went to the front door and gazed out. Emotionally he hovered

between the world aboveground and the world underground. He longed
to go out, but sober judgment urged him to remain here. Then impulsively he pried the lock loose with one swift twist of the crowbar;
the door swung outward. Through the twilight he saw a white man and
a white woman coming toward him. He held himself tense, waiting
for them to pass; but they came directly to the door and confronted
him.

"I want to buy a pound of grapes," the woman said.

Terrified, he stepped back into the store. The white man stood to one
side and the woman entered.

"Give me a pound of dark ones," the woman said.

The white man came slowly forward, blinking his eyes.

"Where's Nick?" the man asked.

"Were you just closing?" the woman asked.

"Yes, ma'am," he mumbled. For a second he did not breathe, then
he mumbled again: "Yes, ma'am."

"I'm sorry," the woman said.

The street lamps came on, lighting the store somewhat. Ought he
run? But that would raise an alarm. He moved slowly, dreamily, to a
counter and lifted up a bunch of grapes and showed them to the woman.

"Fine," the woman said. "But isn't that more than a pound?"

He did not answer. The man was staring at him intently.

"Put them in a bag for me," the woman said, fumbling with her
purse.

"Yes, ma'am."

He saw a pile of paper bags under a narrow ledge; he opened one and
put the grapes in.

"Thanks," the woman said, taking the bag and placing a dime in his
dark palm.

"Where's Nick?" the man asked again. "At supper?"

"Sir? Yes, sir," he breathed.

They left the store and he stood trembling in the doorway. When
they were out of sight, he burst out laughing and crying. A trolley car
rolled noisily past and he controlled himself quickly. He flung the dime
to the pavement with a gesture of contempt and stepped into the warm
night air. A few shy stars trembled above him. The look of things was
beautiful, yet he felt a lurking threat. He went to an unattended news-
stand and looked at a stack of papers. He saw a headline: HUNT
NEGRO FOR MURDER.

He felt that someone had slipped up on him from behind and was
stripping off his clothes; he looked about wildly, went quickly back into
the store, picked up the meat cleaver where he had left it near the sink,
then made his way through the icebox to the basement. He stood for
a long time, breathing heavily. They know I didn't do anything, he
muttered. But how could he prove it? He had signed a confession.
Though innocent, he felt guilty, condemned. He struck a match and

held it near the steel blade, fascinated and repelled by the dried blotches
of blood. Then his fingers gripped the handle of the cleaver with all
the strength of his body, he wanted to fling the cleaver from him, but
he could not. The match flame wavered and fled; he struggled through
the hole and put the cleaver in the sack with the radio. He was determined to keep it, for what purpose he did not know.

He was about to leave when he remembered the safe. Where was it?
He wanted to give up, but felt that he ought to make one more try.
Opposite the last hole he had dug, he tunneled again, plying the crowbar. Once he was so exhausted that he lay on the concrete floor and
panted. Finally he made another hole. He wriggled through and his
nostrils filled with the fresh smell of coal. He struck a match; yes, the
usual steps led upward. He tiptoed to a door and eased it open. A fair-
haired white girl stood in front of a steel cabinet, her blue eyes wide
upon him. She turned chalky and gave a high-pitched scream. He
bounded down the steps and raced to his hole and clambered through,
replacing the bricks with nervous haste. He paused, hearing loud voices.

"What's the matter, Alice?"

"A man . . ."

"What man? Where?"

"A man was at that door . . ."

"Oh nonsense!"

"He was looking at me through the door!"

"Aw, you're dreaming."

"I *did* see a man!"

The girl was crying now.

"There's nobody here."

Another man's voice sounded.

"What is it, Bob?"

"Alice says she saw a man in here, in that door!"

"Let's take a look."

He waited, poised for flight. Footsteps descended the stairs.

"There's nobody down here."

"The window's locked."

"And there's no door."

"You ought to fire that dame."

"Oh, I don't know. Women are that way."

"She's too hysterical."

The men laughed. Footsteps sounded again on the stairs. A door
slammed. He sighed, relieved that he had escaped. But he had not done
what he had set out to do; his glimpse of the room had been too brief
to determine if the safe was there. He had to know. Boldly he groped
through the hole once more; he reached the steps and pulled off his
shoes and tiptoed up and peered through the keyhole. His head ac-
cidentally touched the door and it swung silently in a fraction of an
inch; he saw the girl bent over the cabinet, her back to him. Beyond

her was the safe. He crept back down the steps, thinking exultingly: I found it!

Now he had to get the combination. Even if the window in the area way was locked and bolted, he could gain entrance when the office closed. He scoured through the hole he had dug and stood again in the basement where he had left the radio and the cleaver. Again he crawled out of the window and lifted himself up the rain pipe and peered. The steel dial showed lonely and bright, reflecting the yellow glow of an unseen light. Resigned to a long wait, he sat and leaned against a wall. From far off came the faint sounds of life aboveground; once he looked with a baffled expression at the dark sky. Frequently he rose and climbed the pipe to see the white hand spin the dial, but nothing happened. He bit his lip with impatience. It was not the money that was luring him, but the mere fact that he could get it with impunity. Was the hand now twirling the dial? He rose and looked, but the white hand was not in sight.

Perhaps it would be better to watch continuously? Yes; he clung to the pipe and watched the dial until his eyes thickened with tears. Exhausted, he stood again in the areaway. He heard a door being shut and he clawed up the pipe and looked. He jerked tense as a vague figure passed in front of him. He stared unblinkingly, hugging the pipe with one hand and holding the screwdriver with the other, ready to etch the combination upon the wall. His ears caught: Dong . . . Dong . . . Dong . . . Dong . . . Dong . . . Dong . . . Dong . . . Seven o'clock, he whispered. Maybe they were closing now? What kind of a store would be open as late as this? he wondered. Did anyone live in the rear? Was there a night watchman? Perhaps the safe was *already* locked for the night! Goddamn! While he had been eating in that shop, they had locked up everything . . . Then, just as he was about to give up, the white hand touched the dial and turned it once to the right and stopped at six. With quivering fingers, he etched 1—R—6 upon the brick wall with the tip of the screwdriver. The hand twirled the dial twice to the left and stopped at two, and he engraved 2—L—2 upon the wall. The dial was spun four times to the right and stopped at six again; he wrote 4—R—6. The dial rotated three times to the left and was centered straight up and down; he wrote 3—L—0. The door swung open and again he saw the piles of green money and the rows of wrapped coins. I got it, he said grimly.

Then he was stone still, astonished. There were two hands now. A right hand lifted a wad of green bills and deftly slipped it up the sleeve of a left arm. The hands trembled; again the right hand slipped a packet of bills up the left sleeve. He's stealing, he said to himself. He grew indignant, as if the money belonged to him. Though *he* had planned to steal the money, he despised and pitied the man. He felt that his stealing the money and the man's stealing were two entirely different things. He wanted to steal the money merely for the sensation involved in getting it, and he had no intention whatever of spending a penny of it; but he knew that the man who was now stealing it was going to spend it, perhaps for pleasure. The huge steel door closed with a soft click.

Though angry, he was somewhat satisfied. The office would close soon. I'll clean the place out, he mused. He imagined the entire office staff cringing with fear; the police would question everyone for a crime they had not committed, just as they had questioned him. And they would have no idea of how the money had been stolen until they discovered the holes he had tunneled in the walls of the basements. He lowered himself and laughed mischievously, with the abandoned glee of an adolescent.

He flattened himself against the wall as the window above him closed with rasping sound. He looked; somebody was bolting the window securely with a metal screen. That won't help you, he snickered to himself. He clung to the rain pipe until the yellow light in the office went out. He went back into the basement, picked up the sack containing the radio and cleaver, and crawled through the two holes he had dug and groped his way into the basement of the building that held the safe. He moved in slow motion, breathing softly. Be careful now, he told himself. There might be a night watchman . . . In his memory was the combination written in bold white characters as upon a blackboard. Eel-like he squeezed through the last hole and crept up the steps and put his hand on the knob and pushed the door in about three inches. Then his courage ebbed; his imagination wove dangers for him.

Perhaps the night watchman was waiting in there, ready to shoot. He dangled his cap on a forefinger and poked it past the jamb of the door. If anyone fired, they would hit his cap; but nothing happened. He widened the door, holding the crowbar high above his head, ready to beat off an assailant. He stood like that for five minutes; the rumble of a streetcar brought him to himself. He entered the room. Moonlight floated in from a wide window. He confronted the safe, then checked himself. Better take a look around first . . . He stepped about and found a closed door. Was the night watchman in there? He opened it and saw a washbowl, a faucet, and a commode. To the left was still another door that opened into a huge dark room that seemed empty; on the far side of that room he made out the shadow of still another door. Nobody's here, he told himself.

He turned back to the safe and fingered the dial; it spun with ease. He laughed and twirled it just for fun. Get to work, he told himself. He turned the dial to the figures he saw on the blackboard of his memory; it was so easy that he felt that the safe had not been locked at all. The heavy door eased loose and he caught hold of the handle and pulled hard, but the door swung open with a slow momentum of its own. Breathless, he gaped at wads of green bills, rows of wrapped coins, curious glass jars full of white pellets, and many oblong green metal boxes. He glanced guiltily over his shoulder; it seemed impossible that someone should not call to him to stop.

They'll be surprised in the morning, he thought. He opened the top of the sack and lifted a wad of compactly tied bills; the money was crisp and new. He admired the smooth, clean-cut edges. The fellows in Washington sure know how to make this stuff, he mused. He rubbed the money with his fingers, as though expecting it to reveal hidden qualities. He lifted the wad to his nose and smelled the fresh odor of ink. Just like any other paper, he mumbled. He dropped the wad into the sack and picked up another. Holding the bag, he thought and laughed.

There was in him no sense of possessiveness; he was intrigued with the form and color of the money, with the manifold reactions which he knew that men aboveground held toward it. The sack was one-third full when it occurred to him to examine the denominations of the bills; without realizing it, he had put many wads of one-dollar bills into the sack. Aw, nuts, he said in disgust. Take the big ones . . . He dumped the one-dollar bills onto the floor and swept all the hundred-dollar bills he could find into the sack, then he raked in rolls of coins with crooked fingers.

He walked to a desk upon which sat a typewriter, the same machine which the blond girl had used. He was fascinated by it; never in his life had he used one of them. It was a queer instrument of business, something beyond the rim of his life. Whenever he had been in an office where a girl was typing, he had almost always spoken in whispers. Remembering vaguely what he had seen others do, he inserted a sheet of paper into the machine; it went in lopsided and he did not know how to straighten it. Spelling in a soft diffident voice, he pecked out his name on the keys: *freddaniels*. He looked at it and laughed. He would learn to type correctly one of these days.

Yes, he would take the typewriter too. He lifted the machine and placed it atop the bulk of money in the sack. He did not feel that he was stealing, for the cleaver, the radio, the money, and the typewriter were all on the same level of value, all meant the same thing to him. They were the serious toys of the men who lived in the dead world of sunshine and rain he had left, the world that had condemned him, branded him guilty.

But what kind of a place is this? he wondered. What was in that dark room to his rear? He felt for his matches and found that he had only one left. He leaned the sack against the safe and groped forward into the room, encountering smooth, metallic objects that felt like machines. Baffled, he touched a wall and tried vainly to locate an electric switch. Well, he *had* to strike his last match. He knelt and struck it, cupping the flame near the floor with his palms. The place seemed to be a factory, with benches and tables. There were bulbs with green shades spaced about the tables; he turned on a light and twisted it low so that the glare was limited. There were stools at the benches and he concluded that men worked here at some trade. He wandered and found a few half-used folders of matches. If only he could find more cigarettes! But there were none.

But what kind of a place was this? On a bench he saw a pad of paper captioned: PEER'S—MANUFACTURING JEWELERS. His lips formed an "O," then he snapped off the light and ran back to the safe and lifted one of the glass jars and stared at the tiny white pellets. Gingerly he picked up one and found that it was wrapped in tissue paper. He peeled the paper and saw a glittering stone that looked like glass, glinting white and blue sparks. Diamonds, he breathed.

Roughly he tore the paper from the pellets and soon his palm quivered with precious fire. Trembling, he took all four glass jars from the safe and put them into the sack. He grabbed one of the metal boxes, shook it, and heard a tinny rattle. He pried off the lid with the screwdriver. Rings! Hundreds of them . . . Were they worth anything? He scooped up a handful and jets of fire shot fitfully from the stones. These are diamonds too, he said. He pried open another box. Watches! A chorus of soft, metallic ticking filled his ears. For a moment he could not move, then he dumped all the boxes into the sack.

He shut the safe door, then stood looking around, anxious not to overlook anything. Oh! He had seen a door in the room where the machines were. What was in there? More valuables? He re-entered the room, crossed the floor, and stood undecided before the door. He finally caught hold of the knob and pushed the door in; the room beyond was dark. He advanced cautiously inside and ran his fingers along the wall for the usual switch, then he was stark still. *Something had moved in the room!* What was it? Ought he to creep out, taking the rings and diamonds and money? Why risk what he already had? He waited and the ensuing silence gave him confidence to explore further. Dare he strike a match? Would not a match flame make him a good target? He tensed again as he heard a faint sigh; he was now convinced that there was something alive near him, something that lived and breathed. On tiptoe he felt slowly along the wall, hoping that he would not collide with anything. Luck was with him; he found the light switch.

No; don't turn the light on . . . Then suddenly he realized that he did not know in what direction the door was. Goddamn! He had to turn the light on or strike a match. He fingered the switch for a long time, then thought of an idea. He knelt upon the floor, reached his arm up to the switch and flicked the button, hoping that if anyone shot, the bullet would go above his head. The moment the light came on he narrowed his eyes to see quickly. He sucked in his breath and his body gave a violent twitch and was still. In front of him, so close that it made him want to bound up and scream, was a human face.

He was afraid to move lest he touch the man. If the man had opened his eyes at that moment, there was no telling what he might have done. The man—long and rawboned—was stretched out on his back upon a little cot, sleeping in his clothes, his head cushioned by a dirty pillow; his face, clouded by a dark stubble of beard, looked straight up to the ceiling. The man sighed, and he grew tense to defend himself; the man mumbled and turned his face away from the light. I've got to turn off that light, he thought. Just as he was about to rise, he saw a gun and cartridge belt on the floor at the man's side. Yes, he would take the gun and cartridge belt, not to use them, but just to keep them, as one takes a memento from a country fair. He picked them up and was about to click off the light when his eyes fell upon a photograph perched upon a chair near the man's head; it was the picture of a woman, smiling, shown against a background of open fields; at the woman's side were two young children, a boy and a girl. He smiled indulgently; he could send a bullet into that man's brain and time would be over for him . . .

He clicked off the light and crept silently back into the room where the safe stood; he fastened the cartridge belt about him and adjusted the holster at his right hip. He strutted about the room on tiptoe, lolling his head nonchalantly, then paused abruptly, pulled the gun, and pointed it with grim face toward an imaginary foe. "Boom!" he whispered fiercely. Then he bent forward with silent laughter. That's just like they do it in the movies, he said.

He contemplated his loot for a long time, then got a towel from the washroom and tied the sack securely. When he looked up he was momentarily frightened by his shadow looming on the wall before him. He lifted the sack, dragged it down the basement steps, lugged it across the basement, gasping for breath. After he had struggled through the hole, he clumsily replaced the bricks, then tussled with the sack until he got it to the cave. He stood in the dark, wet with sweat, brooding about the diamonds, the rings, the watches, the money; he remembered the singing in the church, the people yelling in the movie, the dead baby, the nude man stretched out upon the white table . . . He saw these items hovering before his eyes and felt that some dim meaning linked them together, that some magical relationship made them kin. He stared with vacant eyes, convinced that all of these images, with their tongueless reality, were striving to tell him something . . .

Later, seeing with his fingers, he untied the sack and set each item neatly upon the dirt floor. Exploring, he took the bulb, the socket, and the wire out of the tool chest; he was elated to find a double socket at one end of the wire. He crammed the stuff into his pockets and hoisted himself upon the rusty pipes and squinted into the church; it was dim and empty. Somewhere in this wall were live electric wires; but where? He lowered himself, groped and tapped the wall with the butt of the screwdriver, listening vainly for hollow sounds. I'll just take a chance and dig, he said.

For an hour he tried to dislodge a brick, and when he struck a match, he found that he had dug a depth of only an inch! No use in digging here, he sighed. By the flickering light of a match, he looked upward, then lowered his eyes, only to glance up again, startled. Directly above his head, beyond the pipes, was a wealth of electric wiring. I'll be damned, he snickered.

He got an old dull knife from the chest and, seeing again with his fingers, separated the two strands of wire and cut away the insulation. Twice he received a slight shock. He scraped the wiring clean and managed to join the two twin ends, then screwed in the bulb. The sudden illumination blinded him and he shut his lids to kill the pain in his eyeballs. I've got that much done, he thought jubilantly.

He placed the bulb on the dirt floor and the light cast a blatant glare on the bleak clay walls. Next he plugged one end of the wire that dangled from the radio into the light socket and bent down and switched on the button; almost at once there was the harsh sound of static, but no words or music. Why won't it work? he wondered. Had he damaged the mechanism in any way? Maybe it needed grounding? Yes . . . He rummaged in the tool chest and found another length of wire, fastened it to the ground of the radio, and then tied the opposite end to a pipe. Rising and growing distinct, a slow strain of music entranced him with its measured sound. He sat upon the chest, deliriously happy.

Later he searched again in the chest and found a half-gallon can of glue; he opened it and smelled a sharp odor. Then he recalled that he had not even looked at the money. He took a wad of green bills and weighed it in his palm, then broke the seal and held one of the bills up to the light and studied it closely. *The United States of America will pay to the bearer on demand one hundred dollars,* he read in slow speech; then: *This note is legal tender for all debts, public and private.* . . . He broke into a musing laugh, feeling that he was reading of the doings of people who lived on some far-off planet. He turned the bill over and saw on the other side of it a delicately beautiful building gleaming with paint and set amidst green grass. He had no desire whatever to count the money; it was what it stood for—the various currents of life swirling aboveground—that captivated him. Next he opened the rolls of coins and let them slide from their paper wrappings to the ground; the bright, new gleaming pennies and nickels and dimes piled high at his feet, a glowing mound of shimmering copper and silver. He sifted them through his fingers, listening to their tinkle as they struck the conical heap.

Oh, yes! He had forgotten. He would now write his name on the typewriter. He inserted a piece of paper and poised his fingers to write. But what was his name? He stared, trying to remember. He stood and glared about the dirt cave, his name on the tip of his lips. But it would not come to him. Why was he here? Yes, he had been running away from the police. But why? His mind was blank. He bit his lips and sat again, feeling a vague terror. But why worry? He laughed, then pecked slowly: *itwasalonghotday*. He was determined to type the sentence without making any mistakes. How did one make capital letters? He experimented and luckily discovered how to lock the machine for capital letters and then shift it back to lower case. Next he discovered how to make spaces, then he wrote neatly and correctly: *It was a long hot day*. Just why he selected that sentence he did not know; it was merely the ritual of performing the thing that appealed to him. He took the sheet out of the machine and looked around with stiff neck and hard eyes and spoke to an imaginary person:

"Yes, I'll have the contracts ready tomorrow."

He laughed. That's just the way they talk, he said. He grew weary of the game and pushed the machine aside. His eyes fell upon the can of glue, and a mischievous idea bloomed in him, filling him with nervous eagerness. He leaped up and opened the can of glue, then broke the seals on all the wads of money. I'm going to have some wallpaper, he said with a luxurious, physical laugh that made him bend at the knees. He took the towel with which he had tied the sack and balled it into a swab and dipped it into the can of glue and dabbed glue onto the wall; then he pasted one green bill by the side of another. He stepped back and cocked his head. Jesus! That's funny . . . He slapped his thighs and guffawed. He had triumphed over the world aboveground! He was free! If only people could see this! He wanted to run from this cave and yell his discovery to the world.

He swabbed all the dirt walls of the cave and pasted them with green bills; when he had finished the walls blazed with a yellow-green fire. Yes, this room would be his hide-out; between him and the world that had branded him guilty would stand this mocking symbol. He had not stolen the money; he had simply picked it up, just as a man would pick up firewood in a forest. And that was how the world aboveground now seemed to him, a wild forest filled with death.

The walls of money finally palled on him and he looked about for new interests to feed his emotions. The cleaver! He drove a nail into the wall and hung the bloody cleaver upon it. Still another idea welled up. He pried open the metal boxes and lined them side by side on the dirt floor. He grinned at the gold and fire. From one box he lifted up a fistful of ticking gold watches and dangled them by their gleaming chains. He stared with an idle smile, then began to wind them up; he did not attempt to set them at any given hour, for there was no time for him now. He took a fistful of nails and drove them into the papered walls and hung the watches upon them, letting them swing down by their glittering chains, trembling and ticking busily against the backdrop of green with the lemon sheen of the electric light shining upon the metal watch casings, converting the golden disks into blobs of liquid yellow. Hardly had he hung up the last watch than the idea extended itself; he took more nails from the chest and drove them into the green paper and took the boxes of rings and went from nail to nail and hung up the golden bands. The blue and white sparks from the stones filled the cave with brittle laughter, as though enjoying his hilarious secret. People certainly can do some funny things, he said to himself.

He sat upon the tool chest, alternately laughing and shaking his head soberly. Hours later he became conscious of the gun sagging at his hip and he pulled it from the holster. He had seen men fire guns in movies, but somehow his life had never led him into contact with firearms. A desire to feel the sensation others felt in firing came over him. But someone might hear . . . Well, what if they did? They would not know where the shot had come from. Not in their wildest notions would they think that it had come from under the streets! He tightened his finger on the trigger; there was a deafening report and it seemed that the entire underground had caved in upon his eardrums; and in the same instant there flashed an orange-blue spurt of flame that died quickly but lingered on as a vivid after-image. He smelled the acrid stench of burnt powder filling his lungs and he dropped the gun abruptly.

The intensity of his feelings died and he hung the gun and cartridge belt upon the wall. Next he lifted the jars of diamonds and turned them bottom upward, dumping the white pellets upon the ground. One by one he picked them up and peeled the tissue paper from them and piled them in a neat heap. He wiped his sweaty hands on his trousers, lit a cigarette, and commenced playing another game. He imagined that he was a rich man who lived aboveground in the obscene sunshine and he was strolling through a park of a summer morning, smiling, nodding to his neighbors, sucking an after-breakfast cigar. Many times he crossed the floor of the cave, avoiding the diamonds with his feet, yet subtly gauging his footsteps so that his shoes, wet with sewer slime, would strike the diamonds at some undetermined moment. After twenty minutes of sauntering, his right foot smashed into the heap and diamonds lay scattered in all directions, glinting with a million tiny chuckles of icy laughter. Oh, shucks, he mumbled in mock regret, intrigued by the damage he had wrought. He continued walking, ignoring the brittle fire. He felt that he had a glorious victory locked in his heart.

He stooped and flung the diamonds more evenly over the floor and they showered rich sparks, collaborating with him. He went over the floor and trampled the stones just deep enough for them to be faintly visible, as though they were set delicately in the prongs of a thousand rings. A ghostly light bathed the cave. He sat on the chest and frowned. Maybe *anything's* right, he mumbled. Yes, if the world as men had made it was right, then anything else was right, any act a man took to satisfy himself, murder, theft, torture.

He straightened with a start. What was happening to him? He was drawn to these crazy thoughts, yet they made him feel vaguely guilty. He would stretch out upon the ground, then get up; he would want to crawl again through the holes he had dug, but would restrain himself; he would think of going again up into the streets, but fear would hold him still. He stood in the middle of the cave, surrounded by green walls and a laughing floor, trembling. He was going to do something, but what? Yes, he was afraid of himself, afraid of doing some nameless thing.

To control himself, he turned on the radio. A melancholy piece of music rose. Brooding over the diamonds on the floor was like looking up into a sky full of restless stars; then the illusion turned into its opposite: he was high up in the air looking down at the twinkling lights of a sprawling city. The music ended and a man recited news events. In the same attitude in which he had contemplated the city, so now, as he heard the cultivated tone, he looked down upon land and sea as men fought, as cities were razed, as planes scattered death upon open towns, as long lines of trenches wavered and broke. He heard the names of generals and the names of mountains and the names of countries and the names and numbers of divisions that were in action on different battle fronts. He saw black smoke billowing from the stacks of warships as they neared each other over wastes of water and he heard their huge guns thunder as red-hot shells screamed across the surface of night seas. He saw hundreds of planes wheeling and droning in the sky and heard the clatter of machine guns as they fought each other and he saw planes falling in plumes of smoke and blaze of fire. He saw steel tanks rumbling across fields of ripe wheat to meet other tanks and there was a loud clang of steel as numberless tanks collided. He saw troops with fixed bayonets charging in waves against other troops who held fixed bayonets and men groaned as steel ripped into their bodies and they went down to die . . . The voice of the radio faded and he was staring at the diamonds on the floor at his feet.

He shut off the radio, fighting an irrational compulsion to act. He walked aimlessly about the cave, touching the walls with his finger tips. Suddenly he stood still. *What was the matter with him?* Yes, he knew . . . It was these walls; these crazy walls were filling him with a wild urge to climb out into the dark sunshine aboveground. Quickly he doused the light to banish the shouting walls, then sat again upon the tool chest. Yes, he was trapped. His muscles were flexed taut and sweat ran down his face. He knew now that he could not stay here and he could not go out. He lit a cigarette with shaking fingers; the match flame revealed the green-papered walls with militant distinctness; the purple on the gun barrel glinted like a threat; the meat cleaver brooded with its eloquent splotches of blood; the mound of silver and copper smoldered angrily; the diamonds winked at him from the floor; and the gold watches ticked and trembled, crowning time the king of consciousness, defining the limits of living . . . The match blaze died and he bolted from where he stood and collided brutally with the nails upon the walls. The spell was broken. He shuddered, feeling that, in spite of his fear, sooner or later he would go up into that dead sunshine and somehow say something to somebody about all this.

He sat again upon the tool chest. Fatigue weighed upon his forehead and eyes. Minutes passed and he relaxed. He dozed, but his imagination was alert. He saw himself rising, wading again in the sweeping water of the sewer; he came to a manhole and climbed out and was amazed to discover that he had hoisted himself into a room filled with armed policemen who were watching him intently. He jumped awake in the dark; he had not moved. He sighed, closed his eyes, and slept again; this time his imagination designed a scheme of protection for him. His dreaming made him feel that he was standing in a room watching over his own nude body lying stiff and cold upon a white table. At the far end of the room he saw a crowd of people huddled in a corner, afraid of his body. Though lying dead upon the table, he was standing in some mysterious way at his side, warding off the people, guarding his body, and laughing to himself as he observed the situation. They're scared of me, he thought.

He awakened with a start, leaped to his feet, and stood in the center of the black cave. It was a full minute before he moved again. He hovered between sleeping and waking, unprotected, a prey of wild fears. He could neither see nor hear. One part of him was asleep; his blood coursed slowly and his flesh was numb. On the other hand he was roused to a strange, high pitch of tension. He lifted his fingers to his face, as though about to weep. Gradually his hands lowered and he struck a match, looking about, expecting to see a door through which he could walk to safety: but there was no door, only the green walls and the moving floor. The match flame died and it was dark again.

Five minutes later he was still standing when the thought came to him that he had been asleep. Yes . . . But he was not yet fully awake; he was still queerly blind and deaf. How long had he slept? Where was he? Then suddenly he recalled the green-papered walls of the cave and in the same instant he heard loud singing coming from the church beyond the wall. Yes, they woke me up, he muttered. He hoisted himself and lay atop the bed of pipes and brought his face to the narrow slit. Men and women stood here and there between pews. A song ended and a young black girl tossed back her head and closed her eyes and broke plaintively into another hymn:

> Glad, glad, glad, oh, so glad
> I got Jesus in my soul . . .

Those few words were all she sang, but what her words did not say, her emotions said as she repeated the lines, varying the mood and tempo, making her tone express meanings which her conscious mind did not know. Another woman melted her voice with the girl's, and then an old man's voice merged with that of the two women. Soon the entire congregation was singing:

> Glad, glad, glad, oh, so glad
> I got Jesus in my soul . . .

They're wrong, he whispered in the lyric darkness. He felt that their search for a happiness they could never find made them feel that they had committed some dreadful offense which they could not remember or understand. He was now in possession of the feeling that had gripped him when he had first come into the underground. It came to him in a series of questions: Why was this sense of guilt so seemingly innate, so easy to come by, to think, to feel, so verily physical? It seemed that when one felt this guilt one was retracing in one's feelings a faint pattern designed long before; it seemed that one was always trying to remember a gigantic shock that had left a haunting impression upon one's body which one could not forget or shake off, but which had been forgotten by the conscious mind, creating in one's life a state of eternal anxiety.

He had to tear himself away from this; he got down from the pipes. His nerves were so taut that he seemed to feel his brain pushing through his skull. He felt that he had to do something, but he could not figure out what it was. Yet he knew that if he stood here until he made up his mind, he would never move. He crawled through the hole he had made in the brick wall and the exertion afforded him respite from tension. When he entered the basement of the radio store, he stopped in fear, hearing loud voices.

"Come on, boy! Tell us what you did with the radio!"

"Mister, I didn't steal the radio! I swear!"

He heard a dull thumping sound and he imagined a boy being struck violently.

"Please, mister!"

"Did you take it to a pawn shop?"

"No, sir! I didn't steal the radio! I got a radio at home," the boy's voice pleaded hysterically. "Go to my home and look!"

There came to his ears the sound of another blow. It was so funny that he had to clap his hand over his mouth to keep from laughing out loud. They're beating some poor boy, he whispered to himself, shaking his head. He felt a sort of distant pity for the boy and wondered if he ought to bring back the radio and leave it in the basement. No. Perhaps it was a good thing that they were beating the boy; perhaps the beating would bring to the boy's attention, for the first time in his life, the secret of his existence, the guilt that he could never get rid of.

Smiling, he scampered over a coal pile and stood again in the basement of the building where he had stolen the money and jewelry. He
lifted himself into the areaway, climbed the rain pipe, and squinted
through a two-inch opening of window. The guilty familiarity of what
he saw made his muscles tighten. Framed before him in a bright tableau
of daylight was the night watchman sitting upon the edge of a chair,
stripped to the waist, his head sagging forward, his eyes red and puffy.
The watchman's face and shoulders were stippled with red and black
welts. Back of the watchman stood the safe, the steel door wide open
showing the empty vault. Yes, they think he did it, he mused.

Footsteps sounded in the room and a man in a blue suit passed in
front of him, then another, then still another. Policemen, he breathed.
Yes, they were trying to make the watchman confess, just as they had
once made him confess to a crime he had not done. He stared into
the room, trying to recall something. Oh . . . Those were the same
policemen who had beaten him, had made him sign that paper when
he had been too tired and sick to care. Now, they were doing the same
thing to the watchman. His heart pounded as he saw one of the policemen shake a finger into the watchman's face.

"Why don't you admit it's an inside job, Thompson?" the policeman
said.

"I've told you all I know," the watchman mumbled through swollen
lips.

"But nobody was here but you!" the policeman shouted.

"I was sleeping," the watchman said. "It was wrong, but I was sleeping all that night!"

"Stop telling us that lie!"

"It's the truth!"

"When did you get the combination?"

"I don't know how to open the safe," the watchman said.

He clung to the rain pipe, tense; he wanted to laugh, but he controlled himself. He felt a great sense of power; yes, he could go back
to the cave, rip the money off the walls, pick up the diamonds and
rings, and bring them here and write a note, telling them where to
look for their foolish toys. No . . . What good would that do? It was
not worth the effort. The watchman was guilty; although he was not
guilty of the crime of which he had been accused, he was guilty, had
always been guilty. The only thing that worried him was that the man
who had been really stealing was not being accused. But he consoled
himself: they'll catch him sometime during his life.

He saw one of the policemen slap the watchman across the mouth.

"Come clean, you bastard!"

"I've told you all I know," the watchman mumbled like a child.

One of the police went to the rear of the watchman's chair and
jerked it from under him; the watchman pitched forward upon his face.

"Get up!" a policeman said.

Trembling, the watchman pulled himself up and sat limply again in the chair.

"Now, are you going to talk?"

"I've told you all I know," the watchman gasped.

"Where did you hide the stuff?"

"I didn't take it!"

"Thompson, your brains are in your feet," one of the policemen said. "We're going to string you up and get them back into your skull."

He watched the policemen clamp handcuffs on the watchman's wrists and ankles; then they lifted the watchman and swung him upside-down and hoisted his feet to the edge of a door. The watchman hung, head down, his eyes bulging. They're crazy, he whispered to himself as he clung to the ridges of the pipe.

"You going to talk?" a policeman shouted into the watchman's ear.

He heard the watchman groan.

"We'll let you hang there till you talk, see?"

He saw the watchman close his eyes.

"Let's take 'im down. He passed out," a policeman said.

He grinned as he watched them take the body down and dump it carelessly upon the floor. The policeman took off the handcuffs.

"Let 'im come to. Let's get a smoke," a policeman said.

The three policemen left the scope of his vision. A door slammed. He had an impulse to yell to the watchman that he could escape through the hole in the basement and live with him in the cave. But he wouldn't understand, he told himself. After a moment he saw the watchman rise and stand swaying from weakness. He stumbled across the room to a desk, opened a drawer, and took out a gun. He's going to kill himself, he thought, intent, eager, detached, yearning to see the end of the man's actions. As the watchman stared vaguely about he lifted the gun to his temple; he stood like that for some minutes, biting his lips until a line of blood etched its way down a corner of his chin. No, he oughtn't do that, he said to himself in a mood of pity.

"Don't!" he half whispered and half yelled.

The watchman looked wildly about; he had heard him. But it did not help; there was a loud report and the watchman's head jerked violently and he fell like a log and lay prone, the gun clattering over the floor.

The three policemen came running into the room with drawn guns. One of the policemen knelt and rolled the watchman's body over and stared at a ragged, scarlet hole in the temple.

"Our hunch was right," the kneeling policeman said. "He was guilty, all right."

"Well, this ends the case," another policeman said.

"He knew he was licked," the third one said with grim satisfaction.

He eased down the rain pipe, crawled back through the holes he had made, and went back into his cave. A fever burned in his bones. He had to act, yet he was afraid. His eyes stared in the darkness as though propped open by invisible hands, as though they had become lidless. His muscles were rigid and he stood for what seemed to him a thousand years.

When he moved again his actions were informed with precision, his muscular system reinforced from a reservoir of energy. He crawled through the hole of earth, dropped into the gray sewer current, and sloshed ahead. When his right foot went forward at a street intersection, he fell backward and shot down into water. In a spasm of terror his right hand grabbed the concrete ledge of a down-curve and he felt the streaking water tugging violently at his body. The current reached his neck and for a moment he was still. He knew that if he moved clumsily he would be sucked under. He held onto the ledge with both hands and slowly pulled himself up. He sighed, standing once more in the sweeping water, thankful that he had missed death.

He waded on through sludge, moving with care, until he came to a web of light sifting down from a manhole cover. He saw steel hooks running up the side of the sewer wall; he caught hold and lifted himself and put his shoulder to the cover and moved it an inch. A crash of sound came to him as he looked into a hot glare of sunshine through which blurred shapes moved. Fear scalded him and he dropped back into the pallid current and stood paralyzed in the shadows. A heavy car rumbled past overhead, jarring the pavement, warning him to stay in his world of dark light, knocking the cover back into place with an imperious clang.

He did not know how much fear he felt, for fear claimed him completely; yet it was not a fear of the police or of people, but a cold dread at the thought of the actions he knew he would perform if he went out into that cruel sunshine. His mind said no; his body said yes; and his mind could not understand his feelings. A low whine broke from him and he was in the act of uncoiling. He climbed upward and heard the faint honking of auto horns. Like a frantic cat clutching a rag, he clung to the steel prongs and heaved his shoulder against the cover and pushed it off halfway. For a split second his eyes were drowned in the terror of yellow light and he was in a deeper darkness than he had ever known in the underground.

Partly out of the hole, he blinked, regaining enough sight to make out meaningful forms. An odd thing was happening: No one was rushing forward to challenge him. He had imagined the moment of his emergence as a desperate tussle with men who wanted to cart him off to be killed; instead, life froze about him as the traffic stopped. He pushed the cover aside, stood, swaying in a world so fragile that he expected it to collapse and drop him into some deep void. But nobody seemed to pay him heed. The cars were now swerving to shun him and the gaping hole.

"Why in hell don't you put up a red light, dummy?" a raucous voice yelled.

He understood; they thought that he was a sewer workman. He walked toward the sidewalk, weaving unsteadily through the moving traffic.

"Look where you're going, nigger!"

"That's right! Stay there and get killed!"

"You blind, you bastard?"

"Go home and sleep your drunk off!"

A policeman stood at the curb, looking in the opposite direction. When he passed the policeman, he feared that he would be grabbed, but nothing happened. Where was he? Was this real? He wanted to look about to get his bearings, but felt that something awful would happen to him if he did. He wandered into a spacious doorway of a store that sold men's clothing and saw his reflection in a long mirror: his cheekbones protruded from a hairy black face; his greasy cap was perched askew upon his head and his eyes were red and glassy. His shirt and trousers were caked with mud and hung loosely. His hands were gummed with a black stickiness. He threw back his head and laughed so loudly that passers-by stopped and stared.

He ambled on down the sidewalk, not having the merest notion of where he was going. Yet, sleeping within him, was the drive to go somewhere and say something to somebody. Half an hour later his ears caught the sound of spirited singing.

> The Lamb, the Lamb, the Lamb
> I hear thy voice a-calling
> The Lamb, the Lamb, the Lamb
> I feel thy grace a-falling

A church! he exclaimed. He broke into a run and came to brick steps leading downward to a subbasement. This is it! The church into which he had peered. Yes, he was going in and tell them. What? He did not know; but, once face to face with them, he would think of what to say. Must be Sunday, he mused. He ran down the steps and jerked the door open; the church was crowded and a deluge of song swept over him.

> The Lamb, the Lamb, the Lamb
> Tell me again your story
> The Lamb, the Lamb, the Lamb
> Flood my soul with your glory

He stared at the singing faces with a trembling smile.

"Say!" he shouted.

Many turned to look at him, but the song rolled on. His arm was jerked violently.

"I'm sorry, Brother, but you can't do that in here," a man said.

"But, mister!"

"You can't act rowdy in God's house," the man said.

"He's filthy," another man said.

"But I want to tell 'em," he said loudly.

"He stinks," someone muttered.

The song had stopped, but at once another one began.

> *Oh, wondrous sight upon the cross*
> *Vision sweet and divine*
> *Oh, wondrous sight upon the cross*
> *Full of such love sublime*

He attempted to twist away, but other hands grabbed him and rushed him into the doorway.

"Let me alone!" he screamed, struggling.

"Get out!"

"He's drunk," somebody said. "He ought to be ashamed!"

"He acts crazy!"

He felt that he was failing and he grew frantic.

"But, mister, let me tell—"

"Get away from this door, or I'll call the police!"

He stared, his trembling smile fading in a sense of wonderment.

"The police," he repeated vacantly.

"Now, get!"

He was pushed toward the brick steps and the door banged shut. The waves of song came.

> *Oh, wondrous sight, wondrous sight*
> *Lift my heavy heart above*
> *Oh, wondrous sight, wondrous sight*
> *Fill my weary soul with love*

He was smiling again now. Yes, the police . . . That was it! Why had he not thought of it before? The idea had been deep down in him, and only now did it assume supreme importance. He looked up and saw a street sign: COURT STREET—HARTSDALE AVENUE. He turned and walked northward, his mind filled with the image of the police station. Yes, that was where they had beaten him, accused him, and had made him sign a confession of his guilt. He would go there and clear up everything, make a statement. What statement? He did not know. He was the statement, and since it was all so clear to him, surely he would be able to make it clear to others.

He came to the corner of Hartsdale Avenue and turned westward. Yeah, there's the station . . . A policeman came down the steps and walked past him without a glance. He mounted the stone steps and went through the door, paused; he was in a hallway where several policemen were standing, talking, smoking. One turned to him.

"What do you want, boy?"

He looked at the policeman and laughed.

"What in hell are you laughing about?" the policeman asked.

He stopped laughing and stared. His whole being was full of what he wanted to say to them, but he could not say it.

"Are you looking for the Desk Sergeant?"

"Yes, sir," he said quickly; then: "Oh, no, sir."

"Well, make up your mind, now."

Four policemen grouped themselves around him.

"I'm looking for the men," he said.

"What men?"

Peculiarly, at that moment he could not remember the names of the policemen; he recalled their beating him, the confession he had signed, and how he had run away from them. He saw the cave next to the church, the money on the walls, the guns, the rings, the cleaver, the watches, and the diamonds on the floor.

"They brought me here," he began.

"When?"

His mind flew back over the blur of the time lived in the underground blackness. He had no idea of how much time had elapsed, but the intensity of what had happened to him told him that it could not have transpired in a short space of time, yet his mind told him that time must have been brief.

"It was a long time ago." He spoke like a child relating a dimly remembered dream. "It was a long time," he repeated, following the promptings of his emotions. "They beat me . . . I was scared . . . I ran away."

A policeman raised a finger to his temple and made a derisive circle.

"Nuts," the policeman said.

"Do you know what place this is, boy?"

"Yes, sir. The police station," he answered sturdily, almost proudly.

"Well, who do you want to see?"

"The men," he said again, feeling that surely they knew the men. "You know the men," he said in a hurt tone.

"What's your name?"

He opened his lips to answer and no words came. He had forgotten. But what did it matter if he had? It was not important.

"Where do you live?"

Where did he live? It had been so long ago since he had lived up here in this strange world that he felt it was foolish even to try to remember. Then for a moment the old mood that had dominated him in the underground surged back. He leaned forward and spoke eagerly.

"They said I killed the woman."

"What woman?" a policeman asked.

"And I signed a paper that said I was guilty," he went on, ignoring their questions. "Then I ran off . . ."

"Did you run off from an institution?"

"No, sir," he said, blinking and shaking his head. "I came from under the ground. I pushed off the manhole cover and climbed out . . ."

"All right, now," a policeman said, placing an arm about his shoulder. "We'll send you to the psycho and you'll be taken care of."

"Maybe he's a Fifth Columnist!" a policeman shouted.

There was laughter and, despite his anxiety, he joined in. But the laughter lasted so long that it irked him.

"I got to find those men," he protested mildly.

"Say, boy, what have you been drinking?"

"Water," he said. "I got some water in a basement."

"Were the men you ran away from dressed in white, boy?"

"No, sir," he said brightly. "They were men like you."

An elderly policeman caught hold of his arm.

"Try and think hard. Where did they pick you up?"

He knitted his brows in an effort to remember, but he was blank inside. The policeman stood before him demanding logical answers and he could no longer think with his mind; he thought with his feelings and no words came.

"I was guilty," he said. "Oh, no, sir. I wasn't then, I mean, mister!"

"Aw, talk sense. Now, where did they pick you up?"

He felt challenged and his mind began reconstructing events in reverse; his feelings ranged back over the long hours and he saw the cave, the sewer, the bloody room where it was said that a woman had been killed.

"Oh, yes, sir," he said, smiling. "I was coming from Mrs. Wooten's."

"Who is she?"

"I work for her."

"Where does she live?"

"Next door to Mrs. Peabody, the woman who was killed."

The policemen were very quiet now, looking at him intently.

"What do you know about Mrs. Peabody's death, boy?"

"Nothing, sir. But they said I killed her. But it doesn't make any difference. I'm guilty!"

"What are you talking about, boy?"

His smile faded and he was possessed with memories of the underground; he saw the cave next to the church and his lips moved to speak. But how could he say it? The distance between what he felt and what these men meant was vast. Something told him, as he stood there looking into their faces, that he would never be able to tell them, that they would never believe him even if he told them.

"All the people I saw was guilty," he began slowly.

"Aw, nuts," a policemen muttered.

"Say," another policeman said, "that Peabody woman was killed over on Winewood. That's Number Ten's beat."

"Where's Number Ten?" a policeman asked.

"Upstairs in the swing room," someone answered.

"Take this boy up, Sam," a policeman ordered.

"O.K. Come along, boy."

An elderly policeman caught hold of his arm and led him up a flight of wooden stairs, down a long hall, and to a door.

"Squad Ten!" the policeman called through the door.

"What?" a gruff voice answered.

"Someone to see you!"

"About what?"

The old policeman pushed the door in and then shoved him into the room.

He stared, his lips open, his heart barely beating. Before him were the three policemen who had picked him up and had beaten him to extract the confession. They were seated about a small table, playing cards. The air was blue with smoke and sunshine poured through a high window, lighting up fantastic smoke shapes. He saw one of the policemen look up; the policeman's face was tired and a cigarette drooped limply from one corner of his mouth and both of his fat, puffy eyes were squinting and his hands gripped his cards.

"Lawson!" the man exclaimed.

The moment the man's name sounded he remembered the names of all of them: Lawson, Murphy, and Johnson. How simple it was. He waited, smiling, wondering how they would react when they knew that he had come back.

"Looking for me?" the man who had been called Lawson mumbled, sorting his cards. "For what?"

So far only Murphy, the red-headed one, had recognized him.

"Don't you-all remember me?" he blurted, running to the table.

All three of the policemen were looking at him now. Lawson, who seemed the leader, jumped to his feet.

"Where in hell have you been?"

"Do you know 'im, Lawson?" the old policeman asked.

"Huh?" Lawson frowned. "Oh, yes. I'll handle 'im." The old policeman left the room and Lawson crossed to the door and turned the key in the lock. "Come here, boy," he ordered in a cold tone.

He did not move; he looked from face to face. Yes, he would tell them about his cave.

"He looks batty to me," Johnson said, the one who had not spoken before.

"Why in hell did you come back here?" Lawson said.

"I—I just didn't want to run away no more," he said. "I'm all right, now." He paused; the men's attitude puzzled him.

"You've been hiding, huh?" Lawson asked in a tone that denoted that he had not heard his previous words. "You told us you were sick, and when we left you in the room, you jumped out of the window and ran away."

Panic filled him. Yes, they were indifferent to what he would say! They were waiting for him to speak and they would laugh at him. He had to rescue himself from this bog; he had to force the reality of himself upon them.

"Mister, I took a sackful of money and pasted it on the walls . . ." he began.

"I'll be damned," Lawson said.

"Listen," said Murphy, "let me tell you something for your own good. We don't want you, see? You're free, free as air. Now go home and forget it. It was all a mistake. We caught the guy who did the Peabody job. He wasn't colored at all. He was an Eyetalian."

"Shut up!" Lawson yelled. "Have you no sense!"

"But I want to tell 'im," Murphy said.

"We can't let this crazy fool go," Lawson exploded. "He acts nuts, but this may be a stunt . . ."

"I was down in the basement," he began in a childlike tone as though repeating a lesson learned by heart; "and I went into a movie . . ." His voice failed. He was getting ahead of his story. First, he ought to tell them about the singing in the church, but what words could he use? He looked at them appealingly. "I went into a shop and took a sackful of money and diamonds and watches and rings . . . I didn't steal 'em; I'll give 'em all back. I just took 'em to play with . . ." He paused, stunned by their disbelieving eyes.

Lawson lit a cigarette and looked at him coldly.

"What did you do with the money?" he asked in a quiet, waiting voice.

"I pasted the hundred-dollar bills on the walls."

"What walls?" Lawson asked.

"The walls of the dirt room," he said, smiling, "the room next to the church. I hung up the rings and the watches and I stamped the diamonds into the dirt . . ." He saw that they were not understanding what he was saying. He grew frantic to make them believe, his voice tumbled on eagerly. "I saw a dead baby and a dead man . . ."

"Aw, you're nuts," Lawson snarled, shoving him into a chair.

"But, mister . . ."

"Johnson, where's the paper he signed?" Lawson asked.

"What paper?"

"The confession, fool!"

Johnson pulled out his billfold and extracted a crumpled piece of paper.

"Yes, sir, mister," he said, stretching forth his hand. "That's the paper I signed . . ."

Lawson slapped him and he would have toppled had his chair not struck a wall behind him. Lawson scratched a match and held the paper over the flame; the confession burned down to Lawson's fingertips.

He stared, thunderstruck; the sun of the underground was fleeing and the terrible darkness of the day stood before him. They did not believe him, but he *had* to make them believe him!

"But, mister . . ."

"It's going to be all right, boy," Lawson said with a quiet, soothing laugh. "I've burned your confession, see? You didn't sign anything." Lawson came close to him with the black ashes cupped in his palm. "You don't remember a thing about this, do you?"

"Don't you-all be scared of me," he pleaded, sensing their uneasiness. "I'll sign another paper, if you want me to. I'll show you the cave."

"What's your game, boy?" Lawson asked suddenly.

"What are you trying to find out?" Johnson asked.

"Who sent you here?" Murphy demanded.

"Nobody sent me, mister," he said. "I just want to show you the room . . ."

"Aw, he's plumb bats," Murphy said. "Let's ship 'im to the psycho."

"No," Lawson said. "He's playing a game and I wish to God I knew what it was."

There flashed through his mind a definite way to make them believe him; he rose from the chair with nervous excitement.

"Mister, I saw the night watchman blow his brains out because you accused him of stealing," he told them. "But he didn't steal the money and diamonds. I took 'em."

Tigerishly Lawson grabbed his collar and lifted him bodily.

"*Who told you about that?*"

"Don't get excited, Lawson," Johnson said. "He read about it in the papers."

Lawson flung him away.

"He couldn't have," Lawson said, pulling papers from his pocket. "I haven't turned in the reports yet."

"Then how *did* he find out?" Murphy asked.

"Let's get out of here," Lawson said with quick resolution. "Listen, boy, we're going to take you to a nice, quiet place, see?"

"Yes, sir," he said. "And I'll show you the underground."

"Goddamn," Lawson muttered, fastening the gun at his hip. He narrowed his eyes at Johnson and Murphy. "Listen," he spoke just above a whisper, "say nothing about this, you hear?"

"O.K.," Johnson said.

"Sure," Murphy said.

Lawson unlocked the door and Johnson and Murphy led him down the stairs. The hallway was crowded with policemen.

"What have you got there, Lawson?"

"What did he do, Lawson?"

"He's psycho, ain't he, Lawson?"

Lawson did not answer; Johnson and Murphy led him to the car parked at the curb, pushed him into the back seat. Lawson got behind the steering wheel and the car rolled forward.

"What's up, Lawson?" Murphy asked.

"Listen," Lawson began slowly, "we tell the papers that he spilled about the Peabody job, then he escapes. The Wop is caught and we tell the papers that we steered them wrong to trap the real guy, see? Now this dope shows up and acts nuts. If we let him go, he'll squeal that we framed him, see?"

"I'm all right, mister," he said, feeling Murphy's and Johnson's arms locked rigidly into his. "I'm guilty . . . I'll show you everything in the underground. I laughed and laughed . . ."

"Shut that fool up!" Lawson ordered.

Johnson tapped him across the head with a blackjack and he fell back against the seat cushion, dazed.

"Yes, sir," he mumbled. "I'm all right."

The car sped along Hartsdale Avenue, then swung onto Pine Street and rolled to State Street, then turned south. It slowed to a stop, turned in the middle of a block, and headed north again.

"You're going around in circles, Lawson," Murphy said.

Lawson did not answer; he was hunched over the steering wheel. Finally he pulled the car to a stop at the curb.

"Say, boy, tell us the truth," Lawson asked quietly. "Where did you hide?"

"I didn't hide, mister."

The three policemen were staring at him now; he felt that for the first time they were willing to understand him.

"Then what happened?"

"Mister, when I looked through all of those holes and saw how people were living, I loved 'em. . . ."

"Cut out that crazy talk!" Lawson snapped. "Who sent you back here?"

"Nobody, mister."

"Maybe he's talking straight," Johnson ventured.

"All right," Lawson said. "Nobody hid you. Now, tell us *where* you hid."

"I went underground . . ."

"What goddamn underground do you keep talking about?"

"I just went . . ." He paused and looked into the street, then pointed to a manhole cover. "I went down in there and stayed."

"In the *sewer?*"

"Yes, sir."

The policemen burst into a sudden laugh and ended quickly. Lawson swung the car around and drove to Woodside Avenue; he brought the car to a stop in front of a tall apartment building.

"What're we going to do, Lawson?" Murphy asked.

"I'm taking him up to my place," Lawson said. "We've got to wait until night. There's nothing we can do now."

They took him out of the car and led him into a vestibule.

"Take the steps," Lawson muttered.

They led him up four flights of stairs and into the living room of a small apartment. Johnson and Murphy let go of his arms and he stood uncertainly in the middle of the room.

"Now, listen, boy," Lawson began, "forget those wild lies you've been telling us. Where did you hide?"

"I just went underground, like I told you."

The room rocked with laughter. Lawson went to a cabinet and got a bottle of whisky; he placed glasses for Johnson and Murphy. The three of them drank.

He felt that he could not explain himself to them. He tried to muster all the sprawling images that floated in him; the images stood out sharply in his mind, but he could not make them have the meaning for others that they had for him. He felt so helpless that he began to cry.

"He's nuts, all right," Johnson said. "All nuts cry like that."

Murphy crossed the room and slapped him.

"Stop that raving!"

A sense of excitement flooded him; he ran to Murphy and grabbed his arm.

"Let me show you the cave," he said. "Come on, and you'll see!"

Before he knew it a sharp blow had clipped him on the chin; darkness covered his eyes. He dimly felt himself being lifted and laid out on the sofa. He heard low voices and struggled to rise, but hard hands held him down. His brain was clearing now. He pulled to a sitting posture and stared with glazed eyes. It had grown dark. How long had he been out?

"Say, boy," Lawson said soothingly, "will you show us the underground?"

His eyes shone and his heart swelled with gratitude. Lawson believed him! He rose, glad; he grabbed Lawson's arm, making the policeman spill whisky from the glass to his shirt.

"Take it easy, goddammit," Lawson said.

"Yes, sir."

"O.K. We'll take you down. But you'd better be telling us the truth, you hear?"

He clapped his hands in wild joy.

"I'll show you everything!"

He had triumphed at last! He would now do what he had felt was compelling him all along. At last he would be free of his burden.

"Take 'im down," Lawson ordered.

They led him down to the vestibule; when he reached the sidewalk he saw that it was night and a fine rain was falling.

"It's just like when I went down," he told them.

"What?" Lawson asked.

"The rain," he said, sweeping his arm in a wide arc. "It was raining when I went down. The rain made the water rise and lift the cover off."

"Cut it out," Lawson snapped.

They did not believe him now, but they would. A mood of high selflessness throbbed in him. He could barely contain his rising spirits. They would see what he had seen; they would feel what he had felt. He would lead them through all the holes he had dug and . . . He wanted to make a hymn, prance about in physical ecstasy, throw his arms about the policemen in fellowship.

"Get into the car," Lawson ordered.

He climbed in and Johnson and Murphy sat at either side of him; Lawson slid behind the steering wheel and started the motor.

"Now, tell us where to go," Lawson said.

"It's right around the corner from where the lady was killed," he said.

The car rolled slowly and he closed his eyes, remembering the song he had heard in the church, the song that had wrought him to such a high pitch of terror and pity. He sang softly, lolling his head:

> Glad, glad, glad, oh, so glad
> I got Jesus in my soul . . .

"Mister," he said, stopping his song, "you ought to see how funny the rings look on the wall." He giggled. "I fired a pistol, too. Just once, to see how it felt."

"What do you suppose he's suffering from?" Johnson asked.

"Delusions of grandeur, maybe," Murphy said.

"Maybe it's because he lives in a white man's world," Lawson said.

"Say, boy, what did you eat down there?" Murphy asked, prodding Johnson anticipatorily with his elbow.

"Pears, oranges, bananas, and pork chops," he said.

The car filled with laughter.

"You didn't eat any watermelon?" Lawson asked, smiling.

"No, sir," he answered calmly. "I didn't see any."

The three policemen roared harder and louder.

"Boy, you're sure some case," Murphy said, shaking his head in wonder.

The car pulled to a curb.

"All right, boy," Lawson said. "Tell us where to go."

He peered through the rain and saw where he had gone down. The streets, save for a few dim lamps glowing softly through the rain, were dark and empty.

"Right there, mister," he said, pointing.

"Come on; let's take a look," Lawson said.

"Well, suppose he did hide down there," Johnson said, "what is that supposed to prove?"

"I don't believe he hid down there," Murphy said.

"It won't hurt to look," Lawson said. "Leave things to me."

Lawson got out of the car and looked up and down the street.

He was eager to show them the cave now. If he could show them what he had seen, then they would feel what he had felt and they in turn would show it to others and those others would feel as they had felt, and soon everybody would be governed by the same impulse of pity.

"Take 'im out," Lawson ordered.

Johnson and Murphy opened the door and pushed him out; he stood trembling in the rain, smiling. Again Lawson looked up and down the street; no one was in sight. The rain came down hard, slanting like black wires across the windswept air.

"All right," Lawson said. "Show us."

He walked to the center of the street, stopped and inserted a finger in one of the tiny holes of the cover and tugged, but he was too weak to budge it.

"Did you really go down in there, boy?" Lawson asked; there was a doubt in his voice.

"Yes, sir. Just a minute. I'll show you."

"Help 'im get that damn thing off," Lawson said.

Johnson stepped forward and lifted the cover; it clanged against the wet pavement. The hole gaped round and black.

"I went down in there," he announced with pride.

Lawson gazed at him for a long time without speaking, then he reached his right hand to his holster and drew his gun.

"Mister, I got a gun just like that down there," he said, laughing and looking into Lawson's face. "I fired it once then hung it on the wall. I'll show you."

"Show us how you went down," Lawson said quietly.

"I'll go down first, mister, and then you-all can come after me, hear?" He spoke like a little boy playing a game.

"Sure, sure," Lawson said soothingly. "Go ahead. We'll come."

He looked brightly at the policemen; he was bursting with happiness. He bent down and placed his hands on the rim of the hole and sat on the edge, his feet dangling into watery darkness. He heard the familiar drone of the gray current. He lowered his body and hung for a moment by his fingers, then he went downward on the steel prongs, hand over hand, until he reached the last rung. He dropped and his feet hit the water and he felt the stiff current trying to suck him away. He balanced himself quickly and looked back upward at the policemen.

"Come on, you-all!" he yelled, casting his voice above the rustling at his feet.

The vague forms that towered above him in the rain did not move. He laughed, feeling that they doubted him. But, once they saw the things he had done, they would never doubt again.

"Come on! The cave isn't far!" he yelled. "But be careful when your feet hit the water, because the current's pretty rough down here!"

Lawson still held the gun. Murphy and Johnson looked at Lawson quizzically.

"What are we going to do, Lawson?" Murphy asked.

"We are not going to follow that crazy nigger down into that sewer, are we?" Johnson asked.

"Come on, you-all!" he begged in a shout.

He saw Lawson raise the gun and point it directly at him. Lawson's face twitched, as though he were hesitating.

Then there was a thunderous report and a streak of fire ripped through his chest. He was hurled into the water, flat on his back. He looked in amazement at the blurred white faces looming above him. They shot me, he said to himself. The water flowed past him, blossoming in foam about his arms, his legs, and his head. His jaw sagged and his mouth gaped soundless. A vast pain gripped his head and gradually squeezed out consciousness. As from a great distance he heard hollow voices.

"What did you shoot him for, Lawson?"

"I had to."

"Why?"

"You've got to shoot his kind. They'd wreck things."

As though in a deep dream, he heard a metallic clank; they had replaced the manhole cover, shutting out forever the sound of wind and rain. From overhead came the muffled roar of a powerful motor and the swish of a speeding car. He felt the strong tide pushing him slowly into the middle of the sewer, turning him about. For a split second there hovered before his eyes the glittering cave, the shouting walls, and the laughing floor . . . Then his mouth was full of thick, bitter water. The current spun him around. He sighed and closed his eyes, a whirling object rushing alone in the darkness, veering, tossing, lost in the heart of the earth.

QUESTIONS

1. Why is it significant that the man forgets his name after he goes underground? What other reasons might Wright have had for wanting his character to be nameless?

2. Study Wright's descriptions of the world aboveground and the world underground, noting particularly his references to light and dark. How do the two worlds compare? What conclusions can be drawn from this comparison about the symbolic function of the underground in this story?

3. This story has the effect of a nightmare. How is this effect

achieved? In what way does it underscore the meaning and theme of the story?

4. Wright refers repeatedly to the movie, the church, the dead baby, the nude corpse, the diamonds, and he says the man felt that "some dim meaning linked them together." What "link" has the man found?

5. Having pasted the money on the wall, the man for the first time in his life felt free. He wanted to "run from this cave and yell his discovery to the world." What has he discovered? Why has this discovery given him a sense of freedom?

6. One of the central moral questions raised in this story is that of guilt—what it is and how it affects human lives. Why, for example, does the man feel guilty for the crime he has not committed and yet not feel guilty for stealing the cleaver, the radio, and the money? Why, when he goes to the police at the end, does he say, "All the people I saw was guilty"? What is Wright saying about the real causes and meaning of guilt in the world? Why is this important to the story?

7. Wright says of his underground man that "some part of him was trying to remember the world he had left, and another part of him did not want to remember it. . . . He possessed them now more completely than he had ever possessed them when he had lived above-ground." What has given the man the paradoxical feeling of detachment and fulfillment shown by these statements? How, then, do you interpret his behavior in the last sentence of the story?

8. What elements of realism and naturalism appear in this story? (If you are not certain what the literary terms "realism" and "naturalism" mean, look them up.)

King of the Bingo Game

Ralph Ellison

The woman in front of him was eating roasted peanuts that smelled so good that he could barely contain his hunger. He could not even sleep and wished they'd hurry and begin the bingo game. There, on his right, two fellows were drinking wine out of a bottle wrapped in a paper bag, and he could hear soft gurgling in the dark. His stomach gave a low, gnawing growl. "If this was down South," he thought, "all I'd have to do is lean over and say, 'Lady, gimme a few of those peanuts, please ma'm,' and she'd pass me the bag and never think nothing of it." Or he could ask the fellows for a drink in the same way. Folks down South stuck together that way; they didn't even have to know you. But up here it was different. Ask somebody for something, and they'd think you were crazy. Well, I ain't crazy. I'm just broke, 'cause I got no birth certificate to get a job, and Laura 'bout to die 'cause we got no money for a doctor. But I ain't crazy. And yet a pinpoint of doubt was focused in his mind as he glanced toward the screen and saw the hero stealthily entering a dark room and sending the beam of a flashlight along a wall of bookcases. This is where he finds the trapdoor, he remembered. The man would pass abruptly through the wall and find the girl tied to a bed, her legs and arms spread wide, and her clothing torn to rags. He laughed softly to himself. He had seen the picture three times, and this was one of the best scenes.

On his right the fellow whispered wide-eyed to his companion, "Man, look a-yonder!"

"Damn!"

"Wouldn't I like to have her tied up like that . . ."

"Hey! That fool's letting her loose!"

"Aw, man, he loves her."

"Love or no love!"

The man moved impatiently beside him, and he tried to involve himself in the scene. But Laura was on his mind. Tiring quickly of watching the picture he looked back to where the white beam filtered from the projection room above the balcony. It started small and grew large, specks of dust dancing in its whiteness as it reached the screen. It was strange how the beam always landed right on the screen and didn't mess up and fall somewhere else. But they had it all fixed. Everything was fixed. Now suppose when they showed that girl with her dress torn the girl started taking off the rest of her clothes, and when the guy came in he didn't untie her but kept her there and went to taking off his own clothes? *That* would be something to see. If a picture got out of hand like that those guys up there would go nuts. Yeah, and there'd be so many folks in here you couldn't find a seat for nine months! A strange sensation played over his skin. He shuddered. Yesterday he'd seen a bedbug on a woman's neck as they walked out into the bright street. But exploring his thigh through a hole in his pocket he found only goose pimples and old scars.

The bottle gurgled again. He closed his eyes. Now a dreamy music was accompanying the film and train whistles were sounding in the distance, and he was a boy again walking along a railroad trestle down South, and seeing the train coming, and running back as fast as he could go, and hearing the whistle blowing, and getting off the trestle to solid ground just in time, with the earth trembling beneath his feet, and feeling relieved as he ran down the cinder-strewn embankment onto the highway, and looking back and seeing with terror that the train had left the track and was following him right down the middle of the street, and all the white people laughing as he ran screaming . . .

"Wake up there, buddy! What the hell do you mean hollering like that? Can't you see we trying to enjoy this here picture?"

He stared at the man with gratitude.

"I'm sorry, old man," he said. "I musta been dreaming."

"Well, here, have a drink. And don't be making no noise like that, damn!"

His hands trembled as he tilted his head. It was not wine, but whiskey. Cold rye whiskey. He took a deep swoller, decided it was better not to take another, and handed the bottle back to its owner.

"Thanks, old man," he said.

Now he felt the cold whiskey breaking a warm path straight through the middle of him, growing hotter and sharper as it moved. He had not eaten all day, and it made him light-headed. The smell of the peanuts stabbed him like a knife, and he got up and found a seat in the middle aisle. But no sooner did he sit than he saw a row of intense-faced young girls, and got up again, thinking, "You chicks musta been Lindy-hopping somewhere." He found a seat several rows ahead as the lights came on, and he saw the screen disappear behind a heavy red and gold curtain; then the curtain rising, and the man with the microphone and a uniformed attendant coming on the stage.

He felt for his bingo cards, smiling. The guy at the door wouldn't

like it if he knew about his having *five* cards. Well, not everyone played
the bingo game; and even with five cards he didn't have much of a
chance. For Laura, though, he had to have faith. He studied the cards,
each with its different numerals, punching the free center hole in each
and spreading them neatly across his lap; and when the lights faded he
sat slouched in his seat so that he could look from his cards to the bingo
wheel with but a quick shifting of his eyes.

Ahead, at the end of the darkness, the man with the microphone was
pressing a button attached to a long cord and spinning the bingo wheel
and calling out the number each time the wheel came to rest. And each
time the voice rang out his finger raced over the cards for the number.
With five cards he had to move fast. He became nervous; there were
too many cards, and the man went too fast with his grating voice. Perhaps he should just select one and throw the others away. But he was
afraid. He became warm. Wonder how much Laura's doctor would
cost? Damn that, watch the cards! And with despair he heard the man
call three in a row which he missed on all five cards. This way he'd never
win . . .

When he saw the row of holes punched across the third card, he sat
paralyzed and heard the man call three more numbers before he stumbled forward, screaming,

"Bingo! Bingo!"

"Let that fool up there," someone called.

"Get up there, man!"

He stumbled down the aisle and up the steps to the stage into a light
so sharp and bright that for a moment it blinded him, and he felt that
he had moved into the spell of some strange, mysterious power. Yet it
was as familiar as the sun, and he knew it was the perfectly familiar
bingo.

The man with the microphone was saying something to the audience
as he held out his card. A cold light flashed from the man's finger as
the card left his hand. His knees trembled. The man stepped closer,
checking the card against the numbers chalked on the board. Suppose he
had made a mistake? The pomade on the man's hair made him feel
faint, and he backed away. But the man was checking the card over the
microphone now, and he had to stay. He stood tense, listening.

"Under the O, forty-four," the man chanted. "Under the I, seven.
Under the G, three. Under the B, ninety-six. Under the N, thirteen!"

His breath came easier as the man smiled at the audience.

"Yessir, ladies and gentlemen, he's one of the chosen people!"

The audience rippled with laughter and applause.

"Step right up to the front of the stage."

He moved slowly forward, wishing that the light was not so bright.

"To win tonight's jackpot of $36.90 the wheel must stop between
the double zero, understand?"

He nodded, knowing the ritual from the many days and nights he had watched the winners march across the stage to press the button that controlled the spinning wheel and receive the prizes. And now he followed the instructions as though he'd crossed the slippery stage a million prize-winning times.

The man was making some kind of a joke, and he nodded vacantly. So tense had he become that he felt a sudden desire to cry and shook it away. He felt vaguely that his whole life was determined by the bingo wheel; not only that which would happen now that he was at last before it, but all that had gone before, since his birth, and his mother's birth and the birth of his father. It had always been there, even though he had not been aware of it, handing out the unlucky cards and numbers of his days. The feeling persisted, and he started quickly away. I better get down from here before I make a fool of myself, he thought.

"Here, boy," the man called. "You haven't started yet."

Someone laughed as he went hesitantly back.

"Are you all reet?"

He grinned at the man's jive talk, but no words would come, and he knew it was not a convincing grin. For suddenly he knew that he stood on the slippery brink of some terrible embarrassment.

"Where are you from, boy?" the man asked.

"Down South."

"He's from down South, ladies and gentlemen," the man said. "Where from? Speak right into the mike."

"Rocky Mont," he said. "Rock' Mont, North Car'lina."

"So you decided to come down off that mountain to the U.S.," the man laughed. He felt that the man was making a fool of him, but then something cold was placed in his hand, and the lights were no longer behind him.

Standing before the wheel he felt alone, but that was somehow right, and he remembered his plan. He would give the wheel a short quick twirl. Just a touch of the button. He had watched it many times, and always it came close to double zero when it was short and quick. He steeled himself; the fear had left, and he felt a profound sense of promise, as though he were about to be repaid for all the things he'd suffered all his life. Trembling, he pressed the button. There was a whirl of lights, and in a second he realized with finality that though he wanted to, he could not stop. It was as though he held a high-powered line in his naked hand. His nerves tightened. As the wheel increased its speed it seemed to draw him more and more into its power, as though it held his fate; and with it came a deep need to submit, to whirl, to lose himself in its swirl of color. He could not stop it now, he knew. So let it be.

The button rested snugly in his palm where the man had placed it. And now he became aware of the man beside him, advising him through the microphone, while behind the shadowy audience hummed with noisy voices. He shifted his feet. There was still that feeling of helplessness within him, making part of him desire to turn back, even now that the jackpot was right in his hand. He squeezed the button until his fist ached. Then, like the sudden shriek of a subway whistle, a doubt tore through his head. Suppose he did not spin the wheel long enough? What could he do, and how could he tell? And then he knew, even as he wondered, that as long as he pressed the button, he could control the jackpot. He and only he could determine whether or not it was to be his. Not even the man with the microphone could do anything about it now. He felt drunk. Then, as though he had come down from a high hill into a valley of people, he heard the audience yelling.

"Come down from there, you jerk!"

"Let somebody else have a chance . . ."

"Ole Jack thinks he done found the end of the rainbow . . ."

The last voice was not unfriendly, and he turned and smiled dreamily into the yelling mouths. Then he turned his back squarely on them.

"Don't take too long, boy," a voice said.

He nodded. They were yelling behind him. Those folks did not understand what had happened to him. They had been playing the bingo game day in and night out for years, trying to win rent money or hamburger change. But not one of those wise guys had discovered this wonderful thing. He watched the wheel whirling past the numbers and experienced a burst of exaltation: This is God! This is the really truly God! He said it aloud, "This is God!"

He said it with such absolute conviction that he feared he would fall fainting into the footlights. But the crowd yelled so loud that they could not hear. Those fools, he thought. I'm here trying to tell them the most wonderful secret in the world, and they're yelling like they gone crazy. A hand fell upon his shoulder.

"You'll have to make a choice now, boy. You've taken too long."

He brushed the hand violently away.

"Leave me alone, man. I know what I'm doing!"

The man looked surprised and held on to the microphone for support. And because he did not wish to hurt the man's feelings he smiled, realizing with a sudden pang that there was no way of explaining to the man just why he had to stand there pressing the button forever.

"Come here," he called tiredly.

The man approached, rolling the heavy microphone across the stage.

"Anybody can play this bingo game, right?" he said.

"Sure, but . . ."

He smiled, feeling inclined to be patient with this slick looking white man with his blue sport shirt and his sharp gabardine suit.

"That's what I thought," he said. "Anybody can win the jackpot as long as they get the lucky number, right?"

"That's the rule, but after all . . ."

"That's what I thought," he said. "And the big prize goes to the man who knows how to win it?"

The man nodded speechlessly.

"Well then, go on over there and watch me win like I want to. I ain't going to hurt nobody," he said, "and I'll show you how to win. I mean to show the whole world how it's got to be done."

And because he understood, he smiled again to let the man know that he held nothing against him for being white and impatient. Then he refused to see the man any longer and stood pressing the button, the voices of the crowd reaching him like sounds in distant streets. Let them yell. All the Negroes down there were just ashamed because he was black like them. He smiled inwardly, knowing how it was. Most of the time he was ashamed of what Negroes did himself. Well, let them be ashamed for something this time. Like him. He was like a long thin black wire that was being stretched and wound upon the bingo wheel; wound until he wanted to scream; wound, but this time himself controlling the winding and the sadness and the shame, and because he did, Laura would be all right. Suddenly the lights flickered. He staggered backwards. Had something gone wrong? All this noise. Didn't they know that although he controlled the wheel, it also controlled him, and unless he pressed the button forever and forever and ever it would stop, leaving him high and dry, dry and high on this hard high slippery hill and Laura dead? There was only one chance; he had to do whatever the wheel demanded. And gripping the button in despair, he discovered with surprise that it imparted a nervous energy. His spine tingled. He felt a certain power.

Now he faced the raging crowd with defiance, its screams penetrating his eardrums like trumpets shrieking from a jukebox. The vague faces glowing in the bingo lights gave him a sense of himself that he had never known before. He was running the show, by God! They had to react to him, for he was their luck. This is *me*, he thought. Let the bastards yell. Then someone was laughing inside him, and he realized that somehow he had forgotten his own name. It was a sad, lost feeling to lose your name, and a crazy thing to do. That name had been given him by the white man who had owned his grandfather a long lost time ago down South. But maybe those wise guys knew his name.

"Who am I?" he screamed.

"Hurry up and bingo, you jerk!"

They didn't know either, he thought sadly. They didn't even know their own names, they were all poor nameless bastards. Well, he didn't need that old name; he was reborn. For as long as he pressed the button he was The-man-who-pressed-the-button-who-held-the-prize-who-was-the-King-of-Bingo. That was the way it was, and he'd have to press the button even if nobody understood, even though Laura did not understand.

"Live!" he shouted.

The audience quieted like the dying of a huge fan.

"Live, Laura, baby. I got holt of it now, sugar. Live!"

He screamed it, tears streaming down his face. "I got nobody but YOU!"

The screams tore from his very guts. He felt as though the rush of blood to his head would burst out in baseball seams of small red drop-lets, like a head beaten by police clubs. Bending over he saw a trickle of blood splashing the toe of his shoe. With his free hand he searched his head. It was his nose. God, suppose something has gone wrong? He felt that the whole audience had somehow entered him and was stamp-ing its feet in his stomach, and he was unable to throw them out. They wanted the prize, that was it. They wanted the secret for themselves. But they'd never get it; he would keep the bingo wheel whirling forever, and Laura would be safe in the wheel. But would she? It had to be, because if she were not safe the wheel would cease to turn; it could not go on. He had to get away, *vomit* all, and his mind formed an image of himself running with Laura in his arms down the tracks of the sub-way just ahead of an A train, running desperately *vomit* with people screaming for him to come out but knowing no way of leaving the tracks because to stop would bring the train crushing down upon him and to attempt to leave across the other tracks would mean to run into a hot third rail as high as his waist which threw blue sparks that blinded his eyes until he could hardly see.

He heard singing and the audience was clapping its hands.

> *Shoot the liquor to him, Jim, boy!*
> *Clap-clap-clap*
> *Well a-calla the cop*
> *He's blowing his top!*
> *Shoot the liquor to him, Jim, boy!*

Bitter anger grew within him at the singing. They think I'm crazy. Well let 'em laugh. I'll do what I got to do.

He was standing in an attitude of intense listening when he saw that they were watching something on the stage behind him. He felt weak. But when he turned he saw no one. If only his thumb did not ache so. Now they were applauding. And for a moment he thought that the wheel had stopped. But that was impossible, his thumb still pressed the button. Then he saw them. Two men in uniform beckoned from the end of the stage. They were coming toward him, walking in step, slowly, like a tap-dance team returning for a third encore. But their shoulders shot forward, and he backed away, looking wildly about. There was nothing to fight them with. He had only the long black cord which led to a plug somewhere back stage, and he couldn't use that because it operated the bingo wheel. He backed slowly, fixing the men with his eyes as his lips stretched over his teeth in a tight, fixed grin; moved to-ward the end of the stage and realizing that he couldn't go much fur-ther, for suddenly the cord became taut and he couldn't afford to break the cord. But he had to do something. The audience was howling. Suddenly he stopped dead, seeing the men halt, their legs lifted as in an interrupted step of a slow-motion dance. There was nothing to do but run in the other direction and he dashed forward, slipping and sliding. The men fell back, surprised. He struck out violently going past.

"Grab him!"

He ran, but all too quickly the cord tightened, resistingly, and he turned and ran back again. This time he slipped them, and discovered by running in a circle before the wheel he could keep the cord from tightening. But this way he had to flail his arms to keep the men away. Why couldn't they leave a man alone? He ran, circling.

"Ring down the curtain," someone yelled. But they couldn't do that. If they did the wheel flashing from the projection room would be cut off. But they had him before he could tell them so, trying to pry open his fist, and he was wrestling and trying to bring his knees into the fight and holding on to the button, for it was his life. And now he was down, seeing a foot coming down, crushing his wrist cruelly, down, as he saw the wheel whirling serenely above.

"I can't give it up," he screamed. Then quietly, in a confidential tone, "Boys, I really can't give it up."

It landed hard against his head. And in the blank moment they had it away from him, completely now. He fought them trying to pull him up from the stage as he watched the wheel spin slowly to a stop. Without surprise he saw it rest at double-zero.

"You see," he pointed bitterly.

"Sure, boy, sure, it's O. K.," one of the men said smiling.

And seeing the man bow his head to someone he could not see, he felt very, very happy; he would receive what all the winners received.

But as he warmed in the justice of the man's tight smile he did not see the man's slow wink, nor see the bow-legged man behind him step clear of the swiftly descending curtain and set himself for a blow. He only felt the dull pain exploding in his skull, and he knew even as it slipped out of him that his luck had run out on the stage.

QUESTIONS

1. Discuss Ellison's use of a technique that is both realistic and dreamlike. Why do you think he chose to combine these two qualities in the story?

2. Is it important to the narrative that the young man is from "down South"? If so, why?

3. Of what significance is the description of the movie at the beginning to the rest of the story?

4. The bingo wheel may be taken as a modern form of an ancient symbol such as a fortune wheel. What, then, does the bingo

player mean when he says of it, "This is the God! This is the really truly God!"?

5. Why is the bingo player unable to take his hand off the button, saying, " 'I can't give it up . . . Boys, I really can't give it up.' "?

6. What does Ellison mean when he says of the bingo player: "And because he understood, he smiled again to let the man know that he held nothing against him for being white and impatient"? What does the bingo player understand?

7. During the game the bingo player exclaims, "This is *me*," but he is then unable to recall his name. Why is this significant? In what new sense has he found his identity?

8. What does the final paragraph add to the meaning of the story? Does it have implications that go beyond the *facts* of the story?

Sonny's Blues

James Baldwin

I read about it in the paper, in the subway, on my way to work. I read it, and I couldn't believe it, and I read it again. Then perhaps I just stared at it, at the newsprint spelling out his name, spelling out the story. I stared at it in the swinging lights of the subway car, and in the faces and bodies of the people, and in my own face, trapped in the darkness which roared outside.

It was not to be believed and I kept telling myself that as I walked from the subway station to the high school. And at the same time I couldn't doubt it. I was scared, scared for Sonny. He became real to me again. A great block of ice got settled in my belly and kept melting there slowly all day long, while I taught my classes algebra. It was a special kind of ice. I kept melting, sending trickles of ice water all up and down my veins, but it never got less. Sometimes it hardened and seemed to expand until I felt my guts were going to come spilling out or that I was going to choke or scream. This would always be at a moment when I was remembering some specific thing Sonny had once said or done.

When he was about as old as the boys in my classes his face had been bright and open, there was a lot of copper in it; and he'd had wonderfully direct brown eyes, and great gentleness and privacy. I wondered what he looked like now. He had been picked up, the evening before, in a raid on an apartment downtown, for peddling and using heroin.

I couldn't believe it: but what I mean by that is that I couldn't find any room for it anywhere inside me. I had kept it outside me for a long time. I hadn't wanted to know. I had had suspicions, but I didn't name them, I kept putting them away. I told myself that Sonny was wild, but he wasn't crazy. And he'd always been a good boy, he hadn't ever turned hard or evil or disrespectful, the way kids can, so quick, so quick, especially in Harlem. I didn't want to believe that I'd ever see my brother going down, coming to nothing, all that light in his face gone out, in the condition I'd already seen so many others. Yet it had happened and here I was, talking about algebra to a lot of boys who might, every one of them for all I knew, be popping off needles every time they went to the head. Maybe it did more for them than algebra could.

I was sure that the first time Sonny had ever had horse, he couldn't have been much older than these boys were now. These boys, now, were living as we'd been living then, they were growing up with a rush and their heads bumped abruptly against the low ceiling of their actual possibilities. They were filled with rage. All they really knew were two darknesses, the darkness of their lives, which was now closing in on them, and the darkness of the movies, which had blinded them to that other darkness, and in which they now, vindictively, dreamed, at once more together than they were at any other time, and more alone.

When the last bell rang, the last class ended, I let out my breath. It seemed I'd been holding it for all that time. My clothes were wet —I may have looked as though I'd been sitting in a steam bath, all dressed up, all afternoon. I sat alone in the classroom a long time. I listened to the boys outside, downstairs, shouting and cursing and laughing. Their laughter struck me for perhaps the first time. It was not the joyous laughter which—God knows why—one associates with children. It was mocking and insular, its intent was to denigrate. It was disenchanted, and in this, also, lay the authority of their curses. Perhaps I was listening to them because I was thinking about my brother and in them I heard my brother. And myself.

One boy was whistling a tune, at once very complicated and very simple, it seemed to be pouring out of him as though he were a bird, and it sounded very cool and moving through all that harsh, bright air, only just holding its own through all those other sounds.

I stood up and walked over to the window and looked down into the courtyard. It was the beginning of the spring and the sap was rising in the boys. A teacher passed through them every now and again, quickly, as though he or she couldn't wait to get out of that courtyard, to get those boys out of their sight and off their minds. I started collecting my stuff. I thought I'd better get home and talk to Isabel.

The courtyard was almost deserted by the time I got downstairs. I saw this boy standing in the shadow of a doorway, looking just like Sonny. I almost called his name. Then I saw that it wasn't Sonny, but somebody we used to know, a boy from around our block. He'd been Sonny's friend. He'd never been mine, having been too young for me, and, anyway, I'd never liked him. And now, even though he was a grown-up man, he still hung around that block, still spent hours on the street corners, was always high and raggy. I used to run into him from time to time and he'd often work around to asking me for a quarter or fifty cents. He always had some real good excuse, too, and I always gave it to him, I don't know why.

But now, abruptly, I hated him. I couldn't stand the way he looked at me, partly like a dog, partly like a cunning child. I wanted to ask him what the hell he was doing in the school courtyard.

He sort of shuffled over to me, and he said, "I see you got the papers. So you already know about it."

"You mean about Sonny? Yes, I already know about it. How come they didn't get you?"

He grinned. It made him repulsive and it also brought to mind what he'd looked like as a kid. "I wasn't there. I stay away from them people."

"Good for you." I offered him a cigarette and I watched him through the smoke. "You come all the way down here just to tell me about Sonny?"

"That's right." He was sort of shaking his head and his eyes looked strange, as though they were about to cross. The bright sun deadened his damp dark brown skin and it made his eyes look yellow and showed up the dirt in his conked hair. He smelled funky. I moved a little away from him and I said, "Well, thanks. But I already know about it and I got to get home."

"I'll walk you a little ways," he said. We started walking. There were a couple of kids still loitering in the courtyard and one of them said good night to me and looked strangely at the boy beside me.

"What're you going to do?" he asked me. "I mean, about Sonny?"

"Look. I haven't seen Sonny for over a year, I'm not sure I'm going to do anything. Anyway, what the hell *can* I do?"

"That's right," he said quickly, "ain't nothing you can do. Can't much help old Sonny no more, I guess."

It was what I was thinking and so it seemed to me he had no right to say it.

"I'm surprised at Sonny, though," he went on—he had a funny way of talking, he looked straight ahead as though he were talking to himself —"I thought Sonny was a smart boy, I thought he was too smart to get hung."

"I guess he thought so too," I said sharply, "and that's how he got hung. And how about you? You're pretty goddamn smart, I bet."

Then he looked directly at me, just for a minute. "I ain't smart," he said. "If I was smart, I'd have reached for a pistol a long time ago."

"Look. Don't tell *me* your sad story, if it was up to me, I'd give you one." Then I felt guilty—guilty, probably, for never having supposed that the poor bastard *had* a story of his own, much less a sad one, and I asked, quickly, "What's going to happen to him now?"

He didn't answer this. He was off by himself some place. "Funny thing," he said, and from his tone we might have been discussing the quickest way to get to Brooklyn, "when I saw the papers this morning, the first thing I asked myself was if I had anything to do with it. I felt sort of responsible."

I began to listen more carefully. The subway station was on the corner, just before us, and I stopped. He stopped, too. We were in front of a bar and he ducked slightly, peering in, but whoever he was looking for didn't seem to be there. The juke box was blasting away with something black and bouncy and I half watched the barmaid as she danced her way from the juke box to her place behind the bar. And I watched her face as she laughingly responded to something someone said to her, still keeping time to the music. When she smiled one saw the little girl, one sensed the doomed, still-struggling woman beneath the battered face of the semi-whore.

"I never *give* Sonny nothing," the boy said finally, "but a long time ago I come to school high and Sonny asked me how it felt." He paused, I couldn't bear to watch him, I watched the barmaid, and I listened to the music which seemed to be causing the pavement to shake. "I told him it felt great." The music stopped, the barmaid paused and watched the juke box until the music began again. "It did."

All this was carrying me some place I didn't want to go. I certainly didn't want to know how it felt. It filled everything, the people, the houses, the music, the dark, quicksilver barmaid, with menace; and this menace was their reality.

"What's going to happen to him now?" I asked again.

"They'll send him away some place and they'll try to cure him." He shook his head. "Maybe he'll even think he's kicked the habit. Then they'll let him loose"—he gestured, throwing his cigarette into the gutter. "That's all."

"What do you mean, that's *all?*"

But I knew what he meant.

"I *mean*, that's *all.*" He turned his head and looked at me, pulling down the corners of his mouth. "Don't you know what I mean?" he asked, softly.

"How the hell *would* I know what you mean?" I almost whispered it, I don't know why.

"That's right," he said to the air, "how would *he* know what I mean?" He turned towards me again, patient and calm, and yet I somehow felt him shaking, shaking as though he were going to fall apart. I felt that ice in my guts again, the dread I'd felt all afternoon; and again I watched the barmaid, moving about the bar, washing glasses, and singing. "Listen. They'll let him out and then it'll just start all over again. That's what I mean."

"You mean—they'll let him out. And then he'll just start working his way back in again. You mean he'll never kick the habit. Is that what you mean?"

"That's right," he said, cheerfully. "*You* see what I mean."

"Tell me," I said at last, "why does he want to die? He must want to die, he's killing himself, why does he want to die?"

He looked at me in surprise. He licked his lips. "He don't want to die. He wants to live. Don't nobody want to die, ever."

Then I wanted to ask him—too many things. He could not have answered, or if he had, I could not have borne the answers. I started walking. "Well, I guess it's none of my business."

"It's going to be rough on old Sonny," he said. We reached the subway station. "This is your station?" he asked. I nodded. I took one step down. "Damn!" he said, suddenly. I looked up at him. He grinned again. "Damn it if I didn't leave all my money home. You ain't got a dollar on you, have you? Just for a couple of days, is all."

All at once something inside gave and threatened to come pouring out of me. I didn't hate him any more. I felt that in another moment I'd start crying like a child.

"Sure," I said. "Don't sweat." I looked in my wallet and didn't have a dollar, I only had a five. "Here," I said. "That hold you?"

He didn't look at it—he didn't want to look at it. A terrible, closed look came over his face, as though he were keeping the number on the bill a secret from him and me. "Thanks," he said, and now he was dying to see me go. "Don't worry about Sonny. Maybe I'll write him or something."

"Sure," I said. "You do that. So long."

"Be seeing you," he said. I went on down the steps.

And I didn't write Sonny or send him anything for a long time. When I finally did, it was just after my little girl died, he wrote me back a letter which made me feel like a bastard.

Here's what he said:

Dear brother,

You don't know how much I needed to hear from you. I wanted to write you many a time but I dug how much I must have hurt you and so I didn't write. But now I feel like a man who's been trying to climb up out of some deep, real deep and funky hole and just saw the sun up there, outside. I got to get outside.

I can't tell you much about how I got here. I mean I don't know how to tell you. I guess I was afraid of something or I was trying to escape from something and you know I have never been very strong in the head (smile). I'm glad Mama and Daddy are dead and can't see what's happened to their son and I swear if I'd known what I was doing I would never have hurt you so, you and a lot of other fine people who were nice to me and who believed in me.

I don't want you to think it had anything to do with me being a musician. It's more than that. Or maybe less than that. I can't get anything straight in my head down here and I try not to think about what's going to happen to me when I get outside again. Sometime I think I'm going to flip and *never* get outside and sometime I think I'll come straight back. I tell you one thing, though, I'd rather blow my brains out than go through this again. But that's what they all say, so they tell me. If I tell you when I'm coming to New York and if you could meet me, I sure would appreciate it. Give my love to Isabel and the kids and I was sure sorry to hear about little Gracie. I wish I could be like Mama and say the Lord's will be done, but I don't know it seems to me that trouble is the one thing that never does get stopped and I don't know what good it does to blame it on the Lord. But maybe it does some good if you believe it.

Your brother,
Sonny.

Then I kept in constant touch with him and I sent him whatever I could and I went to meet him when he came back to New York. When I saw him many things I thought I had forgotten came flooding back to me. This was because I had begun, finally, to wonder about Sonny, about the life that Sonny lived inside. This life, whatever it was, had made him older and thinner and it had deepened the distant stillness in which he had always moved. He looked very unlike my baby brother. Yet, when he smiled, when we shook hands, the baby brother I'd never known looked out from the depths of his private life, like an animal waiting to be coaxed into the light.

"How you been keeping?" he asked me.

"All right. And you?"

"Just fine." He was smiling all over his face. "It's good to see you again."

"It's good to see you."

The seven years' difference in our ages lay between us like a chasm: I wondered if these years would ever operate between us as a bridge. I was remembering, and it made it hard to catch my breath, that I had been there when he was born; and I had heard the first words he had ever spoken. When he started to walk, he walked from our mother straight to me. I caught him just before he fell when he took the first steps he ever took in this world.

"How's Isabel?"

"Just fine. She's dying to see you."

"And the boys?"

"They're fine, too. They're anxious to see their uncle."

"Oh, come on. You know they don't remember me."

"Are you kidding? Of course they remember you."

He grinned again. We got into a taxi. We had a lot to say to each other, far too much to know how to begin.

As the taxi began to move, I asked, "You still want to go to India?"

He laughed. "You still remember that. Hell, no. This place is Indian enough for me."

"It used to belong to them," I said.

And he laughed again. "They damn sure knew what they were doing when they got rid of it."

Years ago, when he was around fourteen, he'd been all hipped on the idea of going to India. He read books about people sitting on rocks, naked, in all kinds of weather, but mostly bad, naturally, and walking barefoot through hot coals and arriving at wisdom. I used to say that it sounded to me as though they were getting away from wisdom as fast as they could. I think he sort of looked down on me for that.

"Do you mind," he asked, "if we have the driver drive alongside the park? On the west side—I haven't seen the city in so long."

"Of course not," I said. I was afraid that I might sound as though I were humoring him, but I hoped he wouldn't take it that way.

So we drove along, between the green of the park and the stony, lifeless elegance of hotels and apartment buildings, towards the vivid, killing streets of our childhood. These streets hadn't changed, though housing projects jutted up out of them now like rocks in the middle of a boiling sea. Most of the houses in which we had grown up had vanished, as had the stores from which we had stolen, the basements in which we had first tried sex, the rooftops from which we had hurled tin cans and bricks. But houses exactly like the houses of our past yet dominated the landscape, boys exactly like the boys we once had been found themselves smothering in these houses, came down into the streets for light and air and found themselves encircled by disaster. Some escaped the trap, most didn't. Those who got out always left something of themselves behind, as some animals amputate a leg and leave it in the trap. It might be said, perhaps, that I had escaped, after all, I was a school teacher; or that Sonny had, he hadn't lived in Harlem for years. Yet, as the cab moved uptown through streets which seemed, with a rush, to darken with dark people, and as I covertly studied Sonny's face, it came to me that what we both were seeking through our separate cab windows was that part of ourselves which had been left behind. It's always at the hour of trouble and confrontation that the missing member aches.

We hit 110th Street and started rolling up Lenox Avenue. And I'd known this avenue all my life, but it seemed to me again, as it had seemed on the day I'd first heard about Sonny's trouble, filled with a hidden menace which was its very breath of life.

"We almost there," said Sonny.

"Almost." We were both too nervous to say anything more.

We live in a housing project. It hasn't been up long. A few days after it was up it seemed uninhabitably new, now, of course, it's already rundown. It looks like a parody of the good, clean, faceless life—God knows the people who live in it do their best to make it a parody. The beat-looking grass lying around isn't enough to make their lives green, the hedges will never hold out the streets, and they know it. The big windows fool no one, they aren't big enough to make space out of no space. They don't bother with the windows, they watch the TV screen instead. The playground is most popular with the children who don't play at jacks, or skip rope, or roller skate, or swing, and they can be found in it after dark. We moved in partly because it's not too far from where I teach, and partly for the kids; but it's really just like the houses in which Sonny and I grew up. The same things happen, they'll have the same things to remember. The moment Sonny and I started into the house I had the feeling that I was simply bringing him back into the danger he had almost died trying to escape.

Sonny has never been talkative. So I don't know why I was sure he'd be dying to talk to me when supper was over the first night. Everything went fine, the oldest boy remembered him, and the youngest boy liked him, and Sonny had remembered to bring something for each of them; and Isabel, who is really much nicer than I am, more open and giving, had gone to a lot of trouble about dinner and was genuinely glad to see him. And she's always been able to tease Sonny in a way that I haven't. It was nice to see her face so vivid again and to hear her laugh and watch her make Sonny laugh. She wasn't, or, anyway, she didn't seem to be, at all uneasy or embarrassed. She chatted as though there were no subject which had to be avoided and she got Sonny past his first, faint stiffness. And thank God she was there, for I was filled with that icy dread again. Everything I did seemed awkward to me, and everything I said sounded freighted with hidden meaning. I was trying to remember everything I'd heard about dope addiction and I couldn't help watching Sonny for signs. I wasn't doing it out of malice. I was trying to find out something about my brother. I was dying to hear him tell me he was safe.

"Safe!" my father grunted, whenever Mama suggested trying to move to a neighborhood which might be safer for children. "Safe, hell! Ain't no place safe for kids, nor nobody."

He always went on like this, but he wasn't, ever, really as bad as he sounded, not even on week-ends, when he got drunk. As a matter of fact, he was always on the lookout for "something a little better," but he died before he found it. He died suddenly, during a drunken week-end in the middle of the war, when Sonny was fifteen. He and Sonny hadn't ever got on too well. And this was partly because Sonny was the apple of his father's eye. It was because he loved Sonny so much and was frightened for him, that he was always fighting with him. It doesn't do any good to fight with Sonny. Sonny just moves back, inside himself, where he can't be reached. But the principal reason that they never hit it off is that they were so much alike. Daddy was big and rough and loud-talking, just the opposite of Sonny, but they both had—that same privacy.

Mama tried to tell me something about this, just after Daddy died. I was home on leave from the army.

This was the last time I ever saw my mother alive. Just the same, this picture gets all mixed up in my mind with pictures I had of her when she was younger. The way I always see her is the way she used to be on a Sunday afternoon, say, when the old folks were talking after the big Sunday dinner. I always see her wearing pale blue. She'd be sitting on the sofa. And my father would be sitting in the easy chair, not far from her. And the living-room would be full of church folks and relatives. There they sit, in chairs all around the living-room, and the night is creeping up outside, but nobody knows it yet. You can see the darkness growing against the window-panes and you hear the street noises every now and again, or maybe the jangling beat of a tambourine from one of the churches close by, but it's real quiet in the room. For a moment nobody's talking, but every face looks darkening, like the sky outside. And my mother rocks a little from the waist, and my father's eyes are closed. Everyone is looking at something a child can't see. For a minute they've forgotten the children. Maybe a kid is lying on the rug, half asleep. Maybe somebody's got a kid in his lap and is absent-mindedly stroking the kid's head. Maybe there's a kid, quiet and big-eyed, curled up in a big chair in the corner. The silence, the darkness coming, and the darkness in the faces frightens the child obscurely. He hopes that the hand which strokes his forehead will never stop—will never die. He hopes that there will never come a time when the old folks won't be sitting around the living-room, talking about where they've come from, and what they've seen, and what's happened to them and their kinfolk.

But something deep and watchful in the child knows that this is bound to end, is already ending. In a moment someone will get up and turn on the light. Then the old folks will remember the children and they won't talk any more that day. And when the light fills the room, the child is filled with darkness. He knows that every time this happens he's moved just a little closer to that darkness outside. The darkness outside is what the old folks have been talking about. It's what they've come from. It's what they endure. The child knows that they won't talk any more because if he knows too much about what's happened to *them*, he'll know too much too soon, about what's going to happen to *him*.

The last time I talked to my mother, I remember I was restless. I wanted to get out and see Isabel. We weren't married then and we had a lot to straighten out between us.

There Mama sat, in black, by the window. She was humming an old church song, *Lord, you brought me from a long ways off*. Sonny was out somewhere. Mama kept watching the streets.

"I don't know," she said, "if I'll ever see you again, after you go off from here. But I hope you'll remember the things I tried to teach you."

"Don't talk like that," I said, and smiled. "You'll be here a long time yet."

She smiled, too, but she said nothing. She was quiet for a long time. And I said, "Mama, don't you worry about nothing. I'll be writing all the time, and you be getting the checks. . . ."

"I want to talk to you about your brother," she said, suddenly. "If anything happens to me he ain't got to have nobody to look out for him."

"Mama," I said, "ain't nothing going to happen to you or Sonny. Sonny's all right. He's a good boy and he's got good sense."

"It ain't a question of his being a good boy," Mama said, "nor of his having good sense. It ain't only the bad ones, nor yet the dumb ones that gets sucked under." She stopped, looking at me. "Your Daddy once had a brother," she said, and she smiled in a way that made me feel she was in pain. "You didn't never know that, did you?"

"No," I said, "I never knew that," and I watched her face.

"Oh, yes," she said, "your Daddy had a brother." She looked out of the window again. "I know you never saw your Daddy cry. But I did—many a time, through all these years."

I asked her, "What happened to his brother? How come nobody's ever talked about him?"

This was the first time I ever saw my mother look old.

"His brother got killed," she said, "when he was just a little younger than you are now. I knew him. He was a fine boy. He was maybe a little full of the devil, but he didn't mean nobody no harm."

Then she stopped and the room was silent, exactly as it had sometimes been on those Sunday afternoons. Mama kept looking out into the streets.

"He used to have a job in the mill," she said, "and, like all young folks, he just liked to perform on Saturday nights. Saturday nights, him and your father would drift around to different places, go to dances and things like that, or just sit around with people they knew and your father's brother would sing, he had a fine voice, and play along with himself on his guitar. Well, this particular Saturday night, him and your father was coming home from some place, and they were both a little drunk and there was a moon that night, it was bright like day. Your father's brother was feeling kind of good, and he was whistling to himself, and he had his guitar slung over his shoulder. They was coming down a hill and beneath them was a road that turned off from the highway. Well, your father's brother, being always kind of frisky, decided to run down this hill, and he did, with that guitar banging and clanging behind him, and he ran across the road, and he was making water behind a tree. And your father was sort of amused at him and he was still coming down the hill, kind of slow. Then he heard a car motor and that same minute his brother stepped from behind the tree, into the road, in the moonlight. And he started to cross the road. And your father started to run down the hill, he says he don't know why. This car was full of white men. They was all drunk, and when they seen your father's brother they let out a great whoop and holler and they aimed the car straight at him. They was having fun, they just wanted to scare him, the way they do sometimes, you know. But they was drunk. And I guess the boy, being drunk, too, and scared, kind of lost his head. By the time he jumped it was too late. Your father says he heard his brother scream when the car rolled over him, and he heard the wood of that guitar when it give, and he heard them strings go flying, and he heard them white men shouting, and the car kept on a-going and it ain't stopped till this day. And, time your father got down the hill, his brother weren't nothing but blood and pulp."

Tears were gleaming on my mother's face. There wasn't anything I could say.

"He never mentioned it," she said, "because I never let him mention it before you children. Your Daddy was like a crazy man that night and for many a night thereafter. He says he never in his life seen anything as dark as that road after the lights of that car had gone away. Weren't nothing, weren't nobody on that road, just your Daddy and his brother and that busted guitar. Oh, yes. Your Daddy never did really get right again. Till the day he died he weren't sure but that every white man he saw was the man that killed his brother."

She stopped and took out her handkerchief and dried her eyes and looked at me.

"I ain't telling you all this," she said, "to make you scared or bitter or to make you hate nobody. I'm telling you this because you got a brother. And the world ain't changed."

I guess I didn't want to believe this. I guess she saw this in my face. She turned away from me, towards the window again, searching those streets.

"But I praise my Redeemer," she said at last, "that He called your Daddy home before me. I ain't saying it to throw no flowers at myself, but, I declare, it keeps me from feeling too cast down to know I helped your father get safely through this world. Your father always acted like he was the roughest, strongest man on earth. And everybody took him to be like that. But if he hadn't had *me* there—to see his tears!"

She was crying again. Still, I couldn't move. I said, "Lord, Lord, Mama, I didn't know it was like that."

"Oh, honey," she said, "there's a lot that you don't know. But you are going to find it out." She stood up from the window and came over to me. "You got to hold on to your brother," she said, "and don't let him fall, no matter what it looks like is happening to him and no matter how evil you gets with him. You going to be evil with him many a time. But don't you forget what I told you, you hear?"

"I won't forget," I said. "Don't you worry, I won't forget. I won't let nothing happen to Sonny."

My mother smiled as though she were amused at something she saw in my face. Then, "You may not be able to stop nothing from happening. But you got to let him know you's *there*."

Two days later I was married, and then I was gone. And I had a lot of things on my mind and I pretty well forgot my promise to Mama until I got shipped home on a special furlough for her funeral.

And, after the funeral, with just Sonny and me alone in the empty kitchen, I tried to find out something about him.

"What do you want to do?" I asked him.

"I'm going to be a musician," he said.

For he had graduated, in the time I had been away, from dancing to the juke box to finding out who was playing what, and what they were doing with it, and he had bought himself a set of drums.

"You mean, you want to be a drummer?" I somehow had the feeling that being a drummer might be all right for other people but not for my brother Sonny.

"I don't think," he said, looking at me very gravely, "that I'll ever be a good drummer. But I think I can play a piano."

I frowned. I'd never played the role of the older brother quite so seriously before, had scarcely ever, in fact, *asked* Sonny a damn thing. I sensed myself in the presence of something I didn't really know how to handle, didn't understand. So I made my frown a little deeper as I asked: "What kind of musician do you want to be?"

He grinned. "How many kinds do you think there are?"

"Be *serious*," I said.

He laughed, throwing his head back, and then looked at me. "I *am* serious."

"Well, then, for Christ's sake, stop kidding around and answer a serious question. I mean, do you want to be a concert pianist, you want to play classical music and all that, or—or what?" Long before I finished he was laughing again. "For Christ's *sake*, Sonny!"

He sobered, but with difficulty. "I'm sorry. But you sound so—*scared!*" and he was off again.

"Well, you may think it's funny now, baby, but it's not going to be so funny when you have to make your living at it, let me tell you *that*." I was furious because I knew he was laughing at me and I didn't know why.

"No," he said, very sober now, and afraid, perhaps, that he'd hurt me, "I don't want to be a classical pianist. That isn't what interests me. I mean"—he paused, looking hard at me, as though his eyes would help me to understand, and then gestured helplessly, as though perhaps his hand would help—"I mean, I'll have a lot of studying to do, and I'll have to study *everything*, but, I mean, I want to play *with*—jazz musicians." He stopped. "I want to play jazz," he said.

Well, the word had never before sounded as heavy, as real, as it sounded that afternoon in Sonny's mouth. I just looked at him and I was probably frowning a real frown by this time. I simply couldn't see why on earth he'd want to spend his time hanging around night-clubs, clowning around on bandstands, while people pushed each other around on a dance floor. It seemed—beneath him, somehow. I had never thought about it before, had never been forced to, but I suppose I had always put jazz musicians in a class with what Daddy called "good-time people."

"Are you *serious?*"

"Hell, *yes*, I'm serious."

He looked more helpless than ever, and annoyed, and deeply hurt.

I suggested, helpfully: "You mean—like Louis Armstrong?"

His face closed as though I'd struck him. "No. I'm not talking about none of that old-time, down home crap."

"Well, look, Sonny, I'm sorry, don't get mad. I just don't altogether get it, that's all. Name somebody—you know, a jazz musician you admire."

"Bird."

"Who?"

"Bird! Charlie Parker! Don't they teach you nothing in the goddamn army?"

I lit a cigarette. I was surprised and then a little amused to discover that I was trembling. "I've been out of touch," I said. "You'll have to be patient with me. Now. Who's this Parker character?"

"He's just one of the greatest jazz musicians alive," said Sonny, sullenly, his hands in his pockets, his back to me. "Maybe *the* greatest," he added, bitterly, "that's probably why *you* never heard of him."

"All right," I said, "I'm ignorant. I'm sorry. I'll go out and buy all the cat's records right away, all right?"

"It don't," said Sonny, with dignity, "make any difference to me. I don't care what you listen to. Don't do me no favors."

I was beginning to realize that I'd never seen him so upset before. With another part of my mind I was thinking that this would probably turn out to be one of those things kids go through and that I shouldn't make it seem important by pushing it too hard. Still, I didn't think it would do any harm to ask: "Doesn't all this take a lot of time? Can you make a living at it?"

He turned back to me and half leaned, half sat, on the kitchen table. "Everything takes time," he said, "and—well, yes, sure, I can make a living at it. But what I don't seem to be able to make you understand is that it's the only thing I want to do."

"Well, Sonny," I said, gently, "you know people can't always do exactly what they *want* to do—"

"*No*, I don't know that," said Sonny, surprising me. "I think people *ought* to do what they want to do, what else are they alive for?"

"You getting to be a big boy," I said desperately, "it's time you started thinking about your future."

"I'm thinking about my future," said Sonny, grimly. "I think about it all the time."

I gave up. I decided, if he didn't change his mind, that we could always talk about it later. "In the meantime," I said, "you got to finish school." We had already decided that he'd have to move in with Isabel and her folks. I knew this wasn't the ideal arrangement because Isabel's folks are inclined to be dicey and they hadn't especially wanted Isabel to marry me. But I didn't know what else to do. "And we have to get you fixed up at Isabel's."

There was a long silence. He moved from the kitchen table to the window. "That's a terrible idea. You know it yourself."

"Do you have a *better* idea?"

He just walked up and down the kitchen for a minute. He was as tall as I was. He had started to shave. I suddenly had the feeling that I didn't know him at all.

He stopped at the kitchen table and picked up my cigarettes. Looking at me with a kind of mocking, amused defiance, he put one between his lips. "You mind?"

"You smoking already?"

He lit the cigarette and nodded, watching me through the smoke. "I just wanted to see if I'd have the courage to smoke in front of you." He grinned and blew a great cloud of smoke to the ceiling. "It was easy." He looked at my face. "Come on, now. I bet you was smoking at my age, tell the truth."

I didn't say anything but the truth was on my face, and he laughed. But now there was something very strained in his laugh. "Sure. And I bet that ain't all you was doing."

He was frightening me a little. "Cut the crap," I said. "We already decided that you was going to go and live at Isabel's. Now what's got into you all of a sudden?"

"*You* decided it," he pointed out. "I didn't decide nothing." He stopped in front of me, leaning against the stove, arms loosely folded. "Look, brother. I don't want to stay in Harlem no more, I really don't." He was very earnest. He looked at me, then over towards the kitchen window. There was something in his eyes I'd never seen before, some thoughtfulness, some worry all his own. He rubbed the muscle of one arm. "It's time I was getting out of here."

"Where do you want to *go*, Sonny?"

"I want to join the army. Or the navy, I don't care. If I say I'm old enough, they'll believe me."

Then I got mad. It was because I was so scared. "You must be crazy. You goddamn fool, what the hell do you want to go and join the *army* for?"

"I just told you. To get out of Harlem."

"Sonny, you haven't even finished *school*. And if you really want to be a musician, how do you expect to study if you're in the *army?*"

He looked at me, trapped, and in anguish. "There's ways. I might be able to work out some kind of deal. Anyway, I'll have the G.I. Bill when I come out."

"*If* you come out." We stared at each other. "Sonny, please. Be reasonable. I know the setup is far from perfect. But we got to do the best we can."

"I ain't learning nothing in school," he said. "Even when I go." He turned away from me and opened the window and threw his cigarette out into the narrow alley. I watched his back. "At least, I ain't learning nothing you'd want me to learn." He slammed the window so hard I thought the glass would fly out, and turned back to me. "And I'm sick of the stink of these garbage cans!"

"Sonny," I said, "I know how you feel. But if you don't finish school now, you're going to be sorry later that you didn't." I grabbed him by the shoulders. "And you only got another year. It ain't so bad. And I'll come back and I swear I'll help you do *whatever* you want to do. Just try to put up with it till I come back. Will you please do that? For me?"

He didn't answer and he wouldn't look at me.

"Sonny. You hear me?"

He pulled away. "I hear you. But you never hear anything *I* say."

I didn't know what to say to that. He looked out of the window and then back at me. "O.K.," he said, and sighed. "I'll try."

Then I said, trying to cheer him up a little, "They got a piano at Isabel's. You can practice on it."

And as a matter of fact, it did cheer him up for a minute. "That's right," he said to himself. "I forgot that." His face relaxed a little. But the worry, the thoughtfulness, played on it still, the way shadows play on a face which is staring into the fire.

But I thought I'd never hear the end of that piano. At first, Isabel would write me, saying how nice it was that Sonny was so serious about his music and how, as soon as he came in from school, or wherever he had been when he was supposed to be at school, he went straight to that piano and stayed there until suppertime. And, after supper, he went back to that piano and stayed there until everybody went to bed. He was at the piano all day Saturday and all day Sunday. Then he bought a record player and started playing records. He'd play one record over and over again, all day long sometimes, and he'd improvise along with it on the piano. Or he'd play one section of the record, one chord, one change, one progression, then he'd do it on the piano. Then back to the record. Then back to the piano.

Well, I really don't know how they stood it. Isabel finally confessed that it wasn't like living with a person at all, it was like living with sound. And the sound didn't make any sense to her, didn't make any sense to any of them—naturally. They began, in a way, to be afflicted by this presence that was living in their home. It was as though Sonny were some sort of god, or monster. He moved in an atmosphere which wasn't like theirs at all. They fed him and he ate, he washed himself, he walked in and out of their door; he certainly wasn't nasty or unpleasant or rude, Sonny isn't any of those things; but it was as though he were all wrapped up in some cloud, some fire, some vision all his own; and there wasn't any way to reach him.

At the same time, he wasn't really a man yet, he was still a child, and they had to watch out for him in all kinds of ways. They certainly couldn't throw him out. Neither did they dare to make a great scene about that piano because even they dimly sensed, as I sensed, from so many thousands of miles away, that Sonny was at that piano playing for his life.

But he hadn't been going to school. One day a letter came from the school board and Isabel's mother got it—there had, apparently, been other letters but Sonny had torn them up. This day, when Sonny came in, Isabel's mother showed him the letter and asked where he'd been spending his time. And she finally got it out of him that he'd been down in Greenwich Village, with musicians and other characters, in a white girl's apartment. And this scared her and she started to scream at him and what came up, once she began—though she denies it to this day—was what sacrifices they were making to give Sonny a decent home and how little he appreciated it.

Sonny didn't play the piano that day. By evening, Isabel's mother had calmed down but then there was the old man to deal with, and Isabel herself. Isabel says she did her best to be calm but she broke down and started crying. She says she just watched Sonny's face. She could tell, by watching him, what was happening with him. And what was happening was that they penetrated his cloud, they had reached him. Even if their fingers had been a thousand times more gentle than human fingers ever are, he could hardly help feeling that they had stripped him naked and were spitting on that nakedness. For he also had to see that his presence, that music, which was life or death to him, had been torture for them and that they had endured it, not at all for his sake, but only for mine. And Sonny couldn't take that. He can take it a little better today than he could then but he's still not very good at it and, frankly, I don't know anybody who is.

The silence of the next few days must have been louder than the sound of all the music ever played since time began. One morning, before she went to work, Isabel was in his room for something and she suddenly realized that all of his records were gone. And she knew for certain that he was gone. And he was. He went as far as the navy would carry him. He finally sent me a postcard from some place in Greece and that was the first I knew that Sonny was still alive. I didn't see him any more until we were both back in New York and the war had long been over.

He was a man by then, of course, but I wasn't willing to see it. He came by the house from time to time, but we fought almost every time we met. I didn't like the way he carried himself, loose and dreamlike all the time, and I didn't like his friends, and his music seemed to be merely an excuse for the life he led. It sounded just that weird and disordered.

Then we had a fight, a pretty awful fight, and I didn't see him for months. By and by I looked him up, where he was living, in a furnished room in the Village, and I tried to make it up. But there were lots of other people in the room and Sonny just lay on his bed, and he wouldn't come downstairs with me, and he treated these other people as though they were his family and I weren't. So I got mad and then he got mad, and then I told him that he might just as well be dead as live the way he was living. Then he stood up and he told me not to worry about him any more in life, that he *was* dead as far as I was concerned. Then he pushed me to the door and the other people looked on as though nothing were happening, and he slammed the door behind me. I stood in the hallway, staring at the door. I heard somebody laugh in the room and then the tears came to my eyes. I started down the steps, whistling to keep from crying, I kept whistling to myself, *You going to need me, baby, one of these cold, rainy days.*

I read about Sonny's trouble in the spring. Little Grace died in the fall. She was a beautiful little girl. But she only lived a little over two years. She died of polio and she suffered. She had a slight fever for a couple of days, but it didn't seem like anything and we just kept her in bed. And we would certainly have called the doctor, but the fever dropped, she seemed to be all right. So we thought it had just been a cold. Then, one day, she was up, playing, Isabel was in the kitchen fixing lunch for the two boys when they'd come in from school, and she heard Grace fall down in the living-room. When you have a lot of children you don't always start running when one of them falls, unless they start screaming or something. And, this time, Grace was quiet. Yet, Isabel says that when she heard that *thump* and then that silence, something happened in her to make her afraid. And she ran to the living-room and there was little Grace on the floor, all twisted up, and the reason she hadn't screamed was that she couldn't get her breath. And when she did scream, it was the worst sound, Isabel says, that she'd ever heard in all her life, and she still hears it sometimes in her dreams. Isabel will sometimes wake me up with a low, moaning, strangled sound and I have to be quick to awaken her and hold her to me and where Isabel is weeping against me seems a mortal wound.

I think I may have written Sonny the very day that little Grace was buried. I was sitting in the living-room in the dark, by myself, and I suddenly thought of Sonny. My trouble made his real.

One Saturday afternoon, when Sonny had been living with us, or, anyway, been in our house, for nearly two weeks, I found myself wandering aimlessly about the living-room, drinking from a can of beer, and trying to work up the courage to search Sonny's room. He was out, he was usually out whenever I was home, and Isabel had taken the children to see their grandparents. Suddenly I was standing still in front of the living-room window, watching Seventh Avenue. The idea of searching Sonny's room made me still. I scarcely dared to admit to myself what I'd be searching for. I didn't know what I'd do if I found it. Or if I didn't.

On the sidewalk across from me, near the entrance to a barbecue joint, some people were holding an old-fashioned revival meeting. The barbecue cook, wearing a dirty white apron, his conked hair reddish and metallic in the pale sun, and a cigarette between his lips, stood in the doorway, watching them. Kids and older people paused in their errands and stood there, along with some older men and a couple of very tough-looking women who watched everything that happened on the avenue, as though they owned it, or were maybe owned by it. Well, they were watching this, too. The revival was being carried on by three sisters in black, and a brother. All they had were their voices and their Bibles and a tambourine. The brother was testifying and while he testified two of the sisters stood together, seeming to say, amen, and the third sister walked around with the tambourine outstretched and a couple of people dropped coins into it. Then the brother's testimony ended and the sister who had been taking up the collection dumped the coins into her palm and transferred them to the pocket of her long black robe. Then she raised both hands, striking the tambourine against the air, and then against one hand, and she started to sing. And the two other sisters and the brother joined in.

It was strange, suddenly, to watch, though I had been seeing these street meetings all my life. So, of course, had everybody else down there. Yet, they paused and watched and listened and I stood still at the window. "Tis the old ship of Zion," they sang, and the sister with the tambourine kept a steady, jangling beat, "it has rescued many a thousand!" Not a soul under the sound of their voices was hearing this song for the first time, not one of them had been rescued. Nor had they seen much in the way of rescue work being done around them. Neither did they especially believe in the holiness of the three sisters and the brother, they knew too much about them, knew where they lived, and how. The woman with the tambourine, whose voice dominated the air, whose face was bright with joy, was divided by very little from the woman who stood watching her, a cigarette between her heavy, chapped lips, her hair a cuckoo's nest, her face scarred and swollen from many beatings, and her black eyes glittering like coal. Perhaps they both knew this, which was why, when, as rarely, they addressed each other, they addressed each other as Sister. As the singing filled the air the watching, listening faces underwent a change, the eyes focusing on something within; the music seemed to soothe a poison out of them; and time seemed, nearly, to fall away from the sullen, belligerent, battered faces, as though they were fleeing back to their first condition, while dreaming of their last. The barbecue cook half shook his head and smiled, and dropped his cigarette and disappeared into his joint. A man fumbled in his pockets for change and stood holding it in his hand impatiently, as though he had just remembered a pressing appointment further up the avenue. He looked furious. Then I saw Sonny, standing on the edge of the crowd. He was carrying a wide, flat notebook with a green cover, and it made him look, from where I was standing, almost like a school-boy. The coppery sun brought out the copper in his skin, he was very faintly smiling, standing very still. Then the singing stopped, the tambourine turned into a collection plate again. The furious man dropped in his coins and vanished, so did a couple of the women, and Sonny dropped some change in the plate, looking directly at the women with a little smile. He started across the avenue, towards the house. He has a slow, loping walk, something like the way Harlem hipsters walk, only he's imposed on this his own half-beat. I had never really noticed it before.

I stayed at the window, both relieved and apprehensive. As Sonny disappeared from my sight, they began singing again. And they were still singing when his key turned in the lock.

"Hey," he said.

"Hey, yourself. You want some beer?"

"No. Well, maybe." But he came up to the window and stood beside me, looking out. "What a warm voice," he said.

They were singing *If I could only hear my mother pray again!*

"Yes," I said, "and she can sure beat that tambourine."

"But what a terrible song," he said, and laughed. He dropped his notebook on the sofa and disappeared into the kitchen. "Where's Isabel and the kids?"

"I think they went to see their grandparents. You hungry?"

"No." He came back into the living-room with his can of beer. "You want to come some place with me tonight?"

I sensed, I don't know how, that I couldn't possibly say no. "Sure. Where?"

He sat down on the sofa and picked up his notebook and started leafing through it. "I'm going to sit in with some fellows in a joint in the Village."

"You mean, you're going to play, tonight?"

"That's right." He took a swallow of his beer and moved back to the window. He gave me a sidelong look. "If you can stand it."

"I'll try," I said.

He smiled to himself and we both watched as the meeting across the way broke up. The three sisters and the brother, heads bowed, were singing *God be with you till we meet again*. The faces around them were very quiet. Then the song ended. The small crowd dispersed. We watched the three women and the lone man walk slowly up the avenue.

"When she was singing before," said Sonny, abruptly, "her voice reminded me for a minute of what heroin feels like sometimes—when it's in your veins. It makes you feel sort of warm and cool at the same time. And distant. And—and sure." He sipped his beer, very deliberately not looking at me. I watched his face. "It makes you feel—in control. Sometimes you've got to have that feeling."

"Do you?" I sat down slowly in the easy chair.

"Sometimes." He went to the sofa and picked up his notebook again. "Some people do."

"In order," I asked, "to play?" And my voice was very ugly, full of contempt and anger.

"Well"—he looked at me with great, troubled eyes, as though, in fact, he hoped his eyes would tell me things he could never otherwise say —"they *think* so. And *if* they think so—!"

"And what do *you* think?" I asked.

He sat on the sofa and put his can of beer on the floor. "I don't know," he said, and I couldn't be sure if he were answering my question or pursuing his thoughts. His face didn't tell me. "It's not so much to *play*. It's to *stand* it, to be able to make it at all. On any level." He frowned and smiled: "In order to keep from shaking to pieces."

"But these friends of yours," I said, "they seem to shake themselves to pieces pretty goddamn fast."

"Maybe." He played with the notebook. And something told me that I should curb my tongue, that Sonny was doing his best to talk, that I should listen. "But of course you only know the ones that've gone to pieces. Some don't—or at least they haven't *yet* and that's just about all *any* of us can say." He paused. "And then there are some who just live, really, in hell, and they know it and they see what's happening and they go right on. I don't know." He sighed, dropped the notebook, folded his arms. "Some guys, you can tell from the way they play, they on something *all* the time. And you can see that, well, it makes something real for them. But of course," he picked up his beer from the floor and sipped it and put the can down again, "they *want* to, too, you've got to see that. Even some of them that say they don't—*some*, not all."

"And what about you?" I asked—I couldn't help it. "What about you? Do *you* want to?"

He stood up and walked to the window and remained silent for a long time. Then he sighed. "Me," he said. Then: "While I was down-stairs before, on my way here, listening to that woman sing, it struck me all of a sudden how much suffering she must have had to go through —to sing like that. It's *repulsive* to think you have to suffer that much."

I said: "But there's no way not to suffer—is there, Sonny?"

"I believe not," he said and smiled, "but that's never stopped anyone from trying." He looked at me. "Has it?" I realized, with this mocking look, that there stood between us, for ever, beyond the power of time or forgiveness, the fact that I had held silence—so long!—when he had needed human speech to help him. He turned back to the window. "No, there's no way not to suffer. But you try all kinds of ways to keep from drowning in it, to keep on top of it, and to make it seem—well, like *you*. Like you did something, all right, and now you're suffering for it. You know?" I said nothing. "Well you know," he said, impatiently, "why *do* people suffer? Maybe it's better to do something to give it a reason, *any* reason."

"But we just agreed," I said, "that there's no way not to suffer. Isn't it better, then, just to—take it?"

"But nobody just takes it," Sonny cried, "that's what I'm telling you! *Everybody* tries not to. You're just hung up on the *way* some people try—it's not *your* way!"

The hair on my face began to itch, my face felt wet. "That's not true," I said, "that's not true. I don't give a damn what other people do, I don't even care how they suffer. I just care how *you* suffer." And he looked at me. "Please believe me," I said, "I don't want to see you—die —trying not to suffer."

"I won't," he said, flatly, "die trying not to suffer. At least, not any faster than anybody else."

"But there's no need," I said, trying to laugh, "is there? in killing yourself."

I wanted to say more, but I couldn't. I wanted to talk about will power and how life could be—well, beautiful. I wanted to say that it was all within; but was it? or, rather, wasn't that exactly the trouble? And I wanted to promise that I would never fail him again. But it would all have sounded—empty words and lies.

So I made the promise to myself and prayed that I would keep it.

"It's terrible sometimes, inside," he said, "that's what's the trouble. You walk these streets, black and funky and cold, and there's not really a living ass to talk to, and there's nothing shaking, and there's no way of getting it out—that storm inside. You can't talk it and you can't make love with it, and when you finally try to get with it and play it, you realize *nobody's* listening. So *you've* got to listen. You got to find a way to listen."

And then he walked away from the window and sat on the sofa again, as though all the wind had suddenly been knocked out of him. "Sometimes you'll do *anything* to play, even cut your mother's throat." He laughed and looked at me. "Or your brother's." Then he sobered. "Or your own." Then: "Don't worry. I'm all right now and I think I'll *be* all right. But I can't forget—where I've been. I don't mean just the physical place I've been, I mean where I've *been*. And *what* I've been."

"What have you been, Sonny?" I asked.

He smiled—but sat sideways on the sofa, his elbow resting on the back, his fingers playing with his mouth and chin, not looking at me. "I've been something I didn't recognize, didn't know I could be. Didn't know anybody could be." He stopped, looking inward, looking helplessly young, looking old. "I'm not talking about it now because I feel *guilty* or anything like that—maybe it would be better if I did, I don't know. Anyway, I can't really talk about it. Not to you, not to anybody," and now he turned and faced me. "Sometimes, you know, and it was actually when I was most *out* of the world, I felt that I was in it, that I was *with* it, really, and I could play or I didn't really have to *play*, it just came out of me, it was there. And I don't know how I played, thinking about it now, but I know I did awful things, those times, sometimes, to people. Or it wasn't that I *did* anything to them—it was that they weren't real." He picked up the beer can; it was empty; he rolled it between his palms: "And other times—well, I needed a fix, I needed to find a place to lean, I needed to clear a space to *listen*—and I couldn't find it, and I—went crazy, I did terrible things to *me*, I was terrible *for* me." He began pressing the beer can between his hands, I watched the metal begin to give. It glittered, as he played with it, like a knife, and I was afraid he would cut himself, but I said nothing. "Oh well. I can never tell you. I was all by myself at the bottom of something, stinking and sweating and crying and shaking, and I smelled it, you know? *my* stink, and I thought I'd die if I couldn't get away from it and yet, all the same, I knew that everything I was doing was just locking me in with it. And I didn't know," he paused, still flattening the beer can, "I didn't know, I still *don't* know, something kept telling me that maybe it was good to smell your own stink, but I didn't think that *that* was what I'd been trying to do—and—who can stand it?" and he abruptly dropped the ruined beer can, looking at me with a small, still smile, and then rose, walking to the window as though it were the lodestone rock. I watched his face, he watched the avenue. "I couldn't tell you when Mama died—but the reason I wanted to leave Harlem so bad was to get away from drugs. And then, when I ran away, that's what I was running from—really. When I came back, nothing had changed, *I* hadn't changed, I was just—older." And he stopped, drumming with his fingers on the window-pane. The sun had vanished, soon darkness would fall. I watched his face. "It can come again," he said, almost as though speaking to himself. Then he turned to me. "It *can* come again," he repeated. "I just want you to know that."

"All right," I said, at last. "So it can come again, all right."

He smiled, but the smile was sorrowful. "I had to try to tell you," he said.

"Yes," I said. "I understand that."

"You're my brother," he said, looking straight at me, and not smiling at all.

"Yes," I repeated, "yes. I understand that."

He turned back to the window, looking out. "All that hatred down there," he said, "all that hatred and misery and love. It's a wonder it doesn't blow the avenue apart."

We went to the only night-club on a short, dark street, downtown. We squeezed through the narrow, chattering, jam-packed bar to the entrance of the big room, where the bandstand was. And we stood there for a moment, for the lights were very dim in this room and we couldn't see. Then, "Hello, boy," said a voice and an enormous black man, much older than Sonny or myself, erupted out of all that atmospheric lighting and put an arm around Sonny's shoulder. "I been sitting right here," he said, "waiting for you."

He had a big voice, too, and heads in the darkness turned towards us.

Sonny grinned and pulled a little away, and said, "Creole, this is my brother. I told you about him."

Creole shook my hand. "I'm glad to meet you, son," he said, and it was clear that he was glad to meet me *there*, for Sonny's sake. And he smiled, "You got a real musician in *your* family," and he took his arm from Sonny's shoulder and slapped him, lightly, affectionately, with the back of his hand.

"Well. Now I've heard it all," said a voice behind us. This was another musician, and a friend of Sonny's, a coal-black, cheerful-looking man, built close to the ground. He immediately began confiding to me, at the top of his lungs, the most terrible things about Sonny, his teeth gleaming like a lighthouse and his laugh coming up out of him like the beginning of an earthquake. And it turned out that everyone at the bar knew Sonny, or almost everyone; some were musicians, working there, or near by, or not working, some were simply hangers-on, and some were there to hear Sonny play. I was introduced to all of them and they were all very polite to me. Yet, it was clear that, for them, I was only Sonny's brother. Here, I was in Sonny's world. Or, rather: his kingdom. Here, it was not even a question that his veins bore royal blood.

They were going to play soon and Creole installed me, by myself, at a table in a dark corner. Then I watched them, Creole, and the little black man, and Sonny, and the others, while they horsed around, standing just below the bandstand. The light from the bandstand spilled just a little short of them and, watching them laughing and gesturing and moving about, I had the feeling that they, nevertheless, were being most careful not to step into that circle of light too suddenly: that if they moved into the light too suddenly, without thinking, they would perish in flame. Then, while I watched, one of them, the small, black man, moved into the light and crossed the bandstand and started fooling around with his drums. Then—being funny and being, also, extremely ceremonious—Creole took Sonny by the arm and led him to the piano. A woman's voice called Sonny's name and a few hands started clapping. And Sonny, also being funny and being ceremonious, and so touched, I think, that he could have cried, but neither hiding it nor showing it, riding it like a man, grinned, and put both hands to his heart and bowed from the waist.

Creole then went to the bass fiddle and a lean, very bright-skinned brown man jumped up on the bandstand and picked up his horn. So there they were, and the atmosphere on the bandstand and in the room began to change and tighten. Someone stepped up to the microphone and announced them. Then there were all kinds of murmurs. Some people at the bar shushed others. The waitress ran around, frantically getting in the last orders, guys and chicks got closer to each other, and the lights on the bandstand, on the quartet, turned to a kind of indigo. Then they all looked different there. Creole looked about him for the last time, as though he were making certain that all his chickens were in the coop, and then he—jumped and struck the fiddle. And there they were.

All I know about music is that not many people ever really hear it. And even then, on the rare occasions when something opens within, and the music enters, what we mainly hear, or hear corroborated, are personal, private, vanishing evocations. But the man who creates the music is hearing something else, is dealing with the roar rising from the void and imposing order on it as it hits the air. What is evoked in him, then, is of another order, more terrible because it has no words, and triumphant, too, for that same reason. And his triumph, when he triumphs, is ours. I just watched Sonny's face. His face was troubled, he was working hard, but he wasn't with it. And I had the feeling that, in a way, everyone on the bandstand was waiting for him, both waiting for him and pushing him along. But as I began to watch Creole, I realized that it was Creole who held them all back. He had them on a short rein. Up there, keeping the beat with his whole body, wailing on the fiddle, with his eyes half closed, he was listening to everything, but he was listening to Sonny. He was having a dialogue with Sonny. He wanted Sonny to leave the shoreline and strike out for deep water. He was Sonny's witness that deep water and drowning were not the same thing—he had been there, and he knew. And he wanted Sonny to know. He was waiting for Sonny to do the things on the keys which would let Creole know that Sonny was in the water.

And, while Creole listened, Sonny moved, deep within, exactly like someone in torment. I had never before thought of how awful the relationship must be between the musician and his instrument. He has to fill it, this instrument, with the breath of life, his own. He has to make it do what he wants it to do. And a piano is just a piano. It's made out of so much wood and wires and little hammers and big ones, and ivory. While there's only so much you can do with it, the only way to find this out is to try; to try and make it do everything.

And Sonny hadn't been near a piano for over a year. And he wasn't on much better terms with his life, not the life that stretched before him now. He and the piano stammered, started one way, got scared, stopped; started another way, panicked, marked time, started again; then seemed to have found a direction, panicked again, got stuck. And the face I saw on Sonny I'd never seen before. Everything had been burned out of it, and, at the same time, things usually hidden were being burned in, by the fire and fury of the battle which was occurring in him up there.

Yet, watching Creole's face as they neared the end of the first set, I had the feeling that something had happened, something I hadn't heard. Then they finished, there was scattered applause, and then, without an instant's warning, Creole started into something else, it was almost sardonic, it was *Am I Blue*. And, as though he commanded, Sonny began to play. Something began to happen. And Creole let out the reins. The dry, low, black man said something awful on the drums, Creole answered, and the drums talked back. Then the horn insisted, sweet and high, slightly detached perhaps, and Creole listened, commenting now and then, dry, and driving, beautiful and calm and old. Then they all came together again, and Sonny was part of the family again. I could tell this from his face. He seemed to have found, right there beneath his fingers, a damn brand-new piano. It seemed that he couldn't get over it. Then, for awhile, just being happy with Sonny, they seemed to be agreeing with him that brand-new pianos certainly were a gas.

Then Creole stepped forward to remind them that what they were playing was the blues. He hit something in all of them, he hit something in me, myself, and the music tightened and deepened, apprehension began to beat the air. Creole began to tell us what the blues were all about. They were not about anything very new. He and his boys up there were keeping it new, at the risk of ruin, destruction, madness, and death, in order to find new ways to make us listen. For, while the tale of how we suffer, and how we are delighted, and how we may triumph is never new, it always must be heard. There isn't any other tale to tell, it's the only light we've got in all this darkness.

And this tale, according to that face, that body, those strong hands on those strings, has another aspect in every country, and a new depth in every generation. Listen, Creole seemed to be saying, listen. Now these are Sonny's blues. He made the little black man on the drums know it, and the bright, brown man on the horn. Creole wasn't trying any longer to get Sonny in the water. He was wishing him Godspeed. Then he stepped back, very slowly, filling the air with the immense suggestion that Sonny speak for himself.

Then they all gathered around Sonny and Sonny played. Every now and again one of them seemed to say, amen. Sonny's fingers filled the air with life, his life. But that life contained so many others. And Sonny went all the way back, he really began with the spare, flat statement of the opening phrase of the song. Then he began to make it his. It was very beautiful because it wasn't hurried and it was no longer a lament. I seemed to hear with what burning he had made it his, with what burning we had yet to make it ours, how we could cease lamenting. Freedom lurked around us and I understood, at last, that he could help us to be free if we would listen, that he would never be free until we did. Yet, there was no battle in his face now. I heard what he had gone through, and would continue to go through until he came to rest in earth. He had made it his: that long line, of which we knew only Mama and Daddy. And he was giving it back, as everything must be given back, so that, passing through death, it can live for ever. I saw my mother's face again, and felt, for the first time, how the stones of the road she had walked on must have bruised her feet. I saw the moonlit road where my father's brother died. And it brought something else back to me, and carried me past it, I saw my little girl again and felt Isabel's tears again, and I felt my own tears begin to rise. And I was yet aware that this was only a moment, that the world waited outside, as hungry as a tiger, and that trouble stretched above us, longer than the sky.

Then it was over. Creole and Sonny let out their breath, both soaking wet, and grinning. There was a lot of applause and some of it was real. In the dark, the girl came by and I asked her to take drinks to the bandstand. There was a long pause, while they talked up there in the indigo light and after a while I saw the girl put a Scotch and milk on top of the piano for Sonny. He didn't seem to notice it, but just before they started playing again, he sipped from it and looked towards me, and nodded. Then he put it back on top of the piano. For me, then, as they began to play again, it glowed and shook above my brother's head like the very cup of trembling.

QUESTIONS

1. Is the narrator's occupation and family background important to a full understanding of the story? If so, why?

2. What does the mother mean when, having related the details of her brother-in-law's death, she says to her son, " 'I'm telling you this because you got a brother. And the world ain't changed' "?

3. Although revival meetings were not unusual in Harlem, Baldwin indicates that for Sonny the revival meeting took on unusual significance. What new meaning did Sonny perceive in it?

4. Baldwin refers frequently to Sonny's "privacy." Sonny reveals something about his inner world when he is talking to his brother about heroin. What does he say? How does this help explain that "distant stillness in which he always moved"?

5. Baldwin says that Sonny played "for his life," not for a living. How do we come to understand what this means?

6. What is the significance of the description of the musician as a man "dealing with the roar rising from the void and imposing order on it as it hits the air"?

On Trains

James Alan McPherson

The waiters say she got on the train in Chicago, after transferring from Dearborn Station. She was plump and matronly and her glasses were tinted so that she might have been a tourist seeking protection from the sun; but there was neither sun nor fresh air on the train and she was very pale and a little wrinkled, the way clerks or indoor people grow after many years of their protected, colorless kind of life. She was, indeed, that nondescript type of person one might be aware of but never really see in a supermarket or at a bargain basement sale, carefully and methodically fingering each item; or on a busy street corner waiting for the light to change while others, with less conscious respect for the letter of the law, flowed around her. She rode for a whole day before coming into the dining car for a meal: then she had the $1.95 Special. She asked for buttermilk and wanted "lightbread" instead of rolls. The black waiters all grinned at each other in their secret way.

When she finished her meal she sat reading a book and looking out at the yellow and green flatlands of North Dakota until the steward had to ask her to leave so that the waiters could clean up the table for the next setting. She did not protest, but left with an indignant flourish of her dress. The automatic door to the car leading to the Pullman section hissed angrily behind her. The steward called her a bitch between his teeth and the waiter who had served her, standing next to the steward with his tray under his arm, grinned broadly, showing his own smoke-stained teeth. But when he saw that she had left no tip he called her a cheap bitch aloud and the steward scowled at him.

After the last setting the waiters sat down to eat their dinner. Two Pullman Porters came in with their coffee cans, begging for handouts. They were very greedy and, if given one can of free coffee, would continue to come back for more during the length of the trip, as if the first can had entitled them to all that they could drink. They sat down

---

at the waiters' table and watched the waiters eat. The waiters were very greedy too. They ate ravenously. The porters watched the waiters for a while, then one of them closed his eyes and began to doze. The other one, an old fellow with aged and tired eyes like an owl's, looked out at the floating gold of the sunset across the passing wheatfields. He watched until the fields became patterns of black and fading gold. Then he turned to the waiters.

"We got a old Southern gal back there," he said.

"We had her up here," one of the waiters said between huge mouthfuls of beef. "She got good service but she didn't leave no tip."

"She had me polishin' her shoes," the porter said, "but I don't reckon she'll pay off when she gets off. I didn't put much work out on it anyway." He stretched his thin legs under the table. They cracked with the sound of dead autumn branches underfoot.

A woman in pants passed through the car. Her hair was cut somewhat like a little girl's Dutch Boy and a ringlet of it curled against her cheek. She blew at it out of the corner of her mouth and smiled knowingly at the men seated around the table. "Which way to the club car?" she asked. Her lipstick was above the line of her mouth so that it looked like a red moustache. She was not at all pretty and not at all young.

"Two cars ahead," one waiter said.

She turned to go, took a few steps and then looked back at the men. The two waiters were looking her over, one porter was still dozing, and the other, the tired one, was seemingly not aware of her.

"How late does it stay open?"

"Till twelve," the same waiter said.

"Chicago time," the other waiter added.

They watched her move through the door.

"She'll tip big tomorrow," one of them said.

"Yeah."

"That old biddy knows where the club car is. She been in there all day. I seen her battin' them greasy eyes at John Perry on the bar."

"Maybe he'll take care of business for her tonight," the tired Pullman Porter said. But there was no humor in it, and all of their laughs were only polite.

"If he does she'll tip big tomorrow," one of the waiters said again.

The porter with the owl eyes pushed the dozing porter. "Time to get the beds down, Tim," he said. Tim got up slowly and they took their coffee cans and trudged down the aisle toward the Pullman section. As they reached the door it opened and the lady who had transferred from Dearborn came into the car. The two porters stood on either side of the aisle and let her pass between them. They wore white jackets with silver buttons which were embossed: "Pullman Company." Together with their caps with silver plates, which also read "Pullman Porter," and black pants, they looked like two painted black statues before the entrance to some fine suburban home. She did not notice them, but passed directly through the car, leaving behind her a scent of something sweet and strong.

When she entered the club car the woman with the Dutch bob was sitting at the bar talking to John Perry, the bartender, who stood behind the bar leaning with his arms on its waxed red surface. They were very close and the Dutch woman was smiling mysteriously. There was no one else in the car. The Dearborn lady seated herself at a deuce near the far end of the car and began to stare at John Perry as he said something low and soft and smile-provoking to the painted thing on the stool across from him. The Dearborn lady cleared her throat. John Perry placed his dark, thick hand closer to the other, softer hand on the bar and did not look up. The painted woman made a throaty chuckle, like the confusing sound one might hear near a car parked by a frog pond on a summer night.

"I want some service," the lady at the end of the car finally said. "I've been here for ten minutes now and I want some service."

The bartender looked annoyed as he went over to her table. "What'll it be lady?" he said. His voice was deep and smooth and almost as greasy as the painted woman's lips; and it had that familiar ring of professional servitude, which is peculiar to small, serving people who like their work.

"I want a Benedictine and brandy."

"No Benedictine. This is a train, lady."

She paused. "I'll have a crème de menthe then."

"We don't have that neither."

"Try bourbon and water, honey," the woman at the bar said, and she lifted her glass for the woman to see. "He makes it very good. I'm going to have another one myself." She looked at the bartender as she pushed a five-dollar bill across the bar. "Make yourself one too," she told him.

The lady at the deuce looked at her fiercely.

She finally ordered a rosé, paid for it, and settled back, taking turns watching the immediate reflections of the two at the bar in the window next to her face and the darkness of the passing countryside beyond their reflections. The train lumbered on and it made the only noise, save for an occasional giggle and a deep-throated chuckle from the bar. Finally the woman got up from the stool and said, "See you later on" to the bartender. She said it with a contrived, unnatural seductivity and took her time moving out of the car. The Dearborn lady, still seated at the table and facing the window, saw it all through her tinted glasses.

The bartender began to whistle as he washed the glasses. He was a robust fellow but he moved very gracefully behind the bar, like a dancer. Still, he splashed a great deal of water on the floor. He glanced over at the lady once or twice as she, in turn, looked alternately at the darkness beyond the thick window glass and at him. But only her eyes moved Then the man moved out from behind the bar and came toward her.

She stiffened and gathered her purse and got up, all very quickly. He was wiping the tables and whistling as she hurried out of the car.

II

In the Pullman car, the porter was still making the beds. He shuffled from one roomette to the next, not wasting a single step. The occupants came out of their rooms and stood in the hall while he swished and tucked their sheets. Then he knocked on the Dearborn lady's door. "Porter!" he barked, the way a street-corner concessionaire would say "Hot Dogs!" There was no answer, so he went in and began turning down the bed. She came up behind him and watched his back as he moved about the small compartment. She was breathing very hard.

"What time do you lock the doors to the car?" she asked.

"The doors ain't never locked," he said, not turning to face her.

"How do you keep people out?" She paused, and then said: "My luggage is in the hall. It's very expensive."

"I'll watch out for it. I sit up all night."

"Inside the car?"

"Yes ma'am."

"But I . . . we have to sleep. We have to sleep in here," she said. She was very excited now.

"Yes ma'am." He did not stop his work; nor did he look at her, but answered her questions and made the bed with the proficiency and cool detachment of one used to confronting stupidity in the intelligent. It was bargained and paid for in the price of her ticket and his was a patient and polite endurance of her right to be stupid. "I'm a Pullman Porter," he said. "I been a Pullman Porter for forty-three years." He had finished the bed and he smoothed down a light ripple in the red blanket. His hands were rough and wrinkled and the backs of his fingers were very black. "Forty-three years," he repeated reminiscently, half to himself. She could not see his eyes.

"Well, you can't stay in here tonight," she said, and moved into the small compartment as if to possess it entirely with her presence.

The porter backed out. "It's my job," he said.

She was extremely nervous now and ran her hands lightly over the sides of her dress. Her hands stuck to the thin silk. "You go get the Pullman Conductor," she said. "I can talk to him." She began to pace up and down the little length of the roomette.

The porter returned in a few minutes with the Pullman Conductor. The blue-suited conductor entered the compartment while the porter stood outside the door and watched them, his dark old eyes flashing from one face to the other.

"He sits up in the car, lady," the conductor said. "It's his job. He has to be here if anyone rings for him at night." The conductor was very irritated. He had already started to undress for bed and his tie hung loosely about his neck. The lady was perspiring now and the little beads of sweat glistened on her temples in the glare of the white light overhead.

"I can't and I won't sleep in the same car with that . . . that gentleman!"

"That's your business if you don't sleep, lady," the conductor said. "He stays in the car." The conductor was very mad now. The lines in his forehead grew very red and his nose, which was small, grew larger and redder with his controlled breathing.

"We have a *right* to sleep here without these people coming in *doing* things."

"What's he done to you, lady?"

"He's black! He's black!" And she said it with the exasperation and utter defeat of an inexperienced teacher whose patience has been exhausted and who can only stamp the right answer into the mind of a stupid child.

"He's a porter," the conductor said.

The porter, who stood all the while like a child waiting for punishment, seemed to droop and wither and grow smaller; and his eyes, which had only minutes before flashed brightly from the face of the conductor to the enraged face of the lady, now seemed to dull and turn inward as only those who have learned to suffer silently can turn their eyes inward. He was a very old man and he grew older, even older than his occupation or the oldest and most obsequious Pullman Porter.

People were looking out of their compartments and the Dearborn lady, hearing them, raised her voice in a plea. "He sleeps in here. He sleeps in here with us!" she shouted to them. Down the hall, the painted woman opened the door to Compartment G and listened and smiled and shook her head, and then closed the door again. And the rest listened and weighed the thought, which was a new one deserving some consideration. But the conductor said that it was necessary for comfort and they agreed and returned to their rooms. Only the porter stood outside the door looking guilty.

It was finally decided that the Dearborn lady would take a seat in the coaches for the night. She wanted it that way. The porter would sleep as he had always slept: sitting up in the back of the car with his eyes closed and his mind awake and his coffee can by his side and the small bright night-light over his bowed head, and his ear next to the buzzer in case someone should ring. Everyone agreed that it was the way things should be; it was necessary for comfort, and besides, it was his job.

And later that night, when John Perry, the bartender, who danced and splashed a great deal of water when he washed glasses, stole into the dark sleeping car, he paused for a minute before the bent old man on the porter's seat. The coffee can had fallen over on the seat and John Perry picked it up and placed it on the floor next to the old man's feet. Then he knocked very softly on the door to Compartment G. And after a while it was opened and quickly closed behind him.

QUESTIONS

1. Two distinctly different types of women are depicted in this story. How does McPherson use description to make each woman's actions in the latter part of the story seem in keeping with our first impression of their characters?

2. Contrast the reactions of John Perry and the porter to the woman from Dearborn. Why are their different reactions important to the meaning and impact of the story?

3. How do you interpret John Perry's reaction to the Dutch woman?

4. Discuss McPherson's use of irony. Is it a significant part of the story?

5. Can you determine McPherson's judgment of the racial and sexual attitudes of his characters?

part 2

Poetry

Afro-American poetry has had its most luxuriant flowering in the present century. A number of competent versifiers in the nineteenth century, and occasionally an inspired poet, pleaded the Negro cause in conventionally romantic and largely imitative verse, firmly establishing the protest tradition with which black poets are usually associated. Paul Laurence Dunbar (1872–1906) was the most gifted of all these nineteenth-century poets, writing with skill and craftsmanship in dialect and standard English and attracting many imitators. Not a protest poet, he won popularity with his genre pieces, his "lyrics of lowly life." Dunbar's is the only poetry by an Afro-American of this period that has any legitimate claim on our attention as literature.

Although protest continues as a constant amid the variables in the poetry of blacks, its literary value has not gone unquestioned by Afro-American critics and poets themselves. And there seems to be an ongoing controversy over the Afro-American poet's proper function. There are those who believe he should be, above all else, a spokesman for his people, an exhorter, a propagandist. Opponents of this view hold that his only obligation is to speak the truth as he sees it and keep as his objective the creation of genuine poetry that will be universal in its appeal. Both points of view are represented by the poems in this volume.

It is manifestly impossible to discuss all the poets included, and so a few general remarks must suffice. James Weldon Johnson, however, requires specific mention as one whose work foreshadowed much that has developed since he began writing in the latter years of the last century. Like Dunbar, he wrote poems in dialect, later abandoning this kind of poetry because its effects, as he said, were limited to pathos and humor. Perhaps his major poetic achievement was God's Trombones, from which "The Creation" has been selected. In this book Johnson drew on Negro folklore, transcribing "Seven Negro Sermons" in free verse. The importance of this collection is that it reveals Afro-American folklore as a fresh and rich source for the contemporary poet. Johnson's versions of old-time sermons capture the tang of folk-speech in an idiom truer to that actually spoken than the earlier convention of the plantation dialect. Langston Hughes, Sterling A. Brown, Owen Dodson, and Lucille Clifton all seem to have profited from

Johnson's example in their interpretations of the folk experience, whether urban or rural.

If folklore, race consciousness, and protest are typical elements of the poetry written by Afro-Americans, they are by no means its only features. And historically they never have been. From Phillis Wheatley on, black poets, like all other poets worthy of the name, have responded to the uniquely personal aspects of life, as well as to the universals—nature, love, death. Contemporary poetry has been marked by almost ceaseless experimentation and by a great variety of styles, by radical changes in diction, form, and social outlook. The poems that follow show the general directions modern poetry has taken quite as much as they reveal the particular, often divergent, approaches of Afro-American poets to racial experience.

The Creation

James Weldon Johnson

And God stepped out on space,
And he looked around and said:
I'm lonely—
I'll make me a world.

And far as the eye of God could see
Darkness covered everything,
Blacker than a hundred midnights
Down in a cypress swamp.

Then God smiled,
And the light broke,
And the darkness rolled up on one side,
And the light stood shining on the other,
And God said: That's good!

Then God reached out and took the light in his hands,
And God rolled the light around in his hands
Until he made the sun;
And he set that sun a-blazing in the heavens.
And the light that was left from making the sun
God gathered it up in a shining ball
And flung it against the darkness,
Spangling the night with the moon and stars.
Then down between
The darkness and the light

He hurled the world;
And God said: That's good!

Then God himself stepped down—
And the sun was on his right hand,
And the moon was on his left;
The stars were clustered about his head,
And the earth was under his feet.
And God walked, and where he trod
His footsteps hollowed the valleys out
And bulged the mountains up.

Then he stopped and looked and saw
That the earth was hot and barren.
So God stepped over to the edge of the world
And he spat out the seven seas—
He batted his eyes, and the lightnings flashed—
He clapped his hands, and the thunders rolled—
And the waters above the earth came down,
The cooling waters came down.

Then the green grass sprouted,
And the little red flowers blossomed,
The pine tree pointed his finger to the sky,
And the oak spread out his arms,
The lakes cuddled down in the hollows of the ground,
And the rivers ran down to the sea;
And God smiled again,
And the rainbow appeared,
And curled itself around his shoulder.

Then God raised his arm and he waved his hand
Over the sea and over the land,
And he said: Bring forth! Bring forth!
And quicker than God could drop his hand,
Fishes and fowls
And beasts and birds
Swam the rivers and the seas,
Roamed the forests and the woods,
And split the air with their wings.
And God said: That's good!

Then God walked around,
And God looked around
On all that he had made.
He looked at his sun,
And he looked at his moon,
And he looked at his little stars;
He looked on his world
With all its living things,
And God said: I'm lonely still.

Then God sat down—
On the side of a hill where he could think;
By a deep, wide river he sat down;
With his head in his hands,
God thought and thought,
Till he thought: I'll make me a man!

Up from the bed of the river
God scooped the clay;
And by the bank of the river
He kneeled him down;
And there the great God Almighty
Who lit the sun and fixed it in the sky,
Who flung the stars to the most far corner of the night,
Who rounded the earth in the middle of his hand;
This Great God,
Like a mammy bending over her baby,
Kneeled down in the dust
Toiling over a lump of clay
Till he shaped it in his own image;

Then into it he blew the breath of life,
And man became a living soul.
Amen. Amen.

If We Must Die

Claude McKay

If we must die—let it not be like hogs
Hunted and penned in an inglorious spot,
While round us bark the mad and hungry dogs,
Making their mock at our accursed lot.
If we must die—oh, let us nobly die,
So that our precious blood may not be shed
In vain; then even the monsters we defy
Shall be constrained to honor us though dead!
Oh, Kinsmen! We must meet the common foe;
Though far outnumbered, let us show us brave,
And for their thousand blows deal one deathblow!
What though before us lies the open grave?
Like men we'll face the murderous, cowardly pack,
Pressed to the wall, dying, but fighting back!

FROM *Selected Poems of Claude McKay*. Copyright 1953 by Bookman Associates, Inc. Reprinted by permission of Twayne Publishers, Inc.

Outcast

Claude McKay

For the dim regions whence my fathers came
My spirit, bondaged by the body, longs.
Words felt, but never heard, my lips would frame;
My soul would sing forgotten jungle songs.
I would go back to darkness and to peace,
But the great western world holds me in fee,
And I may never hope for full release
While to its alien gods I bend my knee.
Something in me is lost, forever lost,
Some vital thing has gone out of my heart,
And I must walk the way of life a ghost
Among the sons of earth, a thing apart.

For I was born, far from my native clime,
Under the white man's menace, out of time.

FROM *Selected Poems of Claude McKay*. Copyright 1953 by Bookman Associates, Inc. Reprinted by permission of Twayne Publishers, Inc.

Song of the Son

Jean Toomer

Pour O pour that parting soul in song,
O pour it in the sawdust glow of night,
Into the velvet pine-smoke air to-night,
And let the valley carry it along.
And let the valley carry it along.

O land and soil, red soil and sweet-gum tree,
So scant of grass, so profligate of pines,
Now just before an epoch's sun declines
Thy son, in time, I have returned to thee,
Thy son, I have in time returned to thee.

In time, for though the sun is setting on
A song-lit race of slaves, it has not set;
Though late, O soil, it is not too late yet
To catch thy plaintive soul, leaving, soon gone,
Leaving, to catch thy plaintive soul soon gone.

O Negro slaves, dark purple ripened plums,
Squeezed, and bursting in the pine-wood air,
Passing, before they stripped the old tree bare
One plum was saved for me, one seed becomes

An everlasting song, a singing tree,
Caroling softly souls of slavery,
What they were, and what they are to me,
Caroling softly souls of slavery.

The Sea-Turtle and the Shark

Melvin B. Tolson

Strange but true is the story
of the sea-turtle and the shark—
the instinctive drive of the weak to survive
in the oceanic dark.
Driven,
riven
by hunger
from abyss to shoal,
sometimes the shark swallows
the sea-turtle whole.
"The sly reptilian marine
withdraws,
into the shell
of his undersea craft,
his leathery head and the rapacious claws
that can rip
a rhinoceros' hide
or strip
a crocodile to fare-thee-well;
now,
inside the shark,
the sea-turtle begins the churning seesaws
of his descent into pelagic hell;
then . . . *then,*
with ravenous jaws
that can cut sheet steel scrap,
the sea-turtle gnaws

> . . . and gnaws . . . and gnaws . . .
>   his way in a way that appalls—
>   *his* way to freedom,
>   beyond the vomiting dark,
>   beyond the stomach walls
>   of the shark."

Strong Men

Sterling A. Brown

The strong men keep coming—Sandburg

They dragged you from homeland,
They chained you in coffles,
They huddled you spoon-fashion in filthy hatches,
They sold you to give a few gentlemen ease.

They broke you in like oxen,
They scourged you,
They branded you,
They made your women breeders,
They swelled your numbers with bastards . . .
They taught you the religion they disgraced.

You sang:
    Keep a-inchin' along
    Lak a po' inch worm . . .

You sang:
> Bye and bye
> I'm gonna lay down dis heaby load . . .

You sang:
> Walk togedder, chillen,
> Dontcha git weary . . .
>> *The strong men keep a-comin' on*
>> *The strong men git stronger.*

They point with pride to the roads you built for them,
They ride in comfort over the rails you laid for them.
They put hammers in your hands
And said—Drive so much before sundown.

You sang:
> Ain't no hammah
> In dis lan',
> Strikes lak mine, bebby,
> Strikes lak mine.

They cooped you in their kitchens,
They penned you in their factories,
They gave you the jobs that they were too good for,
They tried to guarantee happiness to themselves
By shunting dirt and misery to you.

You sang:
> Me an' muh baby gonna shine, shine
> Me an' muh baby gonna shine.
>> *The strong men keep a-comin' on*
>> *The strong men git stronger . . .*

They bought off some of your leaders
You stumbled, as blind men will . . .
They coaxed you, unwontedly soft-voiced . . .
You followed a way.
Then laughed as usual.

They heard the laugh and wondered;
Uncomfortable;
Unadmitting a deeper terror . . .

The strong men keep a-comin' on
Gittin' stronger . . .

What, from the slums
Where they have hemmed you,
What, from the tiny huts
They could not keep from you—
What reaches them
Making them ill at ease, fearful?
Today they shout prohibition at you
"Thou shalt not this"
"Thou shalt not that"
"Reserved for whites only"
You laugh.

One thing they cannot prohibit—
 The strong men . . . coming on
 The strong men gittin' stronger.
 Strong men . . .
 STRONGER . . .

Theme for English B

Langston Hughes

The instructor said,

 Go home and write
 a page tonight.
 And let that page come out of you—
 Then, it will be true.

FROM *Montage of a Dream Deferred* by Langston Hughes. Copyright 1951 by Langston Hughes. Reprinted by permission of Harold Ober Associates, Incorporated.

I wonder if it's that simple?

I am twenty-two, colored, born in Winston-Salem.
I went to school there, then Durham, then here
to this college on the hill above Harlem.
I am the only colored student in my class.
The steps from the hill lead down into Harlem,
through a park, then I cross St. Nicholas,
Eighth Avenue, Seventh, and I come to the Y,
the Harlem Branch Y, where I take the elevator
up to my room, sit down, and write this page:

It's not easy to know what is true for you or me
at twenty-two, my age. But I guess I'm what
I feel and see and hear, Harlem, I hear you:
hear you, hear me—we two—you, me, talk on this page.
(I hear New York, too.) Me—who?
Well, I like to eat, sleep, drink, and be in love.
I like to work, read, learn, and understand life.
I like a pipe for a Christmas present,
or records—Bessie, bop, or Bach.
I guess being colored doesn't make me *not* like
the same things other folks like who are other races.
So will my page be colored that I write?
Being me, it will not be white.
But it will be
a part of you, instructor.
You are white—
yet a part of me, as I am a part of you.
That's American.
Sometimes perhaps you don't want to be a part of me.
Nor do I often want to be a part of you.
But we are, that's true!
As I learn from you,
I guess you learn from me—
although you're older—and white—
and somewhat more free.

This is my page for English B.

The Negro
Speaks of Rivers

(To W. E. B. DuBois)

Langston Hughes

I've known rivers:
I've known rivers ancient as the world and older than the flow of
human blood in human veins.

My soul has grown deep like the rivers.

I bathed in the Euphrates when dawns were young.
I built my hut near the Congo and it lulled me to sleep.
I looked upon the Nile and raised the pyramids above it.
I heard the singing of the Mississippi when Abe Lincoln went down
to New Orleans, and I've seen its muddy bosom turn all golden in
the sunset.
I've known rivers:
Ancient, dusky rivers.

My soul has grown deep like the rivers.

FROM *Selected Poems* by Langston Hughes. Copyright 1926 by Alfred A. Knopf, Inc.,
and renewed 1954 by Langston Hughes. Reprinted by permission of the publisher.

I, Too, Sing America

Langston Hughes

I, too, sing America.

I am the darker brother.
They send me to eat in the kitchen
When company comes,
But I laugh,
And eat well,
And grow strong.

Tomorrow,
I'll be at the table
When company comes.
Nobody'll dare
Say to me,
"Eat in the kitchen,"
Then.

Besides,
They'll see how beautiful I am
And be ashamed—

I, too, am America.

Close Your Eyes!

Arna Bontemps

Go through the gates with closed eyes.
Stand erect and let your black face front the west.

Drop the axe and leave the timber where it lies;
A woodman on the hill must have his rest.

Go where leaves are lying brown and wet.
Forget her warm arms and her breast who mothered you,
And every face you ever loved forget.
Close your eyes; walk bravely through.

Southern Mansion

Arna Bontemps

Poplars are standing there still as death
And ghosts of dead men
Meet their ladies walking

FROM *Personals* by Arna Bontemps. Copyright © 1963 by Arna Bontemps. Reprinted by permission of Harold Ober Associates, Incorporated.

Two by two beneath the shade
And standing on the marble steps.

There is a sound of music echoing
Through the open door
And in the field there is
Another sound tinkling in the cotton:
Chains of bondmen dragging on the ground.

The years go back with an iron clank,
A hand is on the gate,
A dry leaf trembles on the wall.
Ghosts are walking.
They have broken roses down
And poplars stand there still as death.

From the Dark Tower

(*To Charles S. Johnson*)

Countee Cullen

We shall not always plant while others reap
The golden increment of bursting fruit,
Not always countenance, abject and mute,
That lesser men should hold their brothers cheap;
Not everlastingly while others sleep
Shall we beguile their limbs with mellow flute,
Not always bend to some more subtle brute;
We were not made eternally to weep.

FROM *On These I Stand* by Countee Cullen. Copyright 1927 by Harper & Brothers; renewed 1955 by Ida M. Cullen. Reprinted by permission of Harper & Row, Publishers, Incorporated.

The night whose sable breast relieves the stark,
White stars is no less lovely being dark,
And there are buds that cannot bloom at all
In light, but crumble, piteous, and fall;
So in the dark we hide the heart that bleeds,
And wait, and tend our agonizing seeds.

Heritage

(*For Harold Jackman*)

Countee Cullen

What is Africa to me:
Copper sun or scarlet sea,
Jungle star or jungle track,
Strong bronzed men, or regal black
Women from whose loins I sprang
When the birds of Eden sang?
One three centuries removed
From the scenes his fathers loved,
Spicy grove, cinnamon tree,
What is Africa to me?

So I lie, who all day long
Want no sound except the song
Sung by wild barbaric birds
Goading massive jungle herds,
Juggernauts of flesh that pass
Trampling tall defiant grass

FROM *On These I Stand* by Countee Cullen. Copyright 1925 by Harper & Brothers renewed 1953 by Ida M. Cullen. Reprinted by permission of Harper & Row, Publishers, Incorporated.

Where young forest lovers lie,
Plighting troth beneath the sky.
So I lie, who always hear,
Though I cram against my ear
Both my thumbs, and keep them there,
Great drums throbbing through the air.
So I lie, whose fount of pride,
Dear distress, and joy allied,
Is my somber flesh and skin,
With the dark blood dammed within
Like great pulsing tides of wine
That, I fear, must burst the fine
Channels of the chafing net
Where they surge and foam and fret.

Africa? A book one thumbs
Listlessly, till slumber comes.
Unremembered are her bats
Circling through the night, her cats
Crouching in the river reeds,
Stalking gentle flesh that feeds
By the river brink; no more
Does the bugle-throated roar
Cry that monarch claws have leapt
From the scabbards where they slept.
Silver snakes that once a year
Doff the lovely coats you wear,
Seek no covert in your fear
Lest a mortal eye should see;
What's your nakedness to me?
Here no leprous flowers rear
Fierce corollas in the air;
Here no bodies sleek and wet,
Dripping mingled rain and sweat,
Tread the savage measures of
Jungle boys and girls in love.
What is last year's snow to me,
Last year's anything? The tree
Budding yearly must forget
How its past arose or set—
Bough and blossom, flower, fruit,
Even what shy bird with mute

Wonder at her travail there,
Meekly labored in its hair.
One three centuries removed
From the scenes his fathers loved,
Spicy grove, cinnamon tree,
What is Africa to me?

So I lie, who find no peace
Night or day, no slight release
From the unremittant beat
Made by cruel padded feet
Walking through my body's street.
Up and down they go, and back,
Treading out a jungle track.
So I lie, who never quite
Safely sleep from rain at night—
I can never rest at all
When the rain begins to fall;
Like a soul gone mad with pain
I must match its weird refrain;
Ever must I twist and squirm,
Writhing like a baited worm,
While its primal measures drip
Through my body, crying, "Strip!
Doff this new exuberance.
Come and dance the Lover's Dance!"
In an old remembered way
Rain works on me night and day.

Quaint, outlandish heathen gods
Black men fashion out of rods,
Clay, and brittle bits of stone,
In a likeness like their own,
My conversion came high-priced;
I belong to Jesus Christ,
Preacher of humility;
Heathen gods are naught to me.

Father, Son, and Holy Ghost,
So I make an idle boast;
Jesus of the twice-turned cheek,
Lamb of God, although I speak

With my mouth thus, in my heart
Do I play a double part.
Ever at Thy glowing altar
Must my heart grow sick and falter,
Wishing He I served were black,
Thinking then it would not lack
Precedent of pain to guide it,
Let who would or might deride it;
Surely then this flesh would know
Yours had borne a kindred woe.
Lord, I fashion dark gods, too,
Daring even to give You
Dark despairing features where,
Crowned with dark rebellious hair,
Patience wavers just so much as
Mortal grief compels, while touches
Quick and hot, of anger, rise
To smitten cheek and weary eyes.
Lord, forgive me if my need
Sometimes shapes a human creed.
All day long and all night through,
One thing only must I do:
Quench my pride and cool my blood,
Lest I perish in the flood.
Lest a hidden ember set
Timber that I thought was wet
Burning like the dryest flax,
Melting like the merest wax,
Lest the grave restore its dead.
Not yet has my heart or head
In the least way realized
They and I are civilized.

Incident

(*For Eric Walrond*)

Countee Cullen

Once riding in old Baltimore,
 Heart-filled, head-filled with glee,
I saw a Baltimorean
 Keep looking straight at me.

Now I was eight and very small,
 And he was no whit bigger,
And so I smiled, but he poked out
 His tongue, and called me, "Nigger."

I saw the whole of Baltimore
 From May until December;
Of all the things that happened there
 That's all that I remember.

Middle Passage

Robert Hayden

I

Jesús, Estrella, Esperanza, Mercy:

Sails flashing to the wind like weapons,
sharks following the moans the fever and the dying;
horror the corposant and compass rose.

Middle Passage:
  voyage through death
    to life upon these shores.

"10 April 1800—
Blacks rebellious. Crew uneasy. Our linguist says
their moaning is a prayer for death,
ours and their own. Some try to starve themselves.
Lost three this morning leaped with crazy laughter
to the waiting sharks, sang as they went under."

Desire, Adventure, Tartar, Ann:

Standing to America, bringing home
black gold, black ivory, black seed.

  Deep in the festering hold thy father lies,
  of his bones New England pews are made,
  those are altar lights that were his eyes.

Jesus Saviour Pilot Me
Over Life's Tempestuous Sea

We pray that Thou wilt grant, O Lord,
safe passage to our vessels bringing
heathen souls unto Thy chastening.

Jesus Saviour

"8 bells. I cannot sleep, for I am sick
with fear, but writing eases fear a little
since still my eyes can see these words take shape
upon the page & so I write, as one
would turn to exorcism. 4 days scudding,
but now the sea is calm again. Misfortune
follows in our wake like sharks (our grinning
tutelary gods). Which one of us
has killed an albatross? A plague among
our blacks—Ophthalmia: blindness—& we
have jettisoned the blind to no avail.
It spreads, the terrifying sickness spreads.
Its claws have scratched sight from the Capt.'s eyes
& there is blindness in the fo'c'sle
& we must sail 3 weeks before we come
to port."

What port awaits us, Davy Jones'
or home? I've heard of slavers drifting, drifting,
playthings of wind and storm and chance, their crews
gone blind, the jungle hatred
crawling up on deck.

Thou Who Walked On Galilee

"Deponent further sayeth *The Bella J*
left the Guinea Coast
with cargo of five hundred blacks and odd
for the barracoons of Florida:

"That there was hardly room 'tween-decks for half
the sweltering cattle stowed spoon-fashion there;
that some went mad of thirst and tore their flesh
and sucked the blood:

"That Crew and Captain lusted with the comeliest
of the savage girls kept naked in the cabins;
that there was one they called The Guinea Rose
and they cast lots and fought to lie with her:

"That when the Bo's'n piped all hands, the flames
spreading from starboard already were beyond
control, the negroes howling and their chains
entangled with the flames:

"That the burning blacks could not be reached,
that the Crew abandoned ship,
leaving their shrieking negresses behind,
that the Captain perished drunken with the wenches:

"Further Deponent sayeth not."

Pilot Oh Pilot Me

II

Aye, lad, and I have seen those factories,
Gambia, Rio Pongo, Calabar;
have watched the artful mongos baiting traps
of war wherein the victor and the vanquished

Were caught as prizes for our barracoons.
Have seen the nigger kings whose vanity
and greed turned wild black hides of Fellatah,
Mandingo, Ibo, Kru to gold for us.

And there was one—King Anthracite we named him—
fetish face beneath French parasols
of brass and orange velvet, impudent mouth
whose cups were carven skulls of enemies:

He'd honor us with drum and feast and conjo
and palm-oil-glistening wenches deft in love,
and for tin crowns that shone with paste,
red calico and German-silver trinkets

Would have the drums talk war and send
his warriors to burn the sleeping villages
and kill the sick and old and lead the young
in coffles to our factories.

Twenty years a trader, twenty years,
for there was wealth aplenty to be harvested
from those black fields, and I'd be trading still
but for the fevers melting down my bones.

III

Shuttles in the rocking loom of history,
the dark ships move, the dark ships move,
their bright ironical names
like jests of kindness on a murderer's mouth;
plough through thrashing glister toward
fata morgana's lucent melting shore,
weave toward New World littorals that are
mirage and myth and actual shore.

Voyage through death,
$\qquad$ voyage whose chartings are
$\qquad\qquad$ unlove.
A charnel stench, effluvium of living death
spreads outward from the hold,
where the living and the dead, the horribly dying,
lie interlocked, lie foul with blood and excrement.

> *Deep in the festering hold thy father lies,*
> *the corpse of mercy rots with him,*
> *rats eat love's rotten gelid eyes.*

> *But, oh, the living look at you*
> *with human eyes whose suffering accuses you,*
> *whose hatred reaches through the swill of dark*
> *to strike you like a leper's claw.*

> *You cannot stare that hatred down*
> *or chain the fear that stalks the watches*
> *and breathes on you its fetid scorching breath;*

cannot kill the deep immortal human wish,
the timeless will.

"But for the storm that flung up barriers
of wind and wave, *The Amistad*, señores,
would have reached the port of Príncipe in two,
three days at most; but for the storm we should
have been prepared for what befell.
Swift as the puma's leap it came. There was
that interval of moonless calm filled only
with the water's and the rigging's usual sounds,
then sudden movement, blows and snarling cries
and they had fallen on us with machete
and marlinspike. It was as though the very
air, the night itself were striking us.
Exhausted by the rigors of the storm,
we were no match for them. Our men went down
before the murderous Africans. Our loyal
Celestino ran from below with gun
and lantern and I saw, before the cane-
knife's wounding flash, Cinquez,
that surly brute who calls himself a prince,
directing, urging on the ghastly work.
He hacked the poor mulatto down, and then
he turned on me. The decks were slippery
when daylight finally came. It sickens me
to think of what I saw, of how these apes
threw overboard the butchered bodies of
our men, true Christians all, like so much jetsam.
Enough, enough. The rest is quickly told:
Cinquez was forced to spare the two of us
you see to steer the ship to Africa,
and we like phantoms doomed to rove the sea
voyaged east by day and west by night,
deceiving them, hoping for rescue,
prisoners on our own vessel, till
at length we drifted to the shores of this
your land, America, where we were freed
from our unspeakable misery. Now we
demand, good sirs, the extradition of
Cinquez and his accomplices to La
Havana. And it distresses us to know

there are so many here who seem inclined
to justify the mutiny of these blacks.
We find it paradoxical indeed
that you whose wealth, whose tree of liberty
are rooted in the labor of your slaves
should suffer the august John Quincy Adams
to speak with so much passion of the right
of chattel slaves to kill their lawful masters
and with his Roman rhetoric weave a hero's
garland for Cinquez. I tell you that
we are determined to return to Cuba
with our slaves and there see justice done.
  Cinquez—
or let us say 'the Prince'—Cinquez shall die."

The deep immortal human wish,
the timeless will:

  Cinquez its deathless primaveral image,
  life that transfigures many lives.

Voyage through death
       to life upon these shores.

Runagate Runagate

Robert Hayden

I

Runs falls rises stumbles on from darkness into darkness
and the darkness thicketed with shapes of terror

FROM *Selected Poems* by Robert Hayden. Copyright © 1966 by Robert Hayden. Reprinted by permission of October House, Inc.

and the hunters pursuing and the hounds pursuing
and the night cold and the night long and the river
to cross and the jack-muh-lanterns beckoning beckoning
and blackness ahead and when shall I reach that
    somewhere
morning and keep on going and never turn back
    and keep on going.

    Runagate

          Runagate

              Runagate

Many thousands rise and go
many thousands crossing over

                      O mythic North
              O star-shaped yonder Bible city

Some go weeping and some rejoicing
some in coffins and some in carriages
some in silks and some in shackles

    Rise and go fare you well

No more auction block for me
no more driver's lash for me

    If you see my Pompey, 30 yrs of age,
    new breeches, plain stockings, negro shoes;
    if you see my Anna, likely young mulatto
    branded E on the right cheek, R on the left,
    catch them if you can and notify subscriber.
    Catch them if you can, but it won't be easy.
    They'll dart underground when you try to catch them,
    plunge into quicksand, whirlpools, mazes,
    turn into scorpions when you try to catch them.

And before I'll be a slave
I'll be buried in my grave

    North star and bonanza gold

I'm bound for the freedom, freedom-bound
and oh Susyanna don't you cry for me

                    Runagate
                              Runagate

II

Rises from their anguish and their power,

                    Harriet Tubman,

                    woman of earth, whipscarred,
                    a summoning, a shining

                    Mean to be free

, And this was the way of it, brethren brethren,
   way we journeyed from Can't to Can.
   Moon so bright and no place to hide,
   the cry up and the patterollers riding,
   hound dogs belling in bladed air.
   And fear starts a-murbling, Never make it,
   we'll never make it. *Hush that now,*
   and she's turned upon us, leveled pistol
   glinting in the moonlight:
   Dead folks can't jaybird-talk, she says;
   you keep on going now or die, she says.

Wanted Harriet Tubman alias The General
alias Moses Stealer of Slaves

In league with Garrison Alcott Emerson
Garrett Douglass Thoreau John Brown

Armed and known to be Dangerous

Wanted Reward Dead or Alive

   Tell me, Ezekiel, oh tell me do you see
   mailed Jehovah coming to deliver me?

Hoot-owl calling in the ghosted air,
five times calling to the hants in the air.
Shadow of a face in the scary leaves,
shadow of a voice in the talking leaves:

Come ride-a my train

Oh that train, ghost-story train
through swamp and savanna movering movering,
over trestles of dew, through caves of the wish,
Midnight Special on a saber track movering movering
first stop Mercy and the last Hallelujah.

Come ride-a my train

Mean mean mean to be free.

A Ballad of Remembrance

Robert Hayden

Quadroon mermaids, Afro angels, black saints
balanced upon the switchblades of that air
and sang. Tight streets unfolding to the eye
like fans of corrosion and elegiac lace
crackled with their singing: Shadow of time. Shadow of blood.

Shadow, echoed the Zulu king, dangling
from a cluster of balloons. Blood,
whined the gun-metal priestess, floating
over the courtyard where dead men diced.

FROM *Selected Poems* by Robert Hayden. Copyright © 1966 by Robert Hayden. Reprinted by permission of October House, Inc.

What will you have? she inquired, the sallow vendeuse
of prepared tarnishes and jokes of nacre and ormolu,
what but those gleamings, oldrose graces,
manners like scented gloves? Contrived ghosts
rapped to metronome clack of lavalieres.

Contrived illuminations riding a threat
of river, masked Negroes wearing chameleon
satins gaudy now as a fortuneteller's
dream of disaster, lighted the crazy flopping
dance of love and hate among joys, rejections.

Accommodate, muttered the Zulu king,
toad on a throne of glaucous poison jewels.
Love, chimed the saints and the angels and the mermaids.
Hate, shrieked the gun-metal priestess
from her spiked bellcollar curved like a fleur-de-lis:

As well have a talon as a finger, a muzzle as a mouth,
as well have a hollow as a heart. And she pinwheeled
away in coruscations of laughter, scattering
those others before her like foil stars.

But, the dance continued—now among metaphorical
doors, coffee cups floating poised
hysterias, decors of illusion; now among
mazurka dolls offering death's-heads
of cocaine roses and real violets.

Then you arrived, meditative, ironic,
richly human; and your presence was shore where I rested
released from the hoodoo of that dance, where I spoke
with my true voice again.

And therefore this is not only a ballad of remembrance
for the down-South arcane city with death
in its jaws like gold teeth and archaic cusswords;
not only a token for the troubled generous friends
held in the fists of that schizoid city like flowers,
but also, Mark Van Doren,
a poem of remembrance, a gift, a souvenir for you.

Sorrow Is the Only Faithful One

Owen Dodson

Sorrow is the only faithful one:
The lone companion clinging like a season
To its original skin no matter what the variations.

If all the mountains paraded
Eating the valleys as they went
And the sun were a cliffure on the highest peak,

Sorrow would be there between
The sparkling and the giant laughter
Of the enemy when the clouds come down to swim.

But I am less, unmagic, black,
Sorrow clings to me more than to doomsday mountains
Or erosion scars on a palisade.

Sorrow has a song like a leech
Crying because the sand's blood is dry
And the stars reflected in the lake

Are water for all their twinkling
And bloodless for all their charm.
I have blood, and a song.
SORROW IS THE ONLY FAITHFUL ONE.

FROM *Powerful Long Ladder* by Owen Dodson. Copyright 1946 by Owen Dodson. Reprinted by permission of Farrar, Straus & Giroux, Inc.

George

Dudley Randall

When I was a boy desiring the title of man
And toiling to earn it
In the inferno of the foundry knockout,
I watched and admired you working by my side,
As, goggled, with mask on your mouth and shoulders bright with sweat,
You mastered the monstrous, lumpish cylinder blocks,
And when they clotted the line and plunged to the floor
With force enough to tear your foot in two,
You calmly stepped aside.

One day when the line broke down and the blocks reared up
Groaning, grinding, and mounted like an ocean wave
And then rushed thundering down like an avalanche,
And we frantically dodged, then braced our heads together
To form an arch to life and stack them,
You gave me your highest accolade:
You said: "You not afraid of sweat. You strong as a mule."

Now, here, in the hospital,
In a ward where old men wait to die,
You sit, and watch time go by.
You cannot read the books I bring, not even
Those that are only picture books,
As you sit among the senile wrecks,
The psychopaths, the incontinent.

FROM *Poem Counterpoem* by Margaret Danner and Dudley Randall. Copyright ©
1966 by Dudley Randall. Reprinted by permission of Broadside Press.

The Profile on the Pillow

Dudley Randall

After our fierce loving
in the brief time we found to be together,
you lay in the half light
exhausted, rich,
with your face turned sideways on the pillow,
and I traced the exquisite
line of your profile, dark against the white,
delicate and lovely as a child's.

Perhaps
you will cease to love me,
or we may be consumed in the holocaust,
but I keep, against the ice and the fire,
the memory of your profile on the pillow.

For My People

Margaret Walker

For my people everywhere singing their slave songs repeatedly: their
dirges and their ditties and their blues and jubilees, praying their

prayers nightly to an unknown god, bending their knees humbly to an unseen power;

For my people lending their strength to the years, to the gone years and the now years and the maybe years, washing ironing cooking scrubbing sewing mending hoeing plowing digging planting pruning patching dragging along never gaining never reaping never knowing and never understanding;

For my playmates in the clay and dust and sand of Alabama backyards playing baptizing and preaching and doctor and jail and soldier and school and mama and cooking and playhouse and concert and store and hair and Miss Choomby and company;

For the cramped bewildered years we went to school to learn to know the reasons why and the answers to and the people who and the places where and the days when, in memory of the bitter hours when we discovered we were black and poor and small and different and nobody cared and nobody wondered and nobody understood;

For the boys and girls who grew in spite of these things to be man and woman, to laugh and dance and sing and play and drink their wine and religion and success, to marry their playmates and bear children and then die of consumption and anemia and lynching;

For my people thronging 47th Street in Chicago and Lenox Avenue in New York and Rampart Street in New Orleans, lost disinherited dispossessed and happy people filling the cabarets and taverns and other people's pockets needing bread and shoes and milk and land and money and something—something all our own;

For my people walking blindly spreading joy, losing time being lazy, sleeping when hungry, shouting when burdened, drinking when hopeless, tied and shackled and tangled among ourselves by the unseen creatures who tower over us omnisciently and laugh;

For my people blundering and groping and floundering in the dark of churches and schools and clubs and societies, associations and councils and committees and conventions, distressed and disturbed and deceived and devoured by money-hungry glory-craving leeches, preyed on by facile force of state and fad and novelty, by false prophet and holy believer;

For my people standing staring trying to fashion a better way from confusion, from hypocrisy and misunderstanding, trying to fashion a world that will hold all the people, all the faces, all the adams and eves and their countless generations;

Let a new earth rise. Let another world be born. Let a bloody peace be written in the sky. Let a second generation full of courage issue forth; let a people loving freedom come to growth. Let a beauty full of healing and a strength of final clenching be the pulsing in our spirits and our blood. Let the martial songs be written, let the dirges disappear. Let a race of men now rise and take control.

We Have Been Believers

Margaret Walker

We have been believers believing in the black gods of an old land, believing in the secrets of the seeress and the magic of the charmers and the power of the devil's evil ones.

And in the white gods of a new land we have been believers believing in the mercy of our masters and the beauty of our brothers, believing in the conjure of the humble and the faithful and the pure.

Neither the slavers' whip nor the lynchers' rope nor the bayonet could kill our black belief. In our hunger we beheld the welcome table and in our nakedness the glory of a long white robe. We have been believers in the new Jerusalem.

We have been believers feeding greedy grinning gods, like a Moloch demanding our sons and our daughters, our strength and our wills

---

and our spirits of pain. We have been believers, silent and stolid and stubborn and strong.

We have been believers yielding substance for the world. With our hands have we fed a people and out of our strength have they wrung the necessities of a nation. Our song has filled the twilight and our hope has heralded the dawn.

Now we stand ready for the touch of one fiery iron, for the cleansing breath of many molten truths, that the eyes of the blind may see and the ears of the deaf may hear and the tongues of the people be filled with living fire.

Where are our gods that they leave us asleep? Surely the priests and the preachers and the powers will hear. Surely now that our hands are empty and our hearts too full to pray they will understand. Surely the sires of the people will send us a sign.

We have been believers believing in our burdens and our demigods too long. Now the needy no longer weep and pray; the long-suffering arise, and our fists bleed against the bars with a strange insistency.

Through the Varied Patterned Lace

(*"I salute the divinity in you."* Greeting From a Fellow Baha'i)

Margaret Danner

As I look into each different face,
I am exalted.
I am exalted to recognize His Grace
shimmering through the varied patterned lace.

There is this Good in every man
whether Russian or French, Italian or American
and glowing so in you,
O, Ibo, Yoruba, Zulu, Congolese, Fan.

I look at you and feel It flooding me.
Divinity must win the race. It will not be halted.
We are all small sons of one clan.
I am exalted.

The Chicago *Defender* Sends a Man to Little Rock, Fall, 1957

Gwendolyn Brooks

In Little Rock the people bear
Babes, and comb and part their hair
And watch the want ads, put repair
To roof and latch. While wheat toast burns
A woman waters multiferns.

Time upholds or overturns
The many, tight, and small concerns.

In Little Rock the people sing
Sunday hymns like anything,
Through Sunday pomp and polishing.

And after testament and tunes,
Some soften Sunday afternoons
With lemon tea and Lorna Doones.

I forecast
And I believe
Come Christmas Little Rock will cleave
To Christmas tree and trifle, weave,
From laugh and tinsel, texture fast.

In Little Rock is baseball; Barcarolle.
That hotness in July . . . the uniformed figures raw and implacable
And not intellectual,
Batting the hotness or clawing the suffering dust.
The Open Air Concert, on the special twilight green . . .
When Beethoven is brutal or whispers to ladylike air.
Blanket-sitters are solemn, as Johann troubles to lean
To tell them what to mean . . .
There is love, too, in Little Rock. Soft women softly
Opening themselves in kindness,
Or, pitying one's blindness,
Awaiting one's pleasure
In Azure
Glory with anguished rose at the root . . .
To wash away old semidiscomfitures.
They reteach purple and unsullen blue.
The wispy soils go. And uncertain
Half-havings have they clarified to sures.

In Little Rock they know
Not answering the telephone is a way of rejecting life,
That it is our business to be bothered, is our business
To cherish bores or boredom, be polite
To lies and love and many-faceted fuzziness.

I scratch my head, massage the hate-I-had.
I blink across my prim and pencilled pad.
The saga I was sent for is not down.
Because there is a puzzle in this town.
The biggest News I do not dare
Telegraph to the Editor's chair:
"They are like people everywhere."

The angry Editor would reply
In hundred harryings of Why.

And true, they are hurling spittle, rock,
Garbage and fruit in Little Rock.
And I saw coiling storm a-writhe
On bright madonnas. And a scythe
Of men harassing brownish girls.
(The bows and barrettes in the curls
And braids declined away from joy.)

I saw a bleeding brownish boy . . .
The lariat lynch-wish I deplored.
The loveliest lynchee was our Lord.

Bronzeville Man with a Belt in the Back

Gwendolyn Brooks

In such an armor he may rise and raid
The dark cave after midnight, unafraid,
And slice the shadows with his able sword
Of good broad nonchalance, hashing them down.

And come out and accept the gasping crowd,
Shake off the praises with an airiness.
And, searching, see love shining in an eye,
But never smile.

In such an armor he cannot be slain.

Sadie and Maud

Gwendolyn Brooks

Maud went to college.
Sadie stayed at home.
Sadie scraped life
With a fine-tooth comb.

She didn't leave a tangle in.
Her comb found every strand.
Sadie was one of the livingest chits
In all the land.

Sadie bore two babies
Under her maiden name.
Maud and Ma and Papa
Nearly died of shame.

When Sadie said her last so-long
Her girls struck out from home.
(Sadie had left as heritage
Her fine-tooth comb.)

Maud, who went to college,
Is a thin brown mouse.
She is living all alone
In this old house.

The Sacrifice

Gerald William Barrax

Swing high, Iscariot,
Alone and unmourned
On your tree on the high dark hill.

Even your own ears
Will not hear
The creak of the swinging rope
Above the crash of thunder.

But the lightning is less merciful;
In its flashes you can see
On a hill higher than yours
Three crosses,
One higher than the others.

But the noose is tight:
The dark thunder-lightning tableau
Films red
And you become immortal.

Black Narcissus

Gerald William Barrax

You want to integrate me into your anonymity
because it is my right
you think
to be like you.

I want your right to be like yourself.
Integrate me for this reason:
    Because I will die with you.

But remember
each day I will look into a mirror
and if you have not taken more than you have given
I will laugh when I see that I am still black.

A Negro Soldier's Viet Nam Diary

Herbert Woodward Martin

The day he discovered a mother and child in the river, he wrote.

They had been there a month; the water had begun to tear them apart.
The mother had not relaxed, even in death she held to her child.

I lowered my gun slowly into the water, walked away.
My stomach screamed empty, there was nothing there.
What little warm water I had would not Pilot away the mud or stench.
It was like a dead body we could not discover.
Death hangs on the rice.
The ground is watered with blood.
The land bears no fruit.
Grass is an amenity.
It is a luxury forever to notice so much as a flower,
Or clear water in a stream.
Bullets, here, kill with the same deliberate speed that they do at home.
Fear destroys the thing it is unacquainted with.
I never want to kill again.
Do not celebrate me when and if I come home.
I step around the smallest creatures these days.
I am cautious to pray.
I am cautious to believe the day will come when we can
Take up our sharing again with deliberate speed.
Have you prayed, lately, for that?

A Poem for Black Hearts

LeRoi Jones

For Malcolm's eyes, when they broke
the face of some dumb white man. For
Malcolm's hands raised to bless us
all black and strong in his image
of ourselves, for Malcolm's words
fire darts, the victor's tireless
thrusts, words hung above the world
change as it may, he said it, and

for this he was killed, for saying,
and feeling, and being/ change, all
collected hot in his heart, For Malcolm's
heart, raising us above our filthy cities,
for his stride, and his beat, and his address
to the grey monsters of the world, For Malcolm's
pleas for your dignity, black men, for your life,
black men, for the filling of your minds
with righteousness, For all of him dead and
gone and vanished from us, and all of him which
clings to our speech black god of our time.
For all of him, and all of yourself, look up,
black man, quit stuttering and shuffling, look up,
black man, quit whining and stooping, for all of him,
For Great Malcolm a prince of the earth, let nothing in us rest
until we avenge ourselves for his death, stupid animals
that killed him, let us never breathe a pure breath if
we fail, and white men call us faggots till the end of
the earth.

The Dance

LeRoi Jones

The dance.
            (held up for me by
an older man. He told me how. Showed
me. Not steps, but the fix
of muscle. A position
for myself: to move.

FROM *The Dead Lecturer* by LeRoi Jones. Copyright © 1964 by LeRoi Jones. Reprinted by permission of The Sterling Lord Agency.

Duncan
told of dance. His poems
full of what we called
so long for you to be. A
dance. And all his words
ran out of it. That there
was some bright elegance
the sad meat of the body
made. Some gesture, that
if we became, for one blank moment,
would turn us
into creatures of rhythm.

I want to be sung. I want
all my bones and meat hummed
against the thick floating
winter sky. I want myself
as dance. As what I am
given love, or time, or space
to feel myself.

The time of thought. The space
of actual movement. (Where they
have taken up the sea, and
keep me against my will.) I said, also,
love, being older or younger
than your world. I am given
to lying, love, call you out
now, given to feeling things
I alone create.

And let me once, create
myself. And let you, whoever
sits now breathing on my words
create a self of your own. One
that will love me.

Good Times

Lucille Clifton

My Daddy has paid the rent
and the insurance man is gone
and the lights is back on
and my uncle Brud has hit
for one dollar straight
and they is good times
good times
good times

My Mama has made bread
and Grampaw has come
and everybody is drunk
and dancing in the kitchen
and singing in the kitchen
oh these is good times
good times
good times

oh children think about the
good times

FROM *Good Times* by Lucille Clifton. Copyright © 1969 by Lucille Clifton. Reprinted by permission of Random House, Inc.

I Am a Cowboy in the Boat of Ra[1]

"The devil must be forced to reveal any such physical evil (potions, charms, fetishes, etc.) still outside the body and these must be burned." RITUALE ROMANUM, *published 1947, endorsed by the coat of arms and introduction letter from Francis Cardinal Spellman.*

Ishmael Reed

I am a cowboy in the boat of Ra,
sidewinders in the saloons of fools
bit my forehead   like   O
the untrustworthiness of Egyptologists
Who do not know their trips. Who was that
dog-faced man? they asked, the day I rode
from town.

School marms with halitosis cannot see
the Nefertiti fake chipped on the run by slick
germans, the hawk behind Sonny Rollins' head or
the ritual beard of his axe; a longhorn winding
its bells thru the Field of Reeds.

I am a cowboy in the boat of Ra. I bedded
down with Isis, Lady of the Boogaloo, dove
down deep in her horny, stuck up her Wells-Far-ago
in daring midday get away. "Start grabbing the
blue," i said from top of my double crown.

I am a cowboy in the boat of Ra. Ezzard Charles
of the Chisholm Trail. Took up the bass but they
blew off my thumb. Alchemist in ringmanship but a
sucker for the right cross.

FROM *The New Black Poetry* edited by Clarence Major. Copyright © 1969 by International Publishers Company, Inc.
   [1] Ra, a chief city of ancient Egypt, was the sun-god, the creator, and a vanquisher of evil.

I am a cowboy in the boat of Ra. Vamoosed from
the temple i bide my time. The price on the wanted
poster was a-going down, outlaw alias copped my stance
and moody greenhorns were making me dance; while my mouth's
shooting iron got its chambers jammed.

I am a cowboy in the boat of Ra. Boning-up in
the ol West i bide my time. You should see
me pick off these tin cans whippersnappers. I
write the motown long plays for the comeback of
Osiris. Make them up when stars stare at sleeping
steer out here near the campfire. Women arrive
on the backs of goats and throw themselves on
my Bowie.

I am a cowboy in the boat of Ra. Lord of the lash,
the Loup Garou Kid. Half breed son of Pisces and
Aquarius. I hold the souls of men in my pot. I do
the dirty boogie with scorpions. I make the bulls
keep still and was the first swinger to grape the taste.

I am a cowboy in his boat. Pope Joan of the
Ptah Ra. C/mere a minute willya doll?
Be a good girl and
Bring me my Buffalo horn of black powder
Bring me my headdress of black feathers
Bring me my bones of Ju-Ju snake
Go get my eyelids of red paint.
Hand me my shadow
I'm going into town after Set[2]

I am a cowboy in the boat of Ra
look out Set   here i come Set
to get Set   to sunset Set
to unseat Set   to Set down Set
              usurper of the Royal couch
              imposter RAdio of Moses' bush
              party pooper O hater of dance
              vampire outlaw of the milky way

[2] Set is an ancient Egyptian god, a brother to Osiris (god of vegetation). Sometimes he is identified with evil; sometimes, the protector of the sun-god's boat.

Hymn

Alice Walker

I well remember
A time when
"Amazing Grace" was
All the rage
In the South.
'Happy' black mothers arguing
Agreement with
Illiterate sweating preachers
Hemming and hawing blessedness
Meekness
Inheritance of earth, e.g.,
Mississippi cotton fields?

And in the North
Roy Hamilton singing
"What is America to me?"
Such a good question
From a nice slum
In North Philly.

My God! the songs and
The people and the lives
Started here—
Weaned on 'happy' tears
Black fingers clutching black teats
On black Baptist benches—
Some mother's troubles that everybody's
Seen
And nobody wants to see.

FROM *Once* by Alice Walker. Copyright © 1968 by Alice Walker. Reprinted by permission of Harcourt Brace Jovanovich, Inc.

I can remember the rocking of
The church
And embarrassment
At my mother's shouts
Like it was all—'her happiness'—
Going to kill her.
My father's snores
Punctuating eulogies
His loud singing
Into fluffy grey caskets
A sleepy tear
In his eye.

Amazing Grace
How sweet the sound
That saved a wretch
Like me
I once was lost
But now I'm found
Was blind
But now
I see.

Mahalia Jackson, Clara Ward, Fats Waller,
Ray Charles,
Sitting here embarrassed with me
Watching the birth
Hearing the cries
Bearing witness
To the child,
Music.

Ibe

Lynn Shorter

Ibe, the usher.
land day dark skull, o clay ear of indio corn
housed the voice of singing man,
necklaced in a firewind.
man play sweet on he driftwood guitar
as his song explore a being kingdom.

Ibe, the slave.
land day dark skull, o clay ear of indio corn
charioted singing man
to the temple of pain,
where prayer was his living
and living, another's harvest.

Ibe, the thief.
land day dark skull, o clay ear of indio corn
museum of the toy buffalo
facsimile of the christ head
mine of leaden legends
embryo of a drum.

Ibe, the lover.
land day dark skull, o clay ear of indio corn
laid in the belly of singing man
as he married to spirit.
man play sweet on he driftwood guitar
as his song explore a being kingdom.

Reprinted by permission of Lynn Shorter.

domo's mirror

Lynn Shorter

in the harlem ruins,
domo's stallion with the fish hook tail
grazed on green blades of peace

bees in the pohouse of violets
danced the boogie
with amazing grace

in the mirror,
domo played his flute of herbs
and the ruins sprang to life

QUESTIONS

The following general questions may be asked about each poem. The student should also attempt to frame questions of his own.

1. Does knowing the date of publication add to your understanding of the poem?

2. Does the poem use folk, classical, or biblical materials? If so, explain their significance.

3. Does the poem make use of the black man's African heritage? If so, does this enhance the meaning?

4. Is the poem concerned with the role of the black man in America? How relevant are the ideas in the poem to conditions today?

5. In what ways, if any, does the poem belong to the literature of protest?

6. Does the poem discuss the question of black identity?

7. Is the poem basically narrative, lyric, or dramatic?

8. How appropriate is the poem's form to its theme?

9. What traditional poetic techniques are evident in the poem? In what ways do they depart from traditional techniques?

10. Discuss the imagery.

11. Discuss the use of contrasts, repetitions, and refrains.

12. Does the poet use irony? Explain.

part 3

Drama

The intellectual and political energies released by the civil rights movement during the sixties implemented the development of Black Theater. Opportunities for the Afro-American playwright have in general been extremely limited, although Langston Hughes, Owen Dodson, Louis Peterson, and Theodore Ward had earned recognition as dramatists before this period. And James Baldwin's Blues for Mister Charlie (1959) and Lorraine Hansberry's A Raisin in the Sun (1964), despite didacticism and sentimentality, had reaffirmed the potentialities of drama exploring and interpreting the Negro milieu.

Whether the new playwrights who have since appeared are any closer than their predecessors to realizing these potentialities is a moot point. Although it is hardly possible to discuss these writers as a group, it can be said that on the whole they tend to be experimental and iconoclastic. And they share the aim of portraying Negro life with candor, reacting to what they consider the compromises and half-truths of a theater existing largely for a white audience. The plays of LeRoi Jones, Ed Bullins, Douglas Turner Ward, and Adrienne Kennedy range from the bitterly realistic and political to the fanciful and poetic. A renewed emphasis on cultural nationalism has led some playwrights to "celebrate blackness" in plays that are heavily race conscious, if not chauvinistic. Writers like LeRoi Jones (see his essay in part 5) regard a play as an incitement, as a means of effecting revolutionary thought and action. It is meant to be disturbing, even offensive.

Black Theater in some instances reveals affinities with the Theater of the Absurd, which is characterized, in part, by unexpected juxtapositions of the ordinary and the bizarre, the real and the unreal. Douglas Turner Ward's Day of Absence is a case in point. Fortunately, its brevity makes possible its inclusion in this text as one example of the new drama. Ward's play is a satiric farce, a sardonic commentary on the inherent absurdities of the black-white conflict. The playwright turns stereotypes of the Negro to his own mocking use. Surrealistic fantasy and earthy realism are combined in what Ward describes as "a reverse minstrel show done in white face." It is a play in which thesis does not take precedence over mordant comic invention, and Ward has knowingly employed theatricality to achieve irony and satire.

Day of Absence

A Satirical Fantasy

Douglas Turner Ward

The time is now.

Play opens in unnamed Southern town of medium population on a somnolent cracker morning—meaning no matter the early temperature, it's gonna get hot. The hamlet is just beginning to rouse itself from the sleepy lassitude of night.

NOTES ON PRODUCTION: *No scenery is necessary—only actors shifting in and out on an almost bare stage and freezing into immobility as focuses change or blackouts occur.*

Play is conceived for performance by a Negro cast, a reverse minstrel show done in white face. Logically, it might also be performed by whites—at their own risk. If any producer is faced with choosing between opposite hues, author strongly suggests: "Go 'long wit the blacks —besides all else, they need the work more."

If acted by the latter, race members are urged to go for broke, yet cautioned not to ham it up too broadly. In fact—it just might be more effective if they aspire to serious tragedy. Only qualification needed for Caucasian casting is that the company fit a uniform pattern—insipid white.

Before any horrifying discrimination doubts arise, I hasten to add that a bona fide white actor should be cast as the ANNOUNCER *in all produc-*

tions, likewise a Negro thespian in pure native black as RASTUS. This will truly subvert any charge that the production is unintegrated.

All props, except essential items (chairs, brooms, rags, mop, debris) should be imaginary (phones, switchboard, mikes, eating utensils, food, etc.). Actors should indicate their presence through mime.

The cast of characters develops as the play progresses. In the interest of economical casting, actors should double or triple in roles wherever possible.

PRODUCTION CONCEPT: This is a red-white-and-blue play—meaning that the entire production should be designed around the basic color scheme of our patriotic trinity. Lighting should illustrate, highlight, and detail time, action, and mood—opening scenes stage-lit with white rays of morning, transforming to panic reds of afternoon, flowing into ominous blues of evening. Costuming should be orchestrated around the same color scheme. In addition, subsidiary usage of grays, khakis, yellows, pinks, and patterns of stars and bars should be employed. All actors (ANNOUNCERS and RASTUS excepted, of course) should wear white shoes or sneakers, and all women characters clothed in knee-length frocks should wear white stockings. Blond wigs, both for males and females, can be used in selected instances. Makeup should have uniform consistency, with individual touches thrown in to enhance personal identity.

SAMPLE MODELS OF MAKEUP AND COSTUMING:

MARY   Kewpie-doll face, ruby-red lips painted to valentine pursing, moon-shaped rough circles implanted on each cheek, blond wig of fat flowing ringlets, dazzling ankle-length snow-white nightie.

MAYOR   Seersucker white ensemble, ten-gallon hat, red string tie, and blue belt.

CLEM   Khaki pants, bareheaded, and blond.

LUKE   Blue work jeans, strawhatted.

CLUB WOMAN   Yellow dress patterned with symbols of Dixie, gray hat.

CLAN   A veritable, riotous advertisement of red-white-and-blue combinations with stars and bars tossed in.

PIOUS   White ministerial garb with black cleric's color topping his snow-white shirt.

OPERATORS   All in red with different color wigs.

All other characters should be carefully defined through costuming which typifies their identity.

SCENE: Street.

TIME: Early morning.

CLEM   (sitting under a sign suspended by invisible wires and bold-printed with the lettering: "STORE") Morning, Luke . . .

LUKE (*sitting a few paces away under an identical sign*) Morning, Clem . . .

CLEM Gon be a hot day.

LUKE Looks that way . . .

CLEM Might rain though . . .

LUKE Might.

CLEM Hope it does . . .

LUKE Me too . . .

CLEM Farmers could use a little wet spell for a change . . . How's the Missis?

LUKE Same.

CLEM 'N the kids?

LUKE Them too . . . How's yourns?

CLEM Fine, thank you . . . (*They both lapse into drowsy silence, waving lethargically from time to time at imaginary passersby.*) Hi, Joe . . .

LUKE Joe . . .

CLEM How'd it go yesterday, Luke?

LUKE Fair.

CLEM Same wit me . . . Business don't seem to git no better or no worse. Guess we in a rut, Luke, don't it 'pear that way to you?— Morning, Ma'am.

LUKE Morning . . .

CLEM Tried display, sales, advertisement, stamps—everything—yet merchandising stumbles 'round in the same old groove. . . . But—that's better than plunging downwards, I reckon.

LUKE Guess it is.

CLEM Morning, Bret. How's the family? . . . That's good.

LUKE Bret—

CLEM Morning, Sue.

LUKE How do, Sue.

CLEM (*starting after her*) Fine hunk of woman.

LUKE Sure is.

CLEM Wonder if it's any good?

LUKE Bet it is.

CLEM Sure like to find out!

LUKE So would I.

CLEM You ever try?

LUKE Never did . . .

CLEM Morning, Gus . . .

LUKE Howdy, Gus.

CLEM Fine, thank you. (*They lapse into silence again.* CLEM *rouses himself slowly, begins to look around quizzically.*) Luke . . . ?

LUKE Huh?

CLEM Do you . . . er, er—feel anything—funny . . . ?

LUKE Like what?

CLEM   Like . . . er—something—strange?

LUKE   I dunno . . . haven't thought about it.

CLEM   I mean . . . like something's wrong—outta place, unusual?

LUKE   I don't know . . . What you got in mind?

CLEM   Nothing . . . just that—just that—like somp'um's outta kilter. I got a funny feeling somp'um's not up to snuff. Can't figger out what it is . . .

LUKE   Maybe it's in your haid . . .

CLEM   No, not like that . . . Like somp'um's happened—or happening —gone haywire, loony.

LUKE   Well, don't worry 'bout it, it'll pass.

CLEM   Guess you right (*attempts return to somnolence but doesn't succeed*). I'm sorry, Luke, but you sure you don't feel nothing peculiar . . . ?

LUKE   (*slightly irked*) Toss it out your mind, Clem! We got a long day ahead of us. If something's wrong, you'll know 'bout it in due time. No use worrying about it 'til it comes and if it's coming, it will. Now, relax!

CLEM   All right, you right . . . Hi, Margie . . .

LUKE   Marge.

CLEM   (*unable to control himself*) Luke, I don't give a damn what you say. Somp'um's topsy-turvy, I just know it!

LUKE   (*increasingly irritated*) Now look here, Clem—it's a bright day, it looks like it's gon git hotter. You say the wife and kids are fine and the business is no better or no worse? Well, what else could be wrong? . . . If somp'um's gon happen, it's gon happen anyway and there ain't a damn fool thing you kin do to stop it! So you ain't helping me, yourself or nobody else by thinking 'bout it. It's not gon be no better or no worse when it gits here. It'll come to you when it gits ready to come and it's gon be the same whether you worry about it or not. So stop letting it upset you! (LUKE *settles back in his chair.* CLEM *does likewise.* LUKE *shuts his eyes. After a few moments, they reopen. He forces them shut again. They reopen in greater curiosity. Finally, he rises slowly to an upright position in the chair, looks around frowningly. Turns slowly to* CLEM.) Clem? . . . You know something? . . . Somp'um is peculiar . . .

CLEM   (*vindicated*) I knew it, Luke! I jist knew it! Ever since we been sitting here, I been having that feeling!

(*Scene is blacked out abruptly. Lights rise on another section of the stage where a young couple lie in bed under an invisible-wire suspension sign lettered* "HOME." *Loud, insistent sounds of baby yells are heard.* JOHN, *the husband, turns over trying to ignore the cries;* MARY, *the wife, is undisturbed.* JOHN's *efforts are futile; the cries continue until they cannot be denied. He bolts upright, jumps out of bed, and disappears offstage. Returns quickly and tries to rouse* MARY.)

JOHN Mary . . . (*Nudges her, pushes her, yells into her ear, but she fails to respond.*) Mary, get up . . . Get up!

MARY Ummm . . . (*Shrugs away, still sleeping.*)

JOHN GET UP!

MARY Ummmmmmmmmm!

JOHN Don't you hear the baby's bawling? . . . NOW GET UP!

MARY (*mumbling drowsily*) What baby . . . whose baby . . . ?

JOHN Yours!

MARY Mine? That's ridiculous . . . what'd you say . . . ? Somebody's baby bawling? . . . How could that be so? (*Hearing screams.*) Who's crying? Somebody's crying! . . . What's crying? . . . *Where's Lula?*

JOHN I don't know. You better get up.

MARY That's outrageous! . . . What time is it?

JOHN Late 'nuff! Now rise up!

MARY You must be joking . . . I'm sure I still have four or five hours' sleep in store—even more after that head-splittin' blowout last night . . . (*Tumbles back under covers.*)

JOHN Nobody told you to gulp those last six bourbons—

MARY Don't tell me how many bourbons to swallow, not after you guzzled the whole stinking bar! . . . Get up? . . . You must be cracked . . . Where's Lula? She must be here, she always is . . .

JOHN Well, she ain't here yet, so get up and muzzle that brat before she does drive me cuckoo!

MARY (*springing upright, finally realizing gravity of situation*) Whaddaya mean Lula's not here? She's always here, she must be here . . . Where else kin she be? She supposed to be . . . She just can't *not* be here—call her!

(*Blackout as* JOHN *rushes offstage. Scene shifts to a trio of* TELEPHONE OPERATORS *perched on stools before imaginary switchboards. Chaos and bedlam are taking place to the sound of buzzes. Effect of following dialogue should simulate rising pandemonium.*)

FIRST OPERATOR The line is busy—

SECOND OPERATOR Line is busy—

THIRD OPERATOR Is busy—

FIRST OPERATOR Doing best we can—

SECOND OPERATOR Having difficulty—

THIRD OPERATOR Soon as possible—

FIRST OPERATOR Just one moment—

SECOND OPERATOR Would you hold on—

THIRD OPERATOR Awful sorry, madam—

FIRST OPERATOR Would you hold on, please—

SECOND OPERATOR Just a second, please—

THIRD OPERATOR Please hold on, please—

FIRST OPERATOR The line is busy—

SECOND OPERATOR The line is busy—

THIRD OPERATOR   The line is busy—
FIRST OPERATOR   Doing best we can—
SECOND OPERATOR   Hold on, please—
THIRD OPERATOR   Can't make connections—
FIRST OPERATOR   Unable to put it in—
SECOND OPERATOR   Won't plug through—
THIRD OPERATOR   Sorry, madam—
FIRST OPERATOR   If you'd wait a moment—
SECOND OPERATOR   Doing best we can—
THIRD OPERATOR   Sorry—
FIRST OPERATOR   One moment—
SECOND OPERATOR   Just a second—
THIRD OPERATOR   Hold on—
FIRST OPERATOR   *Yes—*
SECOND OPERATOR   *Stop it!—*
THIRD OPERATOR   *How do I know—*
FIRST OPERATOR   *You another one!*
SECOND OPERATOR   *Hold on, Dammit!*
THIRD OPERATOR   *Up yours, too!*
FIRST OPERATOR   *The line is busy—*
SECOND OPERATOR   *The line is busy—*
THIRD OPERATOR   *The line is busy—*

(*The switchboard clamors a cacophony of buzzes as* OPERATORS *plug connections with the frenzy of a Chaplin movie. Their replies degenerate into a babble of gibberish. At the height of frenzy, the* SUPERVISOR *appears.*)

SUPERVISOR   *What's the snarl-up?*
FIRST OPERATOR   Everybody calling at the same time, Ma'am!
SECOND OPERATOR   Board can't handle it!
THIRD OPERATOR   Like everybody in big New York City is trying to squeeze a call through to lil ole us!
SUPERVISOR   God! . . . Somp'um terrible musta happened! . . . Buzz the emergency frequency hookup to the Mayor's office and find out what the hell's going on!
(*Scene blacks out quickly to* CLEM *and* LUKE.)
CLEM   (*something slowly dawning on him*) Luke . . . ?
LUKE   Yes, Clem?
CLEM   (*eyes roving around in puzzlement*) Luke . . . ?
LUKE   (*irked*) I said what, Clem!
CLEM   Luke . . . ? Where—where is—the—the—?
LUKE   The *what?*
CLEM   Nigras . . . ?
LUKE   What . . . ?

CLEM   Nigras . . . Where is the Nigras, where is they, Luke . . . ? *All the Nigras!* . . . I don't see no Nigras . . . !

LUKE   Whatcha mean . . . ?

CLEM   (*agitatedly*) Luke there ain't a darkey in sight. . . . And if you remember, we ain't seen a nappy hair all morning . . . The Nigras, Luke! We ain't laid eyes on nary a coon this whole morning!

LUKE   You must be crazy or something, Clem!

CLEM   Think about it, Luke, we been sitting here for an hour or more —try and recollect if you remember seeing jist *one* go by!

LUKE   (*confused*) I don't recall . . . But . . . but there musta been some . . . The heat musta got you, Clem! How in hell could that be so?

CLEM   (*triumphantly*) Just think, Luke! . . . Look around ya . . . Now, every morning mosta people walkin 'long this street is colored. They's strolling by going to work, they's waiting for the buses, they's sweeping sidewalks, cleaning stores, starting to shine shoes and wetting the mops—Right? . . . Well, look around you, Luke—Where is they? (LUKE *paces up and down, checking.*) I told you, Luke, they ain't nowheres to be seen.

LUKE   This . . . this . . . some kind of holiday for 'em—or something?

CLEM   I don't know, Luke . . . but . . . but what I do know is they ain't here'n we haven't seen a solitary one . . . It's scarifying, Luke . . . !

LUKE   Well . . . Maybe they's jist standing 'n walking and shining on other streets—Let's go look!

(*Scene blacks out to* JOHN *and* MARY. *Baby cries are as insistent as ever.*)

MARY   (*at end of patience*) Smother it!

JOHN   (*beyond his*) That's a hell of a thing to say 'bout your own child! You should know what to do to hush her up!

MARY   Why don't you try?

JOHN   You had her!

MARY   You shared in borning her!

JOHN   Possibly not!

MARY   Why, you lousy—!

JOHN   What good is a mother who can't shut up her own daughter?

MARY   I told you she yells louder every time I try to lay hands on her —Where's Lula? Didn't you call her?

JOHN   I told you I can't get the call through!

MARY   Try agin—

JOHN   It's no use! I tried numerous times and can't even git through to the switchboard. You've got to quiet her down yourself. (*Firmly.*) Now, go in there and clam her up 'fore I lose my patience! (MARY *exits. Soon, we hear the yells increase. She rushes back in.*)

MARY   She won't let me touch her, just screams louder!

JOHN   Probably wet 'n soppy!

MARY   Yes! Stinks something awful! Phooooey! I can't stand that filth and odor!

JOHN   That's why she's screaming! Needs her didee changed—go change it!

MARY   How you 'spect me to when I don't know how? Suppose I faint?

JOHN   Well let her blast away. I'm getting outta here.

MARY   You can't leave me here like this!

JOHN   Just watch me! . . . See this nice split-level cottage, peachy furniture, multicolored T.V., hi-fi set n' the rest? . . . Well, how you think I scraped 'em together while you curled up on your fat lil fanny? . . . By gitting outta here—not only *on time* . . . but *earlier!* —Beating a frantic crew of nice young executives to the punch— gitting there fustest with the mostest brown-nosing you ever saw! Now if I goof one day—just ONE DAY!—you reckon I'd stay ahead? NO! . . . There'd be a wolf pack trampling over my prostrate body, racing to replace my smiling face against the boss's left rump! . . . *No, mam!* I'm zooming outta here on time, just as I always have, and what's more—you gon fix me some breakfast. *I'm hungry!*

MARY   But—

JOHN   No buts about it! (*Flash blackout as he gags on a mouthful of coffee.*) What you trying to do, STRANGLE ME? (*Jumps up and starts putting on jacket.*)

MARY   (*sarcastically*) What did you expect?

JOHN   (*in biting fury*) That you could possibly boil a pot of water, toast a few slices of bread and fry a coupler eggs! . . . It was a mistaken assumption!

MARY   So they aren't as good as Lula's!

JOHN   That is an overstatement. Your efforts don't result in anything that could possibly be digested by man, mammal, or insect! . . . When I married you, I thought I was fairly acquainted with your faults and weaknesses—I chalked 'em up to human imperfection . . . But now I know I was being extremely generous, overoptimistic and phenomenally deluded!—You have no idea how useless you really are!

MARY   Then why'd you marry me?

JOHN   Decoration!

MARY   You shoulda married Lula!

JOHN   I might've if it wasn't 'gainst the segregation law! . . . But for the sake of my home, my child and my sanity, I will even take a chance on sacrificing my slippery grip on the status pole and drive by her shanty to find out whether she or someone like her kin come over here and prevent some ultimate disaster. (*Storms toward door, stopping abruptly at exit.*) Are you sure you kin make it to the bathroom wit'out Lula backing you up?

(*Blackout. Scene shifts to* MAYOR's *office where a cluttered desk stands center stage amid paper debris.*)

MAYOR   (*striding determinedly toward desk; stopping midway, bellowing*) Woodfence! . . . Woodfence! . . . Woodfence! (*Receiving no reply, completes distance to desk.*) Jack-son! . . . Jackson!

JACKSON   (*entering worriedly*) Yes, sir . . . ?

MAYOR   Where's Vice-Mayor Woodfence, that no-good brother-in-law of mine?

JACKSON   Hasn't come in yet, sir.

MAYOR   *Hasn't come in?* . . . Damn bastard! Knows we have a crucial conference. Soon as he staggers through that door, tell him to shoot in here! (*Angrily focusing on his disorderly desk and littered surroundings.*) And git Mandy here to straighten up this mess—Rufus too! You know he shoulda been waiting to knock dust off my shoes soon as I step in. Get 'em in here! . . . What's the matter wit them lazy Nigras? . . . Already had to dress myself because of J. C., fix my own coffee without May-Belle, drive myself to work 'counta Bubber, feel my old bag's tits after Sapphi—*Never Mind!*—Git 'em in here—*Quick!*

JACKSON   (*meekly*) They aren't . . . they aren't here, sir . . .

MAYOR   Whaddaya mean they aren't here? Find out where they at. We got important business, man! You can't run a town wit laxity like this. Can't allow things to git snafued jist because a bunch of lazy Nigras been out gitting drunk and living it up all night! Discipline, man, discipline!

JACKSON   That's what I'm trying to tell you, sir . . . they didn't come in, can't be found . . . none of 'em.

MAYOR   Ridiculous, boy! Scare 'em up and tell 'em scoot here in a hurry befo' I git mad and fire the whole goddamn lot of 'em!

JACKSON   But we can't find 'em, sir.

MAYOR   Hogwash! Can't nobody in this office do anything right? Do I hafta handle every piddling little matter myself? Git me their numbers, I'll have 'em here befo' you kin shout to—

(THREE MEN *burst into room.*)

ONE   Henry—they vanished!

TWO   Disappeared into thin air!

THREE   Gone wit'out a trace!

TWO   Not a one on the street!

THREE   In the house!

ONE   On the job!

MAYOR   Wait a minute! . . . Hold your water! Calm down—!

ONE   But they've gone, Henry—GONE! All of 'em!

MAYOR   What the hell you talking 'bout? Gone? Who's gone—?

ONE   The Nigras, Henry! They gone!

MAYOR   Gone? . . . Gone where?

TWO   That's what we trying to tell ya—they just disappeared! The Nigras have disappeared, swallowed up, vanished! All of 'em! Every last one!

MAYOR   Has everybody 'round here gone batty? . . . That's impossible, how could the Nigras vanish?

THREE   Beats me, but it's happened!

MAYOR   You mean a whole town of Nigras just evaporated like that—poof!—overnight?

ONE   Right!

MAYOR   Y'all must be drunk! Why, half this town is colored. How could they just sneak out?

TWO   Don't ask me, but there ain't one in sight!

MAYOR   Simmer down 'n put it to me, easy-like.

ONE   Well . . . I first suspected somp'um smelly when Sarah Jo didn't show up this morning and I couldn't reach her—

TWO   Dorothy Jane didn't 'rive at my house—

THREE   Georgia Mae wasn't at mine neither—and SHE sleeps in!

ONE   When I reached the office, I realized I hadn't seen nary one Nigra all morning! Nobody else had either—Wait a minute—Henry, have you?

MAYOR   Now that you mention it . . . no, I haven't . . .

ONE   They gone, Henry . . . Not a one on the street, not a one in our homes, not a single, last living one to be found nowheres in town. What we gon' do?

MAYOR   (*thinking*) Keep heads on your shoulders 'n put clothes on your back . . . They can't be far . . . Must be 'round somewheres . . . Probably playing hide 'n seek, that's it! . . . *Jackson!*

JACKSON   Yessir?

MAYOR   Immediately mobilize our Citizens Emergency Distress Committee!—order a fleet of sound trucks to patrol streets urging the population to remain calm—situation's not as bad as it looks—everything's under control! Then, have another squadron of squawk buggies drive slowly through all Nigra alleys, ordering them to come out wherever they are. If that don't git 'em, organize a vigilante search squad to flush 'em outta hiding! But most important of all, track down that lazy goldbricker Woodfence and tell him to git on top of the situation! By God, we'll find 'em even if we hafta dig 'em outta the ground!

(*Blackout. Scene shifts back to* JOHN *and* MARY *a few hours later. A funereal solemnity pervades their mood.*)

JOHN   Walked up to the shack, knocked on door, didn't git no answer. Hollered: "Lula? lula . . . ?"—not a thing. Went 'round the side, peeped in window—nobody stirred. Next door—nobody there. Crossed other side of street and banged on five or six other doors—not a colored person could be found! Not a man, neither woman or child —not even a black dog could be seen, smelt or heard for blocks around . . . They've gone, Mary.

MARY   What does it all mean, John?

JOHN   I don't know, Mary . . .

MARY   I always had Lula, John. Never missed a day at my side . . . That's why I couldn't accept your wedding proposal until I was sure you'd welcome me and her together as a package. How am I gonna git through the day? Baby don't know *me*, I ain't acquainted wit *it*. I've never lifted cover off pot, swung a mop or broom, dunked a dish or even pushed a dustrag. I'm lost wit'out Lula, I need her, John, I need her. (*Begins to weep softly.* JOHN *pats her consolingly.*)

JOHN   Courage, honey . . . Everybody in town is facing the same dilemma. We mustn't crack up . . .

(*Blackout. Scene shifts back to* MAYOR's *office later in day. Atmosphere and tone resembles a wartime headquarters at the front.* MAYOR *is perched on ladder checking over huge map.*)

INDUSTRIALIST   Half the day is gone already, Henry. On behalf of the factory owners of this town, you've got to bail us out! Seventy-five percent of all production is paralyzed. With the Nigra absent, men are waiting for machines to be cleaned, floors to be swept, crates lifted, equipment delivered and bathrooms deodorized. Why, restrooms and toilets are so filthy until they not only cannot be sat in, but it's virtually impossible to get within hailing distance because of the stench!

MAYOR   Keep your shirt on, Jeb—

BUSINESSMAN   Business is even in worse condition, Henry. The volume of goods moving 'cross counters has slowed down to a trickle—almost negligible. Customers are not only not purchasing—but the absence of handymen, porters, sweepers, stockmovers, deliverers and miscellaneous dirty-work doers is disrupting the smooth harmony of marketing!

CLUBWOMAN   Food poisoning, severe indigestitis, chronic diarrhea, advanced diaper chafings and a plethora of unsanitary household disasters dangerous to life, limb and property! . . . As a representative of the Federation of Ladies' Clubs, I must sadly report that unless the trend is reversed, a complete breakdown in family unity is imminent . . . Just as homosexuality and debauchery signaled the fall of Greece and Rome, the downgrading of Southern Bellesdom might very well prophesy the collapse of our indigenous institutions . . . . Remember—it has always been pure, delicate, lily-white images of Dixie femininity which provided backbone, inspiration and ideology for our male warriors in their defense against the onrushing black horde. If our gallant men are drained of this worship and idolatry—God knows! The cause won't be worth a Confederate nickel!

MAYOR   (*jumping off ladder*) stop this panicky defeatism, y'all hear
me! All machinery at my disposal is being utilized. I assure you wit
great confidence the damage will soon repair itself—Cheerful progress
reports are expected any moment now—Wait! See, here's Jackson
. . . Well, Jackson?

JACKSON   As of now, sir, all efforts are fruitless. Neither hide nor hair
of them has been located. We have not unearthed a single one in our
shack-to-shack search. Not a single one has heeded our appeal. Scoured
every creek and cranny inside their hovels, turning furniture upside
down and inside out, breaking down walls and tearing through ceil-
ings. We made determined efforts to discover where'bouts of our
faithful Uncle Toms and informers—but even they have vanished
without a trace . . . Searching squads are on the verge of panic and
hysteria, sir, wit hotheads among 'em campaigning for scorched earth
policies. Nigras on a whole lack cellars, but there's rising sentiment
favoring burning to find out whether they're underground-dug in!

MAYOR   Absolutely counter such foolhardy suggestions! Suppose they
are tombed in? We'd only accelerate the gravity of the situation using
incendiary tactics! Besides, when they're rounded up where will we
put 'em if we've already burned up their shacks—*in our own bed-
rooms?*

JACKSON   I agree, sir, but the mood of the crowd is becoming irrational.
In anger and frustration, they's forgetting their original purpose was
to *find* the Nigras!

MAYOR   At all costs! Stamp out all burning proposals! Must prevent extremist notions from gaining ascendancy. Git wit it . . . Wait—'n
for Jehovah's sake, find out where the hell is that trifling slacker,
Woodfence!

COURIER   (*rushing in*) Mr. Mayor! . . . We've found some! We've
found some!

MAYOR   (*excitedly*) Where?

COURIER   In the—in the—(*Can't catch breath.*)

MAYOR   (*impatiently*) Where, man? Where?

COURIER   In the colored wing of the city hospital!

MAYOR   The hos—? The hospital! I shoulda known! How could those
helpless, crippled, cut and shot Nigras disappear from a hospital?
Should thought of that! . . . Tell me more, man!

COURIER   I—I didn't wait, sir . . . I—I ran in to report soon as I
heard—

MAYOR   Well git back on the phone, you idiot! Don't'you know what
this means?

COURIER   Yes, sir. (*Races out.*)

MAYOR   Now we gitting somewhere! . . . Gentlemen, if one sole Nigra
is among us, we're well on the road to rehabilitation! Those Nigras
in the hospital must know somp'um 'bout the others where'bouts
. . . Scat back to your colleagues, boost up their morale and inform

'em that things will zip back to normal in a jiffy! (*They start to file out, then pause to observe the* COURIER *re-entering dazedly.*) Well . . . ? Well, man . . . ? What's the matter wit you, ninny? Tell me what else was said!

COURIER   They all . . . they all . . . they all in a—in a—a coma, sir . . .

MAYOR   They all in a what . . . ?

COURIER   In a coma, sir . . .

MAYOR   Talk sense, man! . . . Whaddaya mean, they all in a coma?

COURIER   Doctor says every last one of the Nigras are jist laying in bed . . . *still* . . . not moving . . . neither live or dead . . . laying up there in a coma . . . every last one of 'em . . .

MAYOR   (*splutters, then grabs phone*) Get me Confederate Memorial . . . Put me through to the Staff Chief . . . YES, this is the Mayor . . . Sam? . . . What's this I hear? . . . But how could they be in a coma, Sam? . . . You don't know! Well, what the hell you think the city's paying you for! You've got 'nuff damn hacks and quacks there to find out! . . . How could it be somp'um unknown? You mean Nigras know somp'um 'bout drugs your damn butchers don't? . . . Well, what the crap good are they? . . . All right, all right, I'll be calm. . . . Now, tell me . . . Uh huh, uh huh . . . Well, can't you give 'em some injections or somp'um . . . ?—You did . . . uh huh . . . *Did you try a lil rough treatment?*—that too, huh . . . All right, Sam, keep trying . . . (*Puts phone down deliberately, continuing absently.*) Can't wake 'em up. Just lay there. Them that's sick won't git no sicker, them that's half-well won't git no better, babies that's due won't be born and them that's come won't show no life. Nigras wit cuts won't bleed and them which need blood won't be transfused . . . He say dying Nigras is even refusing to pass away! (*Is silently perplexed for a moment, then suddenly breaks into action.*) Jackson? . . . Call up the police—*the jail!* Find out what's going on there! Them Nigras are captives! If there's one place we got darkies under control, it's there! Them sonsabitches too onery to act right either for colored or white! (JACKSON *exits.*) Keep your fingers crossed, citizens, them Nigras in jail are the most important Nigras we got!

(*All hands are raised conspicuously aloft, fingers prominently crossed. Seconds tick by. Soon* JACKSON *returns crestfallen.*)

JACKSON   Sheriff Bull says they don't know whether they still on premises or not. When they went to rouse Nigra jailbirds this morning, cell block doors refused to swing open. Tried everything—even exploded dynamite charges—but it just wouldn't budge . . . Then they hoisted guards up to peep through barred windows, but couldn't see good 'nuff to tell whether Nigras was inside or not. Finally, gitting desperate, they power-hosed the cells wit water but had to cease 'cause

Sheriff Bull said he didn't wanta jeopardize drowning the Nigras since it might spoil his chance of shipping a record load of cotton pickers to the State Penitentiary for cotton-snatching jubilee . . . Anyway —they ain't heard a Nigra-squeak all day.

MAYOR   That so . . . ? *What 'bout trains 'n busses passing through?* There must be some dinges riding through?

JACKSON   We checked . . . not a one on board.

MAYOR   Did you hear whether any other towns lost their Nigras?

JACKSON   Things are status quo everywhere else.

MAYOR   (*angrily*) Then what they picking on us for?

COURIER   (*rushing in*) Mr. Mayor! Your sister jist called—*hysterical!* She says Vice-Mayor Woodfence went to bed with her last night, but when she woke up this morning he was gone! Been missing all day!

MAYOR   Could Nigras be holding him hostage?

COURIER   No, sir. Besides him—investigations reveal that dozens or more prominent citizens—two City Council members, the chairman of the Junior Chamber of Commerce, our City College All-Southern halfback, the chairlady of the Daughters of the Confederate Rebellion, Miss Cotton Sack Festival of the Year and numerous other miscellaneous nobodies—are absent wit'out leave. Dangerous evidence points to the conclusion that they been infiltrating!

MAYOR   Infiltrating?

COURIER   Passing all along!

MAYOR   *What?*

COURIER   Secret Nigras all the while!

MAYOR   *Naw!*

(CLUBWOMAN *keels over in faint.* JACKSON, BUSINESSMAN *and* INDUSTRIALIST *begin to eye each other suspiciously.*)

COURIER   Yessir!

MAYOR   *Passing?*

COURIER   Yessir!

MAYOR   *Secret Nig—?*

COURIER   Yessir!

MAYOR   (*momentarily stunned to silence*) The dirty mongrelizers! . . . Gentlemen, this is a grave predicament indeed . . . It pains me to surrender priority of our states rights credo, but it is my solemn task and frightening duty to inform you that we have no other recourse but to seek outside help for deliverance.

(*Blackout. Lights rise again on Huntley-Brinkley-Murrow-Severeid-Cronkite-Reasoner-type* ANNOUNCER *grasping a hand-held microphone* [*imaginary*] *a few hours later. He is vigorously, excitedly mouthing his commentary, but no sound escapes his lips. During this dumb, wordless section of his broadcast, a bedraggled assortment of figures marching with picket signs occupies his attention. On their picket signs are inscribed various appeals and slogans.* "CINDY LOU UNFAIR TO BABY JOE"

. . . "CAP'N SAM MISS BIG BOY" . . . "RETURN LIL BLUE TO MARS JIM"
. . . "INFORMATION REQUESTED BOUT MAMMY GAIL." . . . "BOSS NATHAN
PROTEST TO FAST LEROY." *Trailing behind the* MARCHERS, *forcibly iso-
lated, is a* WOMAN *dressed in widow black holding a placard which
reads:* "WHY DIDN'T YOU TELL US—YOUR DEFILED WIFE AND 11 ABSENT
MONGRELS.")

ANNOUNCER (*who has been silently mouthing his delivery during the
picketing procession, is suddenly heard as if caught in the midst of
commentary*) Factories standing idle from the loss of nonessential
workers. Stores remaining shuttered from the absconding of uncrucial
personnel. Fruit, vegetables and other edible foodstuffs rotting in
warehouses, with uncollected garbage threatening pestilence and pol-
lution . . . Also, each second somewheres in this former utopia below the Mason and Dixon, dozens of decrepit old men and women
usually tended by faithful nurses and servants are popping off like
flies—abandoned by sons, daughters and grandchildren whose refusal
to provide these doddering souls with bedpans and other soothing
necessities results in their hasty, nasty, messy departures . . .

An equally wretched fate lurks in wait for juveniles of the town as
hundreds of new born infants HUNGER for the comforting em-
braces of devoted nannies while being forced to endure the presence
of strange parents . . .

But most critically affected of all by this complete drought of Afro-
American resources are policemen and other public safety guardians
denied their daily quota of Negro arrests. One officer known affectionately as "Two-a-Day-Pete" because of his unblemished record of
TWO Negro headwhippings per day has already been carted off to
the County Insane Asylum—strait-jacketed, screaming and biting, unable to withstand the shock of having his spotless slate sullied by
interruption . . . It is feared that similar attacks are soon expected
among municipal judges prevented for the first time in years of distinguished bench-sitting from sentencing one single Negro to corrective institutions . . .

Ladies and gentlemen, as you trudge in from the joys and head-
aches of workday chores and dusk begins to descend on this sleepy
Southern hamlet, we *repeat*—today—before early morning dew had
dried upon magnolia blossoms, your comrade citizens of this lovely
Dixie village awoke to the realization that some—pardon me! not
some but *all*—of their Negroes were missing . . . Absent, vamoosed,
departed, at bay, fugitive, away, gone and so far unretrieved . . .

In order to dispel your incredulity, gauge the temper of your suffering compatriots and just possibly prepare you for the likelihood of an
equally nightmarish eventuality, we have gathered a cross section of
this city's most distinguished leaders for exclusive interviews . . .
First, Mr. Council Clan, grand dragoon of this area's most active civic

organizations and staunch bellwether of the political opposition . . .
Mr. Clan, how do you *account* for this incredible disappearance?

CLAN   A *plot*, plain and simple, that's what it is, as plain as the corns
on your feet!

ANNOUNCER   Whom would you consider responsible?

CLAN   I could go on all night.

ANNOUNCER   Cite a few.

CLAN   Too numerous.

ANNOUNCER   Just one?

CLAN   Name names when time comes.

ANNOUNCER   Could you be referring to native Negroes?

CLAN   Ever try quaranteening lepers from their spots?

ANNOUNCER   Their organizations?

CLAN   Could you slice a nose off a mouth and still keep a face?

ANNOUNCER   Commies?

CLAN   Would you lop off a titty from a chest and still have a breast?

ANNOUNCER   Your city government?

CLAN   Now you talkin'!

ANNOUNCER   State administration?

CLAN   Warming up!

ANNOUNCER   Federal?

CLAN   Kin a blind man see?

ANNOUNCER   The Court?

CLAN   Is a pig clean?

ANNOUNCER   Clergy?

CLAN   Do a polecat stink?!

ANNOUNCER   Well, Mr. Clan, with this massive complicity, how do
you think the plot could've been prevented from succeeding?

CLAN   If I'da been in office, it never woulda happened.

ANNOUNCER   Then you're laying major blame at the doorstep of the
present administration?

CLAN   Damn tooting!

ANNOUNCER   But from your oft-expressed views, Mr. Clan, shouldn't
you and your followers be delighted at the turn of events? After all—
isn't it one of the main policies of your society to *drive* the Negroes
away? *Drive* 'em back where they came from?

CLAN   Drivvve, boy! Driiiivvve! That's right! . . . When we say so and
not befo'. Ain't supposed to do nothing 'til we tell 'em. Got to stay
put until we exercise our God-given right to tell 'em when to git!

ANNOUNCER   But why argue if they've merely jumped the gun? Why
not rejoice at this premature purging of undesirables?

CLAN   The time ain't ripe yet, boy . . . The time ain't ripe yet.

ANNOUNCER   Thank you for being so informative, Mr. Clan—Mrs.
Aide? Mrs. Aide? Over here, Mrs. Aide . . . Ladies and gentlemen,
this city's Social Welfare Commissioner, Mrs. Handy Anna Aide . . .
Mrs. Aide, with all your freeloading Negroes seemingly AWOL,

haven't developments alleviated the staggering demands made upon your Welfare Department? Reduction of relief requests, elimination of case loads, removal of chronic welfare dependents, et cetera?

AIDE Quite the contrary. Disruption of our pilot projects among Nigras saddles our white community with extreme hardship . . . You see, historically, our agencies have always been foremost contributors to the Nigra Git-A-Job movement. We pioneered in enforcing social welfare theories which oppose coddling the fakers. We strenuously believe in helping Nigras help themselves by participating in meaningful labor. "Relief is Out, Work is In," is our motto. We place them as maids, cooks, butlers, and breast-feeders, cesspool-diggers, wash-basin maintainers, shoeshine boys, and so on—mostly on a volunteer self-work basis.

ANNOUNCER Hired at prevailing salaried rates, of course?

AIDE God forbid! Money is unimportant. Would only make 'em worse. Our main goal is to improve their ethical behavior. "Rehabilitation Through Positive Participation" is another motto of ours. All unwed mothers, loose-living malingering fathers, bastard children and shiftless grandparents are kept occupied through constructive muscle therapy. This provides 'em with less opportunity to indulge their pleasure-loving amoral inclinations.

ANNOUNCER They volunteer to participate in these pilot projects?

AIDE Heavens no! They're notorious shirkers. When I said the program is voluntary, I meant white citizens in overwhelming majorities do the volunteering. Placing their homes, offices, appliances and persons at our disposal for use in "Operation Uplift" . . . We would never dare place such a decision in the hands of the Nigra. It would never get off the ground! No, they have no choice in the matter. "Work or Starve" is the slogan we use to stimulate their awareness of what's good for survival.

ANNOUNCER And a good one it is. Thank you, Mrs. Aide, and good luck . . . Rev? . . . Rev? . . . Ladies and gentlemen, this city's foremost spiritual guidance counselor, Reverend Reb Pious . . . How does it look to you, Reb Pious?

PIOUS (continuing to gaze skyward) It's in His hands, son, it's in His hands.

ANNOUNCER How would you assess the disappearance, from a moral standpoint?

PIOUS An immoral act, son, morally wrong and ethically indefensible. A perversion of Christian principles to be condemned from every pulpit of this nation.

ANNOUNCER Can you account for its occurrence after the many decades of the Church's missionary activity among them?

PIOUS It's basically a reversion of the Nigra to his deep-rooted primitivism . . . Now, at last, you can understand the difficulties of the Church in attempting to anchor God's kingdom among ungratefuls.

It's a constant, unrelenting, no-holds-barred struggle against Satan to wrestle away souls locked in his possession for countless centuries! Despite all our aid, guidance, solace and protection, Old Beezlebub still retains tenacious grips upon the Nigras' childish loyalty—comparable to the lure of bright flames to an infant.

ANNOUNCER   But actual physical departure, Reb Pious? How do you explain that?

PIOUS   Voodoo, my son, voodoo . . . With Satan's assist, they have probably employed some heathen magic which we cultivated, sophisticated Christians know absolutely nothing about. However, before long we are confident about counteracting this evil witch-doctory and triumphing in our Holy Savior's name. At this perilous juncture, true believers of all denominations are participating in joint, 'round-the-clock observances, offering prayers for our Master's swiftiest intercession. I'm optimistic about the outcome of His intervention . . . Which prompts me—if I may, sir—to offer these words of counsel to our delinquent Nigras . . . I say to you without rancor or vengeance, quoting a phrase of one of your greatest prophets, Booker T. Washington: "Return your buckets to where they lay and all will be forgiven."

ANNOUNCER   A very inspirational appeal, Reb Pious. I'm certain they will find the tug of its magnet sincerity irresistible. Thank you, Reb Pious . . . All in all—as you have witnessed, ladies and gentlemen—this town symbolizes the face of disaster, suffering as severe a prostration as any city wrecked, ravaged and devastated by the holocaust of war. A vital, lively, throbbing organism brought to a screeching halt by the strange enigma of the missing Negroes . . .

We take you now to offices of the one man into whose hands has been thrust the final responsibility of rescuing this shuddering metropolis from the precipice of destruction . . . We give you the honorable Mayor, Henry R. E. Lee . . . Hello, Mayor Lee.

MAYOR   (jovially) Hello, Jack.

ANNOUNCER   Mayor Lee, we have just concluded interviews with some of your city's leading spokesmen. If I may say so, sir, they don't sound too encouraging about the situation.

MAYOR   Nonsense, Jack! The situation's as well in hand as it could be under the circumstances. Couldn't be better in hand. Underneath every dark cloud, Jack, there's always a ray of sunlight, ha, ha, ha.

ANNOUNCER   Have you discovered one, sir?

MAYOR   Well, Jack, I'll tell you . . . Of course we've been faced wit a little crisis, but look at it like this—we've faced 'em befo': Sherman marched through Georgia—once! Lincoln freed the slaves—momentarily! Carpetbaggers even put Nigras in the Governor's mansion, state legislature, Congress and the Senate of the United States. But what happened? Ole Dixie bounced right on back up . . . At this moment the Supreme Court's trying to put Nigras in our schools and the Nigra has got it in his haid to put hisself everywhere . . . But what you spect gon happen? Ole Dixie will kangaroo back even higher. Southern courage, fortitude, chivalry and superiority always wins out. . . . SHUCKS! We'll have us some Nigras befo' daylight is gone!

ANNOUNCER Mr. Mayor, I hate to introduce this note, but in an earlier interview one of your chief opponents, Mr. Clan, hinted at your own complicity in the affair—

MAYOR A *lot of poppycock!* Clan is politicking! I've beaten him four times outta four and I'll beat him four more times outta four! This is no time for partisan politics! What we need now is level-headedness and across-the-board unity. This typical, rash, mealy-mouth, shooting-off-at-the-lip of Clan and his ilk proves their insincerity, and voters will remember that in the next election! Won't you, voters? (*Has risen to the height of campaign oratory.*)

ANNOUNCER Mr. Mayor! . . . Mr. Mayor! . . . Please—

MAYOR I tell you, I promise you—

ANNOUNCER *Please, Mr. Mayor!*

MAYOR Huh? . . . Oh—yes, carry on.

ANNOUNCER Mr. Mayor, your cheerfulness and infectious good spirits lead me to conclude that startling new developments warrant fresh-found optimism. What concrete, declassified information do you have to support your claim that Negroes will reappear before night-fall?

MAYOR Because we are presently awaiting the payoff of a masterful five-point supra-recovery program which can't help but reap us a bonanza of Nigras 'fore sundown! . . . First: Exhaustive efforts to pinpoint the where'bouts of our own missing darkies continue to zero in on the bull's-eye . . . Second: The President of the United States, following an emergency cabinet meeting, has designated us the prime disaster area of the century—National Guard is already on the way . . . Third: In an unusual, but bold, maneuver we have appealed to the NAACP 'n all other Nigra conspirators to help us git to the bottom of the vanishing act . . . Fourth: We have exercised our non-reciprocal option and requested that all fraternal Southern states express their solidarity by lending us some of their Nigras temporarily on credit . . . Fifth and foremost: We have already gotten consent of the Governor to round up all stray, excess and incorrigible Nigras to be shipped to us under escort of the state militia . . . That's why we've stifled pessimism and are brimming wit confidence that this full-scale concerted mobilization will ring down a jackpot of jigaboos 'fore light vanishes from sky!

ANNOUNCER Congratulations! What happens if it fails?

MAYOR Don't even think *that!* Absolutely no reason to suspect it will . . . (*Peers over shoulder, then whispers confidentially while placing hand over mouth by* ANNOUNCER's *imaginary mike.*) But speculating on the dark side of your question—if we don't turn up some by night-fall, it may be all over. The harm has already been done. You see the South has always been glued together by the uninterrupted presence of its darkies. No telling how unstuck we might git if things keep on like they have—Wait a minute, it musta paid off already! Mission accomplished 'cause here's Jackson 'head a time wit the word . . . Well, Jackson, what's new?

JACKSON Situation on the home front remains static, sir—can't uncover scent or shadow. The NAACP and all other Nigra front groups 'n plotters deny any knowledge or connection wit the missing Nigras. Maintained this even after appearing befo' a Senate Emergency Investigating Committee which subpoenaed 'em to Washington posthaste and threw 'em in jail for contempt. A handful of Nigras who agreed to make spectacular appeals for ours to come back to us have themselves mysteriously disappeared. But, worst news of all, sir, is our sister cities and counties, inside and outside the state, have changed their minds, fallen back on their promises and refused to lend us any Nigras, claiming they don't have 'nuff for themselves.

MAYOR What 'bout Nigras promised by the Governor?

JACKSON Jailbirds and vagrants escorted here from chain gangs and other reservations either revolted and escaped en route or else vanished mysteriously on approaching our city limits . . . Deterioration rapidly escalates, sir. Estimates predict we kin hold out only one more hour before overtaken by anarchistic turmoil . . . Some citizens seeking haven elsewheres have already fled, but on last report were being forcibly turned back by armed sentinels in other cities who wanted no parts of 'em—claiming they carried a jinx.

MAYOR That bad, huh?

JACKSON Worse, sir . . . we've received at least five reports of plots on your life.

MAYOR What?—We've gotta act quickly then!

JACKSON Run out of ideas, sir.

MAYOR Think harder, boy!

JACKSON Don't have much time, sir. One measly hour, then all hell gon break loose.

MAYOR Gotta think of something drastic, Jackson!

JACKSON I'm dry, sir.

MAYOR Jackson! Is there any planes outta here in the next hour?

JACKSON All transportation's been knocked out, sir.

MAYOR I thought so!

JACKSON What were you contemplating, sir?

MAYOR Don't ask me what I was contemplating! I'm still boss 'round here! Don't forgit it!

JACKSON Sorry, sir.

MAYOR Hold the wire! . . . Wait a minute . . . ! Waaaaait a minute —*goddammit!* All this time crapping 'round, diddling and fotsing wit puny lil solutions—all the while neglecting our ace in the hole, our

trump card! Most potent weapon for digging Nigras outta the wood-
pile? All the while right befo' our eyes! . . . Ass! Why didn't you
remind me?

JACKSON   What is it, sir?

MAYOR   *Me—That's what! Me!* a personal appeal from ME! *Directly ·
to them!* . . . Although we wouldn't let 'em march to the polls and
express their affection for me through the ballot box, we've always
known I'm held highest in their esteem. A direct address from their
beloved Mayor! . . . If they's anywheres close within the sound of
my voice, they'll shape up! Or let us know by a sign they's ready to.

JACKSON   You sure *that'll* turn the trick, sir?

MAYOR   As sure as my ancestors befo' me who knew that when they
puckered their lips to whistle, ole Sambo was gonna come a-lickey-
splitting to answer the call! . . . That same chips-down blood courses
through these Confederate gray veins of Henry R. E. Lee! ! !

ANNOUNCER   I'm delighted to offer our network's facilities for such a
crucial public interest address, sir. We'll arrange immediately for your
appearance on an international hookup, placing you in widest prox-
imity to contact them wherever they may be.

MAYOR   Thank you, I'm very grateful . . . Jackson, regrease the machinery and set wheels in motion. Inform townspeople what's being
done. Tell 'em we're all in this together. The next hour is countdown.
I demand absolute cooperation, citywide silence and inactivity. I don't
want the Nigras frightened if they's nearby. This is the most important hour in the town's history. Tell 'em if one single Nigra shows up
during the hour of decision, victory is within sight. I'm gonna git 'em
that one—maybe all! Hurry and crack to it!

(ANNOUNCER *rushes out, followed by* JACKSON. *Blackout. Scene re-
opens, with* MAYOR *seated, eyes front, spotlight illuminating him in
semidarkness. Shadowy figures stand in the background, prepared to
answer phones or aid in any other manner.* MAYOR *waits patiently until
"Go" signal is given.*)

MAYOR   (*voice combining elements of confidence, tremolo and gravity*)
Good evening . . . Despite the fact that millions of you wonderful
people throughout the nation are viewing and listening to this mo-
mentous broadcast—and I thank you for your concern and sympathy
in this hour of our peril—I primarily want to concentrate my attention and address these remarks solely for the benefit of our departed
Nigra friends who may be listening somewhere in our far-flung land
to the sound of my voice . . . If you are—it is with heartfelt emotion and fond memories of our happy association that I ask—"Where
are you . . . ?"

Your absence has left a void in the bosom of every single man,
woman and child of our great city. I tell you—you don't know what
it means for us to wake up in the morning and discover that your

cheerful, grinning, happy-go-lucky faces are missing! . . . From the depths of my heart, I can meekly, humbly suggest what it means to me personally . . . You see—the one face I will never be able to erase from my memory is the face—not of my Ma, not of Pa, neither wife or child—but the image of the first· woman I came to love so well when just a wee lad—the vision of the first human I laid clear sight on at childbirth—the profile—better yet the full face of my dear old . . . Jemimah—God rest her soul . . . Yes! My dear ole mammy, wit her round black moonbeam gleaming down upon me in the crib, teeth shining, blood-red bandanna standing starched, peaked and proud, gazing down on me affectionately as she crooned me a Southern lullaby . . . Oh! It's a memorable picture I will eternally cherish in permanent treasure chambers of my heart, now and forever always . . .

Well, if this radiant image can remain so infinitely vivid to me all these many years after her unfortunate demise in the po' folks' home—*think* of the misery the rest of us must be suffering after being *freshly* denied your soothing presence!

We need ya. If you kin hear me, just contact this station 'n I will welcome you back personally. Let me just tell you that since you eloped, nothing has been the same. How could it? You're part of us, you belong to us. Just give us a sign and we'll be contented that all is well . . .

Now if you've skipped away on a little fun fest, we understand, ha, ha. We know you like a good time and we don't begrudge it to ya. Hell—er, er, we like a good time ourselves—who doesn't . . . In fact, think of all the good times we've had together, huh? We've had some real fun, you and us, yesiree! . . . Nobody knows better than you and I what fun we've had together. You singing us those old Southern coon songs and dancing those Nigra jigs and us clapping, prodding 'n spurring you on! Lots of fun, huh? . . . *Oh boy!* The times we've had together . . . If you've snucked away for a bit of fun by yourself, we'll go 'long wit ya—long as you let us know where you at so we won't be worried about you . . .

We'll go 'long wit you long as you don't take the joke too far. I'll admit a joke is a joke and you've played a *lulu!* . . . I'm warning you, we can't stand much more horsing 'round from you! Business is business 'n fun is fun! You've had your fun so now let's get down to business! Come on back, *you hear me!*

If you been hoodwinked by agents of some foreign government, I've been authorized by the President of these United States to inform you that this liberty-loving Republic is prepared to rescue you from their clutches. Don't pay no 'tention to their sireen songs and atheistic promises! You better off under our control and you know it! . . . If you been bamboozled by rabble-rousing nonsense of your own so-called leaders, we prepared to offer some protection. Just call us up! Just give us a sign! . . . Come on, give us a sign . . . give us a sign—even a teeny weeny one . . . ? (*Glances around checking on possible communications. A bevy of headshakes indicate no success.* MAYOR *returns to address with desperate fervor.*)

Now look—you don't know what you doing! If you persist in this disobedience, you know all too well the consequences! We'll track you to the end of the earth, beyond the galaxy, across the stars! We'll capture you and chastise you with all the vengeance we command! 'N you know only too well how stern we kin be when double-crossed! The city, the state and the entire nation will crucify you for this unpardonable defiance! (*Checks again.*) No call . . . ? No sign . . . ? Time is running out! Deadline slipping past! They gotta respond! They gotta! (*resuming*) Listen to me! I'm begging y'all, you've gotta come back . . . ! Look, George! (*Waves dirty rag aloft.*) I brought the rag you wax the car with . . . Remember, George . . . ? Don't this bring back memories, George, of all the days you spent shining that automobile to shimmering perfection . . . ? And you, Rufus! . . . Here's the polish and the brush! . . . 'Member, Rufus? . . . Remember the happy mornings you spent popping this rag and whisking this brush so furiously 'til it created music that was symphonee to the ear . . . ? And you—*Mandy?* . . . Here's the wastebasket you didn't dump this morning. I saved it just for you! . . . *Look,* all y'all out there . . . (*Signals and a three-person procession parades one after the other before the imaginary camera.*)

DOLL WOMAN (*brandishing a crying baby* [*doll*] *as she strolls past and exits*) She's been crying ever since you left, Caldonia . . .

MOP MAN (*flashing mop*) It's been waiting in the same corner, Buster . . .

MOP MAN (*flashing toilet brush*) It's been dry ever since you left, Washington . . .

MAYOR (*jumping in on the heels of the last exit*) Don't these things mean anything to y'all? By God! Are your memories so short? Is there nothing sacred to ya . . . Please come back, for my sake, please! All of you—even you questionable ones! I promise no harm will be done to you! Revenge is disallowed! We'll forgive everything! Just come on back and I'll git down on my knees—(*Immediately drops to knees.*) I'll be kneeling in the middle of Dixie Avenue to kiss the first shoe of the first one to show up . . . I'll smooch any other spot you request . . . Erase this nightmare 'n we'll concede any demand you make, just come on back—please? . . . *Pleeeeeeeze!*

VOICE (*shouting*) Time!

MAYOR (*remaining on knees, frozen in a pose of supplication. After a brief, deadly silence, he whispers almost inaudibly*) They wouldn't answer . . . they wouldn't answer . . .

(*Blackout as bedlam erupts offstage. Total blackness holds during a sufficient interval where offstage sound effects create the illusion of complete pandemonium, followed by a diminution which trails off into an expressionistic simulation of a city coming to a stricken standstill: industrial machinery clanks to halt, traffic blares to silence, etc. . . . The stage remains dark and silent for a long moment, then lights rise again on the* ANNOUNCER.)

ANNOUNCER   A pitiful sight, ladies and gentlemen. Soon after his unsuccessful appeal, Mayor Lee suffered a vicious pummeling from the mob and barely escaped with his life. National guardsmen and state militia were impotent in quelling the fury of a town venting its frustration in an orgy of destruction—a frenzy of rioting, looting and all other aberrations of a town gone berserk . . . Then—suddenly—as if a magic wand had been waved, madness evaporated and something more frightening replaced it: submission . . .

Even whimpering ceased. The city: exhausted, benumbed—Slowly its occupants slinked off into shadows, and by midnight the town was occupied exclusively by zombies. The fight and life had been drained out . . . Pooped . . . Hope ebbed away as completely as the beloved, absent Negroes . . . As our crew packed gear and crept away silently, we treaded softly—as if we were stealing away from a mausoleum . . . The face of a defeated city.

(*Blackout. Lights rise slowly at the sound of rooster crowing, signaling the approach of a new day, the next morning. Scene is same as opening of play.* CLEM *and* LUKE *are huddled over dazedly, trancelike. They remain so for a long count. Finally, a figure drifts on stage, shuffling slowly.*)

LUKE   (*gazing in silent fascination at the approaching figure*) Clem . . . ? Do you see what I see or am I dreaming . . . ?

CLEM   It's a . . . a Nigra, ain't it, Luke . . . ?

LUKE   Sure looks like one, Clem—but we better make sure—eyes could be playing tricks on us . . . Does he still look like one to you, Clem?

CLEM   He still does, Luke—but I'm scared to believe—

LUKE   Why . . . ? It looks like Rastus, Clem!

CLEM   Sure does, Luke . . . but we better not jump to no hasty conclusion . . .

LUKE   (*in timid softness*) That you, Rastus . . . ?

RASTUS   (*Stepin Fetchit, Willie Best, Nicodemus, Butterfly McQueen and all the rest rolled into one*) Why . . . howdy . . . Mr. Luke . . . Mr. Clem . . .

CLEM   It is him, Luke! It is him!

LUKE   Rastus?

RASTUS   Yas . . . sah?

LUKE   Where was you yesterday?

RASTUS   (*very, very puzzled*) Yes . . . ter . . . day? . . . Yester . . . day . . . ? Why . . . right . . . here . . . Mr. Luke . . .

LUKE   No you warn't, Rastus, don't lie to me! Where was you yestiddy?

RASTUS   Why . . . I'm sure I was . . . Mr. Luke . . . Remember . . . I made . . . that . . . delivery for you . . .

LUKE   That was *Monday*, Rastus, yestiddy was *Tuesday*.

RASTUS   Tues . . . day . . . ? You don't say . . . Well . . . well . . . well . . .

LUKE   Where was you 'n all the other Nigras yesterday, Rastus?

RASTUS   I . . . thought . . . yestiddy . . . was . . . Monday, Mr. Luke —I coulda swore it . . . ! . . . See how . . . things . . . kin git all mixed up? . . . I coulda swore it . . .

LUKE   *Today* is *Wednesday*, Rastus. Where was you *Tuesday*?

RASTUS   Tuesday . . . huh? That's somp'um . . . I . . . don't remember . . . missing . . . a day . . . Mr. Luke . . . but I guess you right . . .

LUKE   Then where was you?

RASTUS   Don't rightly know, Mr. Luke. I didn't know I had skipped a day—But that jist goes to show you how time kin fly, don't it, Mr. Luke . . . Uuh, uuh, uuh . . . (*He starts shuffling off, scratching head, a flicker of a smile playing across his lips.* CLEM *and* LUKE *gaze dumbfoundedly as he disappears.*)

LUKE   (*eyes sweeping around in all directions*) Well . . . There's the others, Clem . . . Back jist like they useta be . . . Everything's same as always . . .

CLEM   Is it . . . Luke . . . ?

(*Slow fade.*)

CURTAIN

QUESTIONS

1. Ward calls his play "a satirical fantasy." It is a fantasy partly because of its major premise that all the blacks in a particular town inexplicably disappear for twenty-four hours. What makes this fantasy satirical? That is, what serious statement or thesis underlies the play?

2. Why do you think Ward selected a Southern rather than a Northern setting?

3. This play contains many stereotypes of Southern behavior and conventions. What are some of the ideas, emotions, and conventions of Southern life that are satirized?

4. Ward's satire is not aimed exclusively at the South. Consider, for example, the characterization of the Mayor, Mrs. Aide, and Reverend Pious. What political issues and qualities of leadership is Ward attacking through these characters?

5. Why does the play conclude with the arrival of a new day, the appearance of Rastus, and a return to what may or may not be a "normal" routine, rather than with the announcer's remark that he and his staff packed their gear and left as if "stealing away from a mausoleum . . . The face of a defeated city"?

6. What is the significance, or purpose, of the last line of the play?

7. How important or useful to your understanding of the drama are the author's production notes? Can you find any topics or themes that are satirized in these notes but are not included in the play itself?

part 4

Autobiography

The autobiographies of Richard Wright, James Baldwin, Malcolm X, and Eldridge Cleaver, though differing in style and temper, have certain large themes in common: becoming, the quest for knowledge, awakened moral and racial consciousness, metamorphosis.

Each writer experiences moments of epiphany when it becomes clear to him that he must choose between "being and nothingness." Wright and Cleaver, in the excerpts presented, tell of the influence of books on their lives. They respond creatively to the power of the written word and turn to writing as a way of release, a way of personal salvation. Their quest for knowledge leads inevitably to self-discovery. For Malcolm X, as well as for Cleaver, self-awareness brings self-analysis, harsh and ruthless, and points to a conclusion: You must change your life. For them, and for Wright and Baldwin, too, a heightened sense of racial identity is crucial to their transformation. They realize they must come to terms with themselves both as human beings and as black men in a society that threatens their individuality, their very existence.

Autobiographies by distinguished Afro-Americans are often more interesting as social commentary than as the revelation of personality. The Life and Times of Frederick Douglass (1881) may be considered prototypal. The culmination of a series of three autobiographies by the great abolitionist and champion of civil rights, this eloquent book is important as an invaluable social document rather than as a personal memoir. Wright, Baldwin, Malcolm X, and Cleaver write with more realism, more daring, of themselves as individuals than the age of Douglass permitted or the memoirist himself would have thought desirable. Their autobiographies are expressions of the modern sensibility. Even so, they are in the old tradition of the life-story as indictment of American racism.

Black Boy

Richard Wright

One morning I arrived early at work and went into the bank lobby where the Negro porter was mopping. I stood at a counter and picked up the Memphis *Commercial Appeal* and began my free reading of the press. I came finally to the editorial page and saw an article dealing with one H. L. Mencken. I knew by hearsay that he was the editor of the *American Mercury*, but aside from that I knew nothing about him. The article was a furious denunciation of Mencken, concluding with one, hot, short sentence: Mencken is a fool.

I wondered what on earth this Mencken had done to call down upon him the scorn of the South. The only people I had ever heard denounced in the South were Negroes, and this man was not a Negro. Then what ideas did Mencken hold that made a newspaper like the *Commercial Appeal* castigate him publicly? Undoubtedly he must be advocating ideas that the South did not like. Were there, then, people other than Negroes who criticized the South? I knew that during the Civil War the South had hated northern whites, but I had not encountered such hate during my life. Knowing no more of Mencken than I did at that moment, I felt a vague sympathy for him. Had not the South, which had assigned me the role of a non-man, cast at him its hardest words?

Now, how could I find out about this Mencken? There was a huge library near the riverfront, but I knew that Negroes were not allowed to patronize its shelves any more than they were the parks and playgrounds of the city. I had gone into the library several times to get books for the white men on the job. Which of them would now help me to get books? And how could I read them without causing concern to the white men with whom I worked? I had so far been successful in hiding my thoughts and feelings from them, but I knew that I would create hostility if I went about this business of reading in a clumsy way.

I weighed the personalities of the men on the job. There was Don, a

Jew; but I distrusted him. His position was not much better than mine and I knew that he was uneasy and insecure; he had always treated me in an offhand, bantering way that barely concealed his contempt. I was afraid to ask him to help me to get books; his frantic desire to demonstrate a racial solidarity with the whites against Negroes might make him betray me.

Then how about the boss? No, he was a Baptist and I had the suspicion that he would not be quite able to comprehend why a black boy would want to read Mencken. There were other white men on the job whose attitudes showed clearly that they were Kluxers or sympathizers, and they were out of the question.

There remained only one man whose attitude did not fit into an anti-Negro category, for I had heard the white men refer to him as a "Pope lover." He was an Irish Catholic and was hated by the white Southerners. I knew that he read books, because I had got him volumes from the library several times. Since he, too, was an object of hatred, I felt that he might refuse me but would hardly betray me. I hesitated, weighing and balancing the imponderable realities.

One morning I paused before the Catholic fellow's desk.

"I want to ask you a favor," I whispered to him.

"What is it?"

"I want to read. I can't get books from the library. I wonder if you'd let me use your card?"

He looked at me suspiciously.

"My card is full most of the time," he said.

"I see," I said and waited, posing my question silently.

"You're not trying to get me into trouble, are you, boy?" he asked, staring at me.

"Oh, no, sir."

"What book do you want?"

"A book by H. L. Mencken."

"Which one?"

"I don't know. Has he written more than one?"

"He has written several."

"I didn't know that."

"What makes you want to read Mencken?"

"Oh, I just saw his name in the newspaper," I said.

"It's good of you to want to read," he said. "But you ought to read the right things."

I said nothing. Would he want to supervise my reading?

"Let me think," he said. "I'll figure out something."

I turned from him and he called me back. He stared at me quizzically.

"Richard, don't mention this to the other white men," he said.

"I understand," I said. "I won't say a word."

A few days later he called me to him.

"I've got a card in my wife's name," he said. "Here's mine."

"Thank you, sir."

"Do you think you can manage it?"

"I'll manage fine," I said.

"If they suspect you, you'll get in trouble," he said.

"I'll write the same kind of notes to the library that you wrote when you sent me for books," I told him. "I'll sign your name."

He laughed.

"Go ahead. Let me see what you get," he said.

That afternoon I addressed myself to forging a note. Now, what were the names of books written by H. L. Mencken? I did not know any of them. I finally wrote what I thought would be a foolproof note: *Dear Madam: Will you please let this nigger boy*—I used the word "nigger" to make the librarian feel that I could not possibly be the author of the note—*have some books by H. L. Mencken?* I forged the white man's name.

I entered the library as I had always done when on errands for whites, but I felt that I would somehow slip up and betray myself. I doffed my hat, stood a respectful distance from the desk, looked as unbookish as possible, and waited for the white patrons to be taken care of. When the desk was clear of people, I still waited. The white librarian looked at me.

"What do you want, boy?"

As though I did not possess the power of speech, I stepped forward and simply handed her the forged note, not parting my lips.

"What books by Mencken does he want?" she asked.

"I don't know, ma'am," I said, avoiding her eyes.

"Who gave you this card?"

"Mr. Falk," I said.

"Where is he?"

"He's at work, at the M—— Optical Company," I said. "I've been in here for him before."

"I remember," the woman said. "But he never wrote notes like this."

Oh, God, she's suspicious. Perhaps she would not let me have the books? If she had turned her back at that moment, I would have ducked out the door and never gone back. Then I thought of a bold idea.

"You can call him up, ma'am," I said, my heart pounding.

"You're not using these books, are you?" she asked pointedly.

"Oh, no, ma'am. I can't read."

"I don't know what he wants by Mencken," she said under her breath.

I knew now that I had won; she was thinking of other things and the race question had gone out of her mind. She went to the shelves. Once or twice she looked over her shoulder at me, as though she was still doubtful. Finally she came forward with two books in her hand.

"I'm sending him two books," she said. "But tell Mr. Falk to come in next time, or send me the names of the books he wants. I don't know what he wants to read."

I said nothing. She stamped the card and handed me the books. Not daring to glance at them, I went out of the library, fearing that the woman would call me back for further questioning. A block away from the library I opened one of the books and read a title: A *Book of Prefaces*. I was nearing my nineteenth birthday and I did not know how to pronounce the word "preface." I thumbed the pages and saw strange words and strange names. I shook my head, disappointed. I looked at the other book; it was called *Prejudices*. I knew what that word meant; I had heard it all my life. And right off I was on guard against Mencken's books. Why would a man want to call a book *Prejudices*? The word was so stained with all my memories of racial hate that I could not conceive of anybody using it for a title. Perhaps I had made a mistake about Mencken? A man who had prejudices must be wrong.

When I showed the books to Mr. Falk, he looked at me and frowned.

"That librarian might telephone you," I warned him.

"That's all right," he said. "But when you're through reading those books, I want you to tell me what you get out of them."

That night in my rented room, while letting the hot water run over my can of pork and beans in the sink, I opened A *Book of Prefaces* and began to read. I was jarred and shocked by the style, the clear, clean, sweeping sentences. Why did he write like that? And how did one write like that? I pictured the man as a raging demon, slashing with his pen, consumed with hate, denouncing everything American, extolling everything European or German, laughing at the weaknesses of people, mocking God, authority. What was this? I stood up, trying to realize what reality lay behind the meaning of the words . . . Yes, this man was fighting, fighting with words. He was using words as a weapon, using them as one would use a club. Could words be weapons? Well, yes, for here they were. Then, maybe, perhaps, I could use them as a weapon? No. It frightened me. I read on and what amazed me was not what he said, but how on earth anybody had the courage to say it.

Occasionally I glanced up to reassure myself that I was alone in the room. Who were these men about whom Mencken was talking so passionately? Who was Anatole France? Joseph Conrad? Sinclair Lewis, Sherwood Anderson, Dostoevski, George Moore, Gustave Flaubert, Maupassant, Tolstoy, Frank Harris, Mark Twain, Thomas Hardy, Arnold Bennett, Stephen Crane, Zola, Norris, Gorky, Bergson, Ibsen, Balzac, Bernard Shaw, Dumas, Poe, Thomas Mann, O. Henry, Dreiser, H. G. Wells, Gogol, T. S. Eliot, Gide, Baudelaire, Edgar Lee Masters, Stendhal, Turgenev, Huneker, Nietzsche, and scores of others? Were these men real? Did they exist or had they existed? And how did one pronounce their names? I ran across many words whose meanings I did not know, and I either looked them up in a dictionary or, before I had a chance to do that, encountered the word in a context that made its meaning clear. But what strange world was this? I concluded the book with the conviction that I had somehow overlooked something terribly important in life. I had once tried to write, had once reveled in feeling, had let my crude imagination roam, but the impulse to dream had been slowly beaten out of me by experience. Now it surged up again and I hungered for books, new ways ,of looking and seeing. It was not a matter of believing or disbelieving what I read, but of feeling something new, of being affected by something that made the look of the world different.

As dawn broke I ate my pork and beans, feeling dopey, sleepy. I went to work, but the mood of the book would not die; it lingered, coloring everything I saw, heard, did. I now felt that I knew what the white men were feeling. Merely because I had read a book that had spoken of how they lived and thought, I identified myself with that book. I felt vaguely guilty. Would I, filled with bookish notions, act in a manner that would make the whites dislike me?

I forged more notes and my trips to the library became frequent. Reading grew into a passion. My first serious novel was Sinclair Lewis's *Main Street*. It made me see my boss, Mr. Gerald, and identify him as an American type. I would smile when I saw him lugging his golf bags into the office. I had always felt a vast distance separating me from the boss, and now I felt closer to him, though still distant. I felt now that I knew him, that I could feel the very limits of his narrow life. And this had happened because I had read a novel about a mythical man called George F. Babbitt.

The plots and stories in the novels did not interest me so much as the point of view revealed. I gave myself over to each novel without reserve, without trying to criticize it; it was enough for me to see and feel something different. And for me, everything was something different. Reading was like a drug, a dope. The novels created moods in which I lived for days. But I could not conquer my sense of guilt, my feeling that the white men around me knew that I was changing, that I had begun to regard them differently.

Whenever I brought a book to the job, I wrapped it in newspaper—a habit that was to persist for years in other cities and under other circumstances. But some of the white men pried into my packages when I was absent and they questioned me.

"Boy, what are you reading those books for?"

"Oh, I don't know, sir."

"That's deep stuff you're reading, boy."

"I'm just killing time, sir."

"You'll addle your brains if you don't watch out."

I read Dreiser's *Jennie Gerhardt* and *Sister Carrie* and they revived in me a vivid sense of my mother's suffering; I was overwhelmed. I grew silent, wondering about the life around me. It would have been impossible for me to have told anyone what I derived from these novels, for it was nothing less than a sense of life itself. All my life had shaped me for the realism, the naturalism of the modern novel, and I could not read enough of them.

Steeped in new moods and ideas, I bought a ream of paper and tried to write; but nothing would come, or what did come was flat beyond telling. I discovered that more than desire and feeling were necessary to write and I dropped the idea. Yet I still wondered how it was possible to know people sufficiently to write about them? Could I ever learn about life and people? To me, with my vast ignorance, my Jim Crow station in life, it seemed a task impossible of achievement. I now knew what being a Negro meant. I could endure the hunger. I had learned to live with hate. But to feel that there were feelings denied me, that the very breath of life itself was beyond my reach, that more than anything else hurt, wounded me. I had a new hunger.

In buoying me up, reading also cast me down, made me see what was possible, what I had missed. My tension returned, new, terrible, bitter, surging, almost too great to be contained. I no longer *felt* that the world about me was hostile, killing; I *knew* it. A million times I asked myself what I could do to save myself, and there were no answers. I seemed forever condemned, ringed by walls.

I did not discuss my reading with Mr. Falk, who had lent me his library card; it would have meant talking about myself and that would have been too painful. I smiled each day, fighting desperately to maintain my old behavior, to keep my disposition seemingly sunny. But some of the white men discerned that I had begun to brood.

"Wake up there, boy!" Mr. Olin said one day.

"Sir!" I answered for the lack of a better word.

"You act like you've stolen something," he said.

I laughed in the way I knew he expected me to laugh, but I resolved to be more conscious of myself, to watch my every act, to guard and hide the new knowledge that was dawning within me.

If I went north, would it be possible for me to build a new life then? But how could a man build a life upon vague, unformed yearnings? I wanted to write and I did not even know the English language. I bought English grammars and found them dull. I felt that I was getting a better sense of the language from novels than from grammars. I read hard, discarding a writer as soon as I felt that I had grasped his point of view. At night the printed page stood before my eyes in sleep.

Mrs. Moss, my landlady, asked me one Sunday morning:

"Son, what is this you keep on reading?"

"Oh, nothing. Just novels."

"What you get out of 'em?"

"I'm just killing time," I said.

"I hope you know your own mind," she said in a tone which implied that she doubted if I had a mind.

I knew of no Negroes who read the books I liked and I wondered if any Negroes ever thought of them. I knew that there were Negro doctors, lawyers, newspapermen, but I never saw any of them. When I read a Negro newspaper I never caught the faintest echo of my preoccupation in its pages. I felt trapped and occasionally, for a few days, I would stop reading. But a vague hunger would come over me for books, books that opened up new avenues of feeling and seeing, and again I would forge another note to the white librarian. Again I would read and wonder as only the naïve and unlettered can read and wonder, feeling that I carried a secret, criminal burden about with me each day.

That winter my mother and brother came and we set up housekeeping, buying furniture on the installment plan, being cheated and yet knowing no way to avoid it. I began to eat warm food and to my surprise found that regular meals enabled me to read faster. I may have lived through many illnesses and survived them, never suspecting that I was ill. My brother obtained a job and we began to save toward the trip north, plotting our time, setting tentative dates for departure. I told none of the white men on the job that I was planning to go north; I knew that the moment they felt I was thinking of the North they would change toward me. It would have made them feel that I did not like the life I was living, and because my life was completely conditioned by what they said or did, it would have been tantamount to challenging them.

I could calculate my chances for life in the South as a Negro fairly clearly now.

I could fight the southern whites by organizing with other Negroes, as my grandfather had done. But I knew that I could never win that way; there were many whites and there were but few blacks. They were strong and we were weak. Outright black rebellion could never win. If I fought openly I would die and I did not want to die. News of lynchings were frequent.

I could submit and live the life of a genial slave, but that was impossible. All of my life had shaped me to live by my own feelings and thoughts. I could make up to Bess and marry her and inherit the house. But that, too, would be the life of a slave; if I did that, I would crush to death something within me, and I would hate myself as much as I knew the whites already hated those who had submitted. Neither could I ever willingly present myself to be kicked, as Shorty had done. I would rather have died than do that.

I could drain off my restlessness by fighting with Shorty and Harrison. I had seen many Negroes solve the problem of being black by transferring their hatred of themselves to others with a black skin and fighting them. I would have to be cold to do that, and I was not cold and I could never be.

I could, of course, forget what I had read, thrust the whites out of my mind, forget them; and find release from anxiety and longing in sex and alcohol. But the memory of how my father had conducted himself made that course repugnant. If I did not want others to violate my life, how could I voluntarily violate it myself?

I had no hope whatever of being a professional man. Not only had I been so conditioned that I did not desire it, but the fulfillment of such an ambition was beyond my capabilities. Well-to-do Negroes lived in a world that was almost as alien to me as the world inhabited by whites.

What, then, was there? I held my life in my mind, in my consciousness each day, feeling at times that I would stumble and drop it, spill it forever. My reading had created a vast sense of distance between me and the world in which I lived and tried to make a living, and that sense of distance was increasing each day. My days and nights were one long, quiet, continuously contained dream of terror, tension, and anxiety. I wondered how long I could bear it.

QUESTIONS

1. In this chapter from his autobiography, Wright recounts his first experience with reading books. He says that he did not care about believing or disbelieving what he read. What did he find in books that mattered most?

2. In speaking of the world reading had opened up for him, Wright says, "In buoying me up, reading also cast me down." He felt that he "carried a secret, criminal burden" around with him each day. What does he mean? In what significant way had reading changed his perception of himself and his world?

3. Wright makes clear the way a black man in the South was forced to play roles according to the conventions established by the white ruling class. What are the examples of "role-playing" Wright describes in this chapter? Specifically, how did Wright's attitude toward his own role in society change?

Notes of a Native Son

James Baldwin

On the 29th of July, in 1943, my father died. On the same day, a few hours later, his last child was born. Over a month before this, while all our energies were concentrated in waiting for these events, there had been, in Detroit, one of the bloodiest race riots of the century. A few hours after my father's funeral, while he lay in state in the under-taker's chapel, a race riot broke out in Harlem. On the morning of the 3rd of August, we drove my father to the graveyard through a wilderness of smashed plate glass.

The day of my father's funeral had also been my nineteenth birthday. As we drove him to the graveyard, the spoils of injustice, anarchy, dis-content, and hatred were all around us. It seemed to me that God him-self had devised, to mark my father's end, the most sustained and brutally dissonant of codas. And it seemed to me, too, that the violence which rose all about us as my father left the world had been devised as a corrective for the pride of his eldest son. I had declined to believe in that apocalypse which had been central to my father's vision; very well, life seemed to be saying, here is something that will certainly pass for an apocalypse until the real thing comes along. I had inclined to be con-temptuous of my father for the conditions of his life, for the conditions of our lives. When his life had ended I began to wonder about that life and also, in a new way, to be apprehensive about my own.

I had not known my father very well. We had got on badly, partly because we shared, in our different fashions, the vice of stubborn pride. When he was dead I realized that I had hardly ever spoken to him. When he had been dead a long time I began to wish I had. It seems to be typical of life in America, where opportunities, real and fancied, are thicker than anywhere else on the globe, that the second generation has no time to talk to the first. No one, including my father, seems to have known exactly how old he was, but his mother had been born during slavery. He was of the first generation of free men. He, along with

FROM *Notes of a Native Son* by James Baldwin. Copyright © 1955 by James Bald-win. Reprinted by permission of the Beacon Press.

thousands of other Negroes, came North after 1919 and I was part of that generation which had never seen the landscape of what Negroes sometimes call the Old Country.

He had been born in New Orleans and had been a quite young man there during the time that Louis Armstrong, a boy, was running errands for the dives and honky-tonks of what was always presented to me as one of the most wicked of cities—to this day, whenever I think of New Orleans, I also helplessly think of Sodom and Gomorrah. My father never mentioned Louis Armstrong, except to forbid us to play his records; but there was a picture of him on our wall for a long time. One of my father's strong-willed female relatives had placed it there and forbade my father to take it down. He never did, but he eventually maneuvered her out of the house and when, some years later, she was in trouble and near death, he refused to do anything to help her.

He was, I think, very handsome. I gather this from photographs and from my own memories of him, dressed in his Sunday best and on his way to preach a sermon somewhere, when I was little. Handsome, proud, and ingrown, "like a toe-nail," somebody said. But he looked to me, as I grew older, like pictures I had seen of African tribal chieftains: he really should have been naked, with war-paint on and barbaric mementos, standing among spears. He could be chilling in the pulpit and indescribably cruel in his personal life and he was certainly the most bitter man I have ever met; yet it must be said that there was something else in him, buried in him, which lent him his tremendous power and, even, a rather crushing charm. It had something to do with his blackness, I think—he was very black—with his blackness and his beauty, and with the fact that he knew that he was black but did not know that he was beautiful. He claimed to be proud of his blackness but it had also been the cause of much humiliation and it had fixed bleak boundaries to his life. He was not a young man when we were growing up and he had already suffered many kinds of ruin; in his outrageously demanding and protective way he loved his children, who were black like him and menaced, like him; and all these things sometimes showed in his face when he tried, never to my knowledge with any success, to establish contact with any of us. When he took one of his children on his knee to play, the child always became fretful and began to cry; when he tried to help one of us with our homework the absolutely unabating tension which emanated from him caused our minds and our tongues to become paralyzed, so that he, scarcely knowing why, flew into a rage and the child, not knowing why, was punished. If it ever entered his head to bring a surprise home for his children, it was, almost unfailingly, the wrong surprise and even the big watermelons he often brought home on his back in the summertime led to the most appalling scenes. I do not remember, in all those years, that one of his children was ever glad to see him come home. From what I was able to gather of his early life, it seemed that this inability to establish contact with other people had always marked him and had been one of the things which had driven him out of New Orleans. There was something in him, therefore, groping and tentative, which was never expressed and which was buried with him. One saw it most clearly when he was facing new people and hoping to impress them. But he never did, not for long. We went from church to smaller and more improbable church, he found himself in less and less demand as a minister, and by the time he died none of his friends had come to see him for a long time. He had lived and died in an intolerable bitterness of spirit and it frightened me, as we drove him to the graveyard through those unquiet, ruined streets, to see how powerful and overflowing this bitterness could be and to realize that this bitterness now was mine.

When he died I had been away from home for a little over a year. In that year I had had time to become aware of the meaning of all my father's bitter warnings, had discovered the secret of his proudly pursed lips and rigid carriage: I had discovered the weight of white people in the world. I saw that this had been for my ancestors and now would be for me an awful thing to live with and that the bitterness which had helped to kill my father could also kill me.

He had been ill a long time—in the mind, as we now realized, reliving instances of his fantastic intransigence in the new light of his affliction and endeavoring to feel a sorrow for him which never, quite, came true. We had not known that he was being eaten up by paranoia, and the discovery that his cruelty, to our bodies and our minds, had been one of the symptoms of his illness was not, then, enough to enable us to forgive him. The younger children felt, quite simply, relief that he would not be coming home any more. My mother's observation that it was he, after all, who had kept them alive all these years meant nothing because the problems of keeping children alive are not real for children. The older children felt, with my father gone, that they could invite their friends to the house without fear that their friends would be insulted or, as had sometimes happened with me, being told that their friends were in league with the devil and intended to rob our family of everything we owned. (I didn't fail to wonder, and it made me hate him, what on earth we owned that anybody else would want.)

His illness was beyond all hope of healing before anyone realized that he was ill. He had always been so strange and had lived, like a prophet, in such unimaginably close communion with the Lord that his long silences which were punctuated by moans and hallelujahs and snatches of old songs while he sat at the living-room window never seemed odd to us. It was not until he refused to eat because, he said, his family was trying to poison him that my mother was forced to accept as a fact what had, until then, been only an unwilling suspicion. When he was committed, it was discovered that he had tuberculosis and, as it turned out, the disease of his mind allowed the disease of his body to destroy him. For the doctors could not force him to eat, either, and, though he was fed intravenously, it was clear from the beginning that there was no hope for him.

In my mind's eye I could see him, sitting at the window, locked up in his terrors; hating and fearing every living soul including his children who had betrayed him, too, by reaching toward the world which had despised him. There were nine of us. I began to wonder what it could have felt like for such a man to have had nine children whom he could barely feed. He used to make little jokes about our poverty, which never, of course, seemed very funny to us; they could not have seemed very funny to him, either, or else our all too feeble response to them would never have caused such rages. He spent great energy and achieved, to our chagrin, no small amount of success in keeping us away from the people who surrounded us, people who had all-night rent parties to which we listened when we should have been sleeping, people who cursed and drank and flashed razor blades on Lenox Avenue. He could not understand why, if they had so much energy to spare, they could not use it to make their lives better. He treated almost everybody on our block with a most uncharitable asperity and neither they, nor, of course, their children were slow to reciprocate.

The only white people who came to our house were welfare workers and bill collectors. It was almost always my mother who dealt with them, for my father's temper, which was at the mercy of his pride, was never to be trusted. It was clear that he felt their very presence in his home to be a violation: this was conveyed by his carriage, almost ludicrously stiff, and by his voice, harsh and vindictively polite. When I was around nine or ten I wrote a play which was directed by a young, white schoolteacher, a woman, who then took an interest in me, and gave me books to read and, in order to corroborate my theatrical bent, decided to take me to see what she somewhat tactlessly referred to as "real" plays. Theater-going was forbidden in our house, but, with the really cruel intuitiveness of a child, I suspected that the color of this woman's skin would carry the day for me. When, at school, she suggested taking me to the theater, I did not, as I might have done if she had been a Negro, find a way of discouraging her, but agreed that she should pick me up at my house one evening. I then, very cleverly, left all the rest to my mother, who suggested to my father, as I knew she would, that it would not be very nice to let such a kind woman make the trip for nothing. Also, since it was a schoolteacher, I imagine that my mother countered the idea of "education," which word, even with my father, carried a kind of bitter weight.

Before the teacher came my father took me aside to ask *why* she was coming, what *interest* she could possibly have in our house, in a boy like me. I said I didn't know but I, too, suggested that it had something to do with education. And I understood that my father was waiting for me to say something—I didn't quite know what; perhaps that I wanted his protection against this teacher and her "education." I said none of these things and the teacher came and we went out. It was clear, during the brief interview in our living room, that my father was agreeing very much against his will and that he would have refused permission if he had dared. The fact that he did not dare caused me to despise him: I had no way of knowing that he was facing in that living room a wholly unprecedented and frightening situation.

Later, when my father had been laid off from his job, this woman became very important to us. She was really a very sweet and generous woman and went to a great deal of trouble to be of help to us, particularly during one awful winter. My mother called her by the highest name she knew: she said she was a "christian." My father could scarcely disagree but during the four or five years of our relatively close association he never trusted her and was always trying to surprise in her open, Midwestern face the genuine, cunningly hidden, and hideous motivation. In later years, particularly when it began to be clear that this "education" of mine was going to lead me to perdition, he became more explicit and warned me that my white friends in high school were not really my friends and that I would see, when I was older, how white people would do anything to keep a Negro down. Some of them could be nice, he admitted, but none of them were to be trusted and most of them were not even nice. The best thing was to have as little to do with them as possible. I did not feel this way and I was certain, in my innocence, that I never would.

But the year which preceded my father's death had made a great change in my life. I had been living in New Jersey, working in defense plants, working and living among southerners, white and black. I knew about the south, of course, and about how southerners treated Negroes and how they expected them to behave, but it had never entered my mind that anyone would look at me and expect *me* to behave that way. I learned in New Jersey that to be a Negro meant, precisely, that one was never looked at but was simply at the mercy of the reflexes the color of one's skin caused in other people. I acted in New Jersey as I had always acted, that is as though I thought a great deal of myself— I had to *act* that way—with results that were, simply, unbelievable. I had scarcely arrived before I had earned the enmity, which was extraordinarily ingenious, of all my superiors and nearly all my co-workers. In the beginning, to make matters worse, I simply did not know what was happening. I did not know what I had done, and I shortly began to wonder what *anyone* could possibly do, to bring about such unanimous, active, and unbearably vocal hostility. I knew about jim-crow but I had never experienced it. I went to the same self-service restaurant three times and stood with all the Princeton boys before the counter, waiting for a hamburger and coffee; it was always an extraordinarily long time before anything was set before me; but it was not until the fourth visit that I learned that, in fact, nothing had ever been set before me: I had simply picked something up. Negroes were not served there, I was told, and they had been waiting for me to realize that I was always the only Negro present. Once I was told this, I determined to go there all the time. But now they were ready for me and, though some dreadful scenes were subsequently enacted in that restaurant, I never ate there again.

It was the same story all over New Jersey, in bars, bowling alleys, diners, places to live. I was always being forced to leave, silently, or with mutual imprecations. I very shortly become notorious and children giggled behind me when I passed and their elders whispered or shouted —they really believed that I was mad. And it did begin to work on my mind, of course; I began to be afraid to go anywhere and to compensate for this I went places to which I really should not have gone and where, God knows, I had no desire to be. My reputation in town naturally enhanced my reputation at work and my working day became one long series of acrobatics designed to keep me out of trouble. I cannot say that these acrobatics succeeded. It began to seem that the machinery of the organization I worked for was turning over, day and night, with but one aim: to eject me. I was fired once, and contrived, with the aid of a friend from New York, to get back on the payroll; was fired again, and bounced back again. It took a while to fire me for the third time, but the third time took. There were no loopholes anywhere. There was not even any way of getting back inside the gates.

That year in New Jersey lives in my mind as though it were the year during which, having an unsuspected predilection for it, I first contracted some dread, chronic disease, the unfailing symptom of which is a kind of blind fever, a pounding in the skull and fire in the bowels. Once this disease is contracted, one can never be really carefree again, for the fever, without an instant's warning, can recur at any moment. It can wreck more important things than race relations. There is not a Negro alive who does not have this rage in his blood—one has the choice, merely, of living with it consciously or surrendering to it. As for me, this fever has recurred in me, and does, and will until the day I die.

My last night in New Jersey, a white friend from New York took me to the nearest big town, Trenton, to go to the movies and have a few drinks. As it turned out, he also saved me from, at the very least, a violent whipping. Almost every detail of that night stands out very clearly in my memory. I even remember the name of the movie we saw because its title impressed me as being so patly ironical. It was a movie about the German occupation of France, starring Maureen O'Hara and Charles Laughton and called *This Land Is Mine*. I remember the name of the diner we walked into when the movie ended: it was the "American Diner." When we walked in the counterman asked what we wanted and I remember answering with the casual sharpness which had become my habit: "We want a hamburger and a cup of coffee, what do you think we want?" I do not know why, after a year of such rebuffs, I so completely failed to anticipate his answer, which was, of course, "We don't serve Negroes here." This reply failed to discompose me, at least for the moment. I made some sardonic comment about the name of the diner and we walked out into the streets.

This was the time of what was called the "brown-out," when the lights in all American cities were very dim. When we re-entered the streets something happened to me which had the force of an optical illusion, or a nightmare. The streets were very crowded and I was facing north. People were moving in every direction but it seemed to me, in that instant, that all of the people I could see, and many more than that, were moving toward me, against me, and that everyone was white. I remember how their faces gleamed. And I felt, like a physical sensation, a *click* at the nape of my neck as though some interior string connecting my head to my body had been cut. I began to walk. I heard my friend call after me, but I ignored him. Heaven only knows what was going on in his mind, but he had the good sense not to touch me —I don't know what would have happened if he had—and to keep me in sight. I don't know what was going on in my mind, either; I certainly had no conscious plan. I wanted to do something to crush these white faces, which were crushing me. I walked for perhaps a block or two until I came to an enormous, glittering, and fashionable restaurant in which I knew not even the intercession of the Virgin would cause me to be served. I pushed through the doors and took the first vacant seat I saw, at a table for two, and waited.

I do not know how long I waited and I rather wonder, until today, what I could possibly have looked like. Whatever I looked like, I frightened the waitress who shortly appeared, and the moment she appeared all of my fury flowed toward her. I hated her for her white face, and for her great, astounded, frightened eyes. I felt that if she found a black man so frightening I would make her fright worth-while.

She did not ask me what I wanted, but repeated, as though she had learned it somewhere, "We don't serve Negroes here." She did not say it with the blunt, derisive hostility to which I had grown so accustomed, but, rather, with a note of apology in her voice, and fear. This made me colder and more murderous than ever. I felt I had to do something with my hands. I wanted her to come close enough for me to get her neck between my hands.

So I pretended not to have understood her, hoping to draw her closer. And she did step a very short step closer, with her pencil poised incongruously over her pad, and repeated the formula: ". . . don't serve Negroes here."

Somehow, with the repetition of that phrase, which was already ringing in my head like a thousand bells of a nightmare, I realized that she would never come any closer and that I would have to strike from a distance. There was nothing on the table but an ordinary water-mug half full of water, and I picked this up and hurled it with all my strength at her. She ducked and it missed her and shattered against the mirror behind the bar. And, with that sound, my frozen blood abruptly thawed, I returned from wherever I had been, I *saw*, for the first time, the restaurant, the people with their mouths open, already, as it seemed to me, rising as one man, and I realized what I had done, and where I was, and I was frightened. I rose and began running for the door. A round, potbellied man grabbed me by the nape of the neck just as I reached the doors and began to beat me about the face. I kicked him and got loose and ran into the streets. My friend whispered, *"Run!"* and I ran.

My friend stayed outside the restaurant long enough to misdirect my pursuers and the police, who arrived, he told me, at once. I do not know what I said to him when he came to my room that night. I could not have said much. I felt, in the oddest, most awful way, that I had somehow betrayed him. I lived it over and over and over again, the way one relives an automobile accident after it has happened and one finds oneself alone and safe. I could not get over two facts, both equally difficult for the imagination to grasp, and one was that I could have been murdered. But the other was that I had been ready to commit murder. I saw nothing very clearly but I did see this: that my life, my *real* life, was in danger, and not from anything other people might do but from the hatred I carried in my own heart.

II

I had returned home around the second week in June—in great haste because it seemed that my father's death and my mother's confinement were both but a matter of hours. In the case of my mother, it soon became clear that she had simply made a miscalculation. This had always been her tendency and I don't believe that a single one of us arrived in the world, or has since arrived anywhere else, on time. But none of us dawdled so intolerably about the business of being born as did my baby sister. We sometimes amused ourselves, during those endless, stifling weeks, by picturing the baby sitting within in the safe, warm dark, bitterly regretting the necessity of becoming a part of our chaos and stubbornly putting it off as long as possible. I understood her perfectly and congratulated her on showing such good sense so soon. Death, however, sat as purposefully at my father's bedside as life stirred within my mother's womb and it was harder to understand why he so lingered in that long shadow. It seemed that he had bent, and for a long time, too, all of his energies toward dying. Now death was ready for him but my father held back.

All of Harlem, indeed, seemed to be infected by waiting. I had never before known it to be so violently still. Racial tensions throughout this country were exacerbated during the early years of the war, partly because the labor market brought together hundreds of thousands of ill-prepared people and partly because Negro soldiers, regardless of where they were born, received their military training in the south. What happened in defense plants and army camps had repercussions, naturally, in every Negro ghetto. The situation in Harlem had grown bad enough for clergymen, policemen, educators, politicians, and social workers to assert in one breath that there was no "crime wave" and to offer, in the very next breath, suggestions as to how to combat it. These suggestions always seemed to involve playgrounds, despite the fact that racial skirmishes were occurring in the playgrounds, too. Playground or not, crime wave or not, the Harlem police force had been augmented in March, and the unrest grew—perhaps, in fact, partly as a result of the ghetto's instinctive hatred of policemen. Perhaps the most revealing news item, out of the steady parade of reports of muggings, stabbings, shootings, assaults, gang wars, and accusations of police brutality, is the item concerning six Negro girls who set upon a white girl in the subway because, as they all too accurately put it, she was stepping on their toes. Indeed she was, all over the nation.

I had never before been so aware of policemen, on foot, on horseback, on corners, everywhere, always two by two. Nor had I ever been so aware of small knots of people. They were on stoops and on corners and in doorways, and what was striking about them, I think, was that they did not seem to be talking. Never, when I passed these groups, did the usual sound of a curse or a laugh ring out and neither did there seem to be any hum of gossip. There was certainly, on the other hand, occurring between them communication extraordinarily intense. Another thing that was striking was the unexpected diversity of the people who made up these groups. Usually, for example, one would see a group of sharpies standing on the street corner, jiving the passing chicks; or a group of older men, usually, for some reason, in the vicinity of a barber shop, discussing baseball scores, or the numbers, or making rather chilling observations about women they had known. Women, in a general way, tended to be seen less often together—unless they were church women, or very young girls, or prostitutes met together for an unprofessional instant. But that summer I saw the strangest combinations: large, respectable, churchly matrons standing on the stoops or the corners with their hair tied up, together with a girl in sleazy satin whose face bore the marks of gin and the razor, or heavy-set, abrupt, no-nonsense older men, in company with the most disreputable and fanatical "race" men, or these same "race" men with the sharpies, or these sharpies with the churchly women. Seventh Day Adventists and Methodists and Spiritualists seemed to be hobnobbing with Holyrollers and they were all, alike, entangled with the most flagrant disbelievers; something heavy in their stance seemed to indicate that they had all, incredibly, seen a common vision, and on each face there seemed to be the same strange, bitter shadow.

The churchly women and the matter-of-fact, no-nonsense men had children in the Army. The sleazy girls they talked to had lovers there, the sharpies and the "race" men had friends and brothers there. It would have demanded an unquestioning patriotism, happily as uncommon in this country as it is undesirable, for these people not to have been disturbed by the bitter letters they received, by the newspaper stories they read, not to have been enraged by the posters, then to be found all over New York, which described the Japanese as "yellow-bellied Japs." It was only the "race" men, to be sure, who spoke ceaselessly of being revenged—how this vengeance was to be exacted was not clear—for the indignities and dangers suffered by Negro boys in uniform; but everybody felt a directionless, hopeless bitterness, as well as that panic which can scarcely be suppressed when one knows that a human being one loves is beyond one's reach, and in danger. This helplessness and this gnawing uneasiness does something, at length, to even the toughest mind. Perhaps the best way to sum all this up is to say that the people I knew felt, mainly, a peculiar kind of relief when they knew that their boys were being shipped out of the south, to do battle overseas. It was, perhaps, like feeling that the most dangerous part of a dangerous journey had been passed and that now, even if death should come, it would come with honor and without the complicity of their countrymen. Such a death would be, in short, a fact with which one could hope to live.

It was on the 28th of July, which I believe was a Wednesday, that I visited my father for the first time during his illness and for the last time in his life. The moment I saw him I knew why I had put off this visit so long. I had told my mother that I did not want to see him because I hated him. But this was not true. It was only that I *had* hated him and I wanted to hold on to this hatred. I did not want to look on him as a ruin: it was not a ruin I had hated. I imagine that one of the reasons people cling to their hates so stubbornly is because they sense, once hate is gone, that they will be forced to deal with pain.

We traveled out to him, his older sister and myself, to what seemed to be the very end of a very Long Island. It was hot and dusty and we wrangled, my aunt and I, all the way out, over the fact that I had recently begun to smoke and, as she said, to give myself airs. But I knew that she wrangled with me because she could not bear to face the fact of her brother's dying. Neither could I endure the reality of her despair, her unstated bafflement as to what had happened to her brother's life, and her own. So we wrangled and I smoked and from time to time she fell into a heavy reverie. Covertly, I watched her face, which was the face of an old woman; it had fallen in, the eyes were sunken and lightless; soon she would be dying, too.

In my childhood—it had not been so long ago—I had thought her beautiful. She had been quick-witted and quick-moving and very generous with all the children and each of her visits had been an event. At one time one of my brothers and myself had thought of running away to live with her. Now she could no longer produce out of her handbag some unexpected and yet familiar delight. She made me feel pity and revulsion and fear. It was awful to realize that she no longer caused me to feel affection. The closer we came to the hospital the more querulous she became and at the same time, naturally, grew more dependent on me. Between pity and guilt and fear I began to feel that there was another me trapped in my skull like a jack-in-the-box who might escape my control at any moment and fill the air with screaming.

She began to cry the moment we entered the room and she saw him lying there, all shriveled and still, like a little black monkey. The great, gleaming apparatus which fed him and would have compelled him to be still even if he had been able to move brought to mind, not benefi-cence, but torture; the tubes entering his arm made me think of pictures I had seen when a child, of Gulliver, tied down by the pygmies on that island. My aunt wept and wept, there was a whistling sound in my father's throat; nothing was said; he could not speak. I wanted to take his hand, to say something. But I do not know what I could have said, even if he could have heard me. He was not really in that room with us, he had at last really embarked on his journey; and though my aunt told me that he said he was going to meet Jesus, I did not hear anything except that whistling in his throat. The doctor came back and we left, into that unbearable train again, and home. In the morning came the telegram saying that he was dead. Then the house was suddenly full of relatives, friends, hysteria, and confusion and I quickly left my mother and the children to the care of those impressive women, who, in Negro communities at least, automatically appear at times of bereavement armed with lotions, proverbs, and patience, and an ability to cook. I went downtown. By the time I returned, later the same day, my mother had been carried to the hospital and the baby had been born.

III

For my father's funeral I had nothing black to wear and this posed a nagging problem all day long. It was one of those problems, simple, or impossible of solution, to which the mind insanely clings in order to avoid the mind's real trouble. I spent most of that day at the downtown apartment of a girl I knew, celebrating my birthday with whiskey and wondering what to wear that night. When planning a birthday celebration one naturally does not expect that it will be up against competition from a funeral and this girl had anticipated taking me out that night, for a big dinner and a night club afterwards. Some-time during the course of that long day we decided that we would go out anyway, when my father's funeral service was over. I imagine I de-cided it, since, as the funeral hour approached, it became clearer and clearer to me that I would not know what to do with myself when it was over. The girl, stifling her very lively concern as to the possible effects of the whiskey on one of my father's chief mourners, concentrated on being conciliatory and practically helpful. She found a black shirt for me somewhere and ironed it and, dressed in the darkest pants and jacket I owned, and slightly drunk, I made my way to my father's funeral.

The chapel was full, but not packed, and very quiet. There were, mainly, my father's relatives, and his children, and here and there I saw faces I had not seen since childhood, the faces of my father's one-time friends. They were very dark and solemn now, seeming somehow to suggest that they had known all along that something like this would happen. Chief among the mourners was my aunt, who had quarreled with my father all his life; by which I do not mean to suggest that her mourning was insincere or that she had not loved him. I suppose that she was one of the few people in the world who had, and their incessant quarreling proved precisely the strength of the tie that bound them. The only other person in the world, as far as I knew, whose relationship to my father rivaled my aunt's in depth was my mother, who was not there.

It seemed to me, of course, that it was a very long funeral. But it was, if anything, a rather shorter funeral than most, nor, since there were no overwhelming, uncontrollable expressions of grief, could it be called— if I dare to use the word—successful. The minister who preached my father's funeral sermon was one of the few my father had still been seeing as he neared his end. He presented to us in his sermon a man whom none of us had even seen—a man thoughtful, patient, and forbearing, a Christian inspiration to all who knew him, and a model for his children. And no doubt the children, in their disturbed and guilty state, were almost ready to believe this; he had been remote enough to be anything and, anyway, the shock of the incontrovertible, that it was really our father lying up there in that casket, prepared the mind for anything. His sister moaned and this grief-stricken moaning was taken as corroboration. The other faces held a dark, non-committal thoughtfulness. This was not the man they had known, but they had scarcely expected to be confronted with *him*; this was, in a sense deeper than questions of fact, the man they had not known, and the man they had not known may have been the real one. The real man, whoever he had been, had suffered and now he was dead: this was all that was sure and all that mattered now. Every man in the chapel hoped that when his hour came he, too, would be eulogized, which is to say forgiven, and that all of his lapses, greeds, errors, and strayings from the truth would be invested with coherence and looked upon with charity. This was perhaps the last thing human beings could give each other and it was what they demanded, after all, of the Lord. Only the Lord saw the midnight tears, only He was present when one of His children, moaning and wringing hands, paced up and down the room. When one slapped one's child in anger the recoil in the heart reverberated through heaven and became part of the pain of the universe. And when the children were hungry and sullen and distrustful and one watched them, daily, growing wilder, and further away, and running headlong into danger, it was the Lord who knew what the charged heart endured as the strap was laid to the backside; the Lord alone who knew what one *would* have said if one had had, like the Lord, the gift of the living word. It was the Lord who knew of the impossibility every parent in that room faced: how to prepare the child for the day when the child would be despised and how to *create* in the child—by what means?—a stronger antidote to this poison than one had found for oneself. The avenues, side streets, bars, billiard halls, hospitals, police stations, and even the playgrounds of Harlem—not to mention the houses of correction, the jails, and the morgue—testified to the potency of the poison while remaining silent as to the efficacy of whatever antidote, irresistibly raising the question of whether or not such an antidote existed; raising, which was worse, the question of whether or not an antidote was desirable; perhaps poison should be fought with poison. With these several schisms in the mind and with more terrors in the heart than could be named, it was better not to judge the man who had gone down under an impossible burden. It was better to remember: *Thou knowest this man's fall; but thou knowest not his wrassling.*

While the preacher talked and I watched the children—years of changing their diapers, scrubbing them, slapping them, taking them to school, and scolding them had had the perhaps inevitable result of making me love them, though I am not sure I knew this then—my mind was busily breaking out with a rash of disconnected impressions. Snatches of popular songs, indecent jokes, bits of books I had read, movie sequences, faces, voices, political issues—I thought I was going mad; all these impressions suspended, as it were, in the solution of the faint nausea produced in me by the heat and liquor. For a moment I had the impression that my alcoholic breath, inefficiently disguised with chewing gum, filled the entire chapel. Then someone began singing one of my father's favorite songs and, abruptly, I was with him, sitting on his knee, in the hot, enormous, crowded church which was the first church we attended. It was the Abyssinian Baptist Church on 138th Street. We had not gone there long. With this image, a host of others came. I had forgotten, in the rage of my growing up, how proud my father had been of me when I was little. Apparently, I had had a voice and my father had liked to show me off before the members of the church. I had forgotten what he had looked like when he was pleased but now I remembered that he had always been grinning with pleasure when my solos ended. I even remembered certain expressions on his face when he teased my mother—had he loved her? I would never know. And when had it all begun to change? For now it seemed that he had not always been cruel. I remembered being taken for a haircut and scraping my knee on the footrest of the barber's chair and I remembered my father's face as he soothed my crying and applied the stinging iodine. Then I remembered our fights, fights which had been of the worst possible kind because my technique had been silence.

I remembered the one time in all our life together when we had really spoken to each other.

It was on a Sunday and it must have been shortly before I left home. We were walking, just the two of us, in our usual silence, to or from church. I was in high school and had been doing a lot of writing and I was, at about this time, the editor of the high school magazine. But I had also been a Young Minister and had been preaching from the pulpit. Lately, I had been taking fewer engagements and preached as rarely as possible. It was said in the church, quite truthfully, that I was "cooling off."

My father asked me abruptly, "You'd rather write than preach, wouldn't you?"

I was astonished at his question—because it was a real question. I answered, "Yes."

That was all we said. It was awful to remember that that was all we had *ever* said.

The casket now was opened and the mourners were being led up the aisle to look for the last time on the deceased. The assumption was that the family was too overcome with grief to be allowed to make this journey alone and I watched while my aunt was led to the casket and, muffled in black, and shaking, led back to her seat. I disapproved of forcing the children to look on their dead father, considering that the shock of his death, or, more truthfully, the shock of death as a reality, was already a little more than a child could bear, but my judgment in this matter had been overruled and there they were, bewildered and frightened and very small, being led, one by one, to the casket. But there is also something very gallant about children at such moments. It has something to do with their silence and gravity and with the fact that one cannot help them. Their legs, somehow, seem *exposed*, so that it is at once incredible and terribly clear that their legs are all they have to hold them up.

I had not wanted to go to the casket myself and I certainly had not wished to be led there, but there was no way of avoiding either of these forms. One of the deacons led me up and I looked on my father's face. I cannot say that it looked like him at all. His blackness had been equivocated by powder and there was no suggestion in that casket of what his power had or could have been. He was simply an old man dead, and it was hard to believe that he had ever given anyone either joy or pain. Yet, his life filled that room. Further up the avenue his wife was holding his newborn child. Life and death so close together, and love and hatred, and right and wrong, said something to me which I did not want to hear concerning man, concerning the life of man.

After the funeral, while I was downtown desperately celebrating my birthday, a Negro soldier, in the lobby of the Hotel Braddock, got into a fight with a white policeman over a Negro girl. Negro girls, white policemen, in or out of uniform, and Negro males—in or out of uniform —were part of the furniture of the lobby of the Hotel Braddock and this was certainly not the first time such an incident had occurred. It was destined, however, to receive an unprecedented publicity, for the fight between the policeman and the soldier ended with the shooting of the soldier. Rumor, flowing immediately to the streets outside, stated that the soldier had been shot in the back, an instantaneous and revealing invention, and that the soldier had died protecting a Negro woman. The facts were somewhat different—for example, the soldier had not been shot in the back, and was not dead, and the girl seems to have been as dubious a symbol of womanhood as her white counterpart in Georgia usually is, but no one was interested in the facts. They preferred the invention because this invention expressed and corroborated their hates and fears so perfectly. It is just as well to remember that people are always doing this. Perhaps many of those legends, including Christianity, to which the world clings began their conquest of the world with just some such concerted surrender to distortion. The effect, in Harlem, of this particular legend was like the effect of a lit match in a tin of gasoline. The mob gathered before the doors of the Hotel Braddock simply began to swell and to spread in every direction, and Harlem exploded.

The mob did not cross the ghetto lines. It would have been easy, for example, to have gone over Morningside Park on the west side or to have crossed the Grand Central railroad tracks at 125th Street on the east side, to wreak havoc in white neighborhoods. The mob seems to have been mainly interested in something more potent and real than the white face, that is, in white power, and the principal damage done during the riot of the summer of 1943 was to white business establishments in Harlem. It might have been a far bloodier story, of course, if, at the hour the riot began, these establishments had still been open. From the Hotel Braddock the mob fanned out, east and west along 125th Street, and for the entire length of Lenox, Seventh, and Eighth avenues. Along each of these avenues, and along each major side street —116th, 125th, 135th, and so on—bars, stores, pawnshops, restaurants, even little luncheonettes had been smashed open and entered and looted —looted, it might be added, with more haste than efficiency. The shelves really looked as though a bomb had struck them. Cans of beans and soup and dog food, along with toilet paper, corn flakes, sardines, and milk tumbled every which way, and abandoned cash registers and cases of beer leaned crazily out of the splintered windows and were strewn along the avenues. Sheets, blankets, and clothing of every description formed a kind of path, as though people had dropped them while running. I truly had not realized that Harlem *had* so many stores until I saw them all smashed open; the first time the word *wealth* ever entered my mind in relation to Harlem was when I saw it scattered in the streets. But one's first, incongruous impression of plenty was countered immediately by an impression of waste. None of this was doing anybody any good. It would have been better to have left the plate glass as it had been and the goods lying in the stores.

It would have been better, but it would also have been intolerable, for Harlem had needed something to smash. To smash something is the ghetto's chronic need. Most of the time it is the members of the ghetto who smash each other, and themselves. But as long as the ghetto walls are standing there will always come a moment when these outlets do not work. That summer, for example, it was not enough to get into a fight on Lenox Avenue, or curse out one's cronies in the barber shops. If ever, indeed, the violence which fills Harlem's churches, pool halls, and bars erupts outward in a more direct fashion, Harlem and its citizens are likely to vanish in an apocalyptic flood. That this is not likely to happen is due to a great many reasons, most hidden and powerful among them the Negro's real relation to the white American. This relation prohibits, simply, anything as uncomplicated and satisfactory as pure hatred. In order really to hate white people, one has to blot so much out of the mind—and the heart—that this hatred itself becomes an exhausting and self-destructive pose. But this does not mean, on the other hand, that love comes easily: the white world is too powerful, too complacent, too ready with gratuitous humiliation, and, above all, too ignorant and too innocent for that. One is absolutely forced to make perpetual qualifications and one's own reactions are always canceling each other out. It is this, really, which has driven so many people mad, both white and black. One is always in the position of having to decide between amputation and gangrene. Amputation is swift but time may prove that the amputation was not necessary—or one may delay the amputation too long. Gangrene is slow, but it is impossible to be sure that one is reading one's symptoms right. The idea of going through life as a cripple is more than one can bear, and equally unbearable is the risk of swelling up slowly, in agony, with poison. And the trouble, finally, is that the risks are real even if the choices do not exist.

"But as for me and my house," my father had said, "we will serve the Lord." I wondered, as we drove him to his resting place, what this line had meant for him. I had heard him preach it many times. I had preached it once myself, proudly giving it an interpretation different from my father's. Now the whole thing came back to me, as though my father and I were on our way to Sunday school and I were memorizing the golden text: *And if it seem evil unto you to serve the Lord, choose you this day whom you will serve; whether the gods which your fathers served that were on the other side of the flood, or the gods of the Amorites, in whose land ye dwell: but as for me and my house, we will serve the Lord.* I suspected in these familiar lines a meaning which had never been there for me before. All of my father's texts and songs, which I had decided were meaningless, were arranged before me at his death like empty bottles, waiting to hold the meaning which life would give them for me. This was his legacy: nothing is ever escaped. That bleakly memorable morning I hated the unbelievable streets and the Negroes and whites who had, equally, made them that way. But I knew that it was folly, as my father would have said, this bitterness was folly. It was necessary to hold on to the things that mattered. The dead man mattered, the new life mattered; blackness and whiteness did not matter; to believe that they did was to acquiesce in one's own destruction. Hatred, which could destroy so much, never failed to destroy the man who hated and this was an immutable law.

It began to seem that one would have to hold in the mind forever two ideas which seemed to be in opposition. The first idea was acceptance, the acceptance, totally without rancor, of life as it is, and men as they are: in the light of this idea, it goes without saying that injustice is a commonplace. But this did not mean that one could be complacent, for the second idea was of equal power: that one must never, in one's own life, accept these injustices as commonplace but must fight them with all one's strength. This fight begins, however, in the heart and it now had been laid to my charge to keep my own heart free of hatred and despair. This intimation made my heart heavy and, now that my father was irrecoverable, I wished that he had been beside me so that I could have searched his face for the answers which only the future would give me now.

QUESTIONS

1. In this essay Baldwin departs from chronological order. Analyze the time structure he uses. Why do you think he chose this method of presentation?

2. A number of Baldwin's themes are implied in his first paragraph. The death of his father, the birth of his sister, the race riots, suggest opposites that are themes throughout: death–birth, parent–child, innocence–experience, hate–love, black–white. Trace Baldwin's treatment of these thematic opposites. In what way is this treatment of thematic material appropriate and effective? How does Baldwin resolve or redefine these themes in the chapter?

3. Baldwin says that after his father's funeral, he found new meaning in the words of the sermon he and his father used to preach. What new meaning did he perceive that enabled him to reevaluate both his father's life and, in a sense, his own?

4. Despite the deep feeling, even bitterness, that gives quality and intensity to this essay, Baldwin would probably say it is not written out of hatred for the white world. What, specifically, does he say about hatred in this essay?

1965

Malcolm X

I must be honest. Negroes—Afro-Americans—showed no inclination to rush to the United Nations and demand justice for themselves here in America. I really had known in advance that they wouldn't. The American white man has so thoroughly brainwashed the black man to see himself as only a domestic "civil rights" problem that it will probably take longer than I live before the Negro sees that the struggle of the American black man is international.

And I had known, too, that Negroes would not rush to follow me into the orthodox Islam which had given me the insight and perspective to see that the black men and white men truly could be brothers. America's Negroes—especially older Negroes—are too indelibly soaked in Christianity's double standard of oppression.

So, in the "public invited" meetings which I began holding each Sunday afternoon or evening in Harlem's well-known Audubon Ballroom, as I addressed predominantly non-Muslim Negro audiences, I did not immediately attempt to press the Islamic religion, but instead to embrace all who sat before me:

"—not Muslim, nor Christian, Catholic, nor Protestant . . . Baptist nor Methodist, Democrat nor Republican, Mason nor Elk! I mean the black people of America—and the black people all over this earth! Because it is as this collective mass of black people that we have been deprived not only of our civil rights, but even of our human rights, the right to human dignity. . . ."

On the streets, after my speeches, in the faces and the voices of the people I met—even those who would pump my hands and want my autograph—I would feel the wait-and-see attitude. I would feel—and I understood—their uncertainty about where I stood. Since the Civil War's "freedom," the black man has gone down so many fruitless paths. His leaders, very largely, had failed him. The religion of Christianity had failed him. The black man was scarred, he was cautious, he was apprehensive.

I understood it better now than I had before. In the Holy World, away from America's race problem, was the first time I ever had been able to think clearly about the basic divisions of white people in America, and how their attitudes and their motives related to, and affected Negroes. In my thirty-nine years on this earth, the Holy City of Mecca had been the first time I had ever stood before the Creator of All and felt like a complete human being.

In that peace of the Holy World—in fact, the very night I have mentioned when I lay awake surrounded by snoring brother pilgrims— my mind took me back to personal memories I would have thought were gone forever . . . as far back, even, as when I was just a little boy, eight or nine years old. Out behind our house, out in the country from Lansing, Michigan, there was an old, grassy "Hector's Hill," we called it—which may still be there. I remembered there in the Holy World how I used to lie on the top of Hector's Hill, and look up at the sky, at the clouds moving over me, and daydream, all kinds of things. And then, in a funny contrast of recollections, I remembered how years later, when I was in prison, I used to lie on my cell bunk—this would be especially when I was in solitary: what we convicts called "The Hole"—and I would picture myself talking to large crowds. I don't have any idea why such previsions came to me. But they did. To tell that to anyone then would have sounded crazy. Even I didn't have, myself, the slightest inkling. . . .

In Mecca, too, I had played back for myself the twelve years I had spent with Elijah Muhammad as if it were a motion picture. I guess it would be impossible for anyone ever to realize fully how complete was my belief in Elijah Muhammad. I believed in him not only as a leader in the ordinary *human* sense, but also I believed in him as a *divine* leader. I believed he had no human weaknesses or faults, and that, therefore, he could make no mistakes and that he could do no wrong. There on a Holy World hilltop, I realized how very dangerous it is for people to hold any human being in such esteem, especially to consider anyone some sort of "divinely guided" and "protected" person.

My thinking had been opened up wide in Mecca. In the long letters I wrote to friends, I tried to convey to them my new insights into the American black man's struggle and his problems, as well as the depths of my search for truth and justice.

"I've had enough of someone else's propaganda," I had written to these friends. "I'm for truth, no matter who tells it. I'm for justice, no matter who it is for or against. I'm a human being first and foremost, and as such I'm for whoever and whatever benefits humanity *as a whole.*"

Largely, the American white man's press refused to convey that I was now attempting to teach Negroes a new direction. With the 1964 "long, hot summer" steadily producing new incidents, I was constantly accused of "stirring up Negroes." Every time I had another radio or television microphone at my mouth, when I was asked about "stirring up Negroes" or "inciting violence," I'd get hot.

"It takes no one to stir up the sociological dynamite that stems from the unemployment, bad housing, and inferior education already in the ghettoes. This explosively criminal condition has existed for so long, it needs no fuse; it fuses itself; it spontaneously combusts from within itself. . . ."

They called me "the angriest Negro in America." I wouldn't deny that charge. I spoke exactly as I felt. "I *believe* in anger. The Bible says there is a *time* for anger." They called me "a teacher, a fomentor of violence." I would say point blank, "That is a lie. I'm not for wanton violence, I'm for justice. I feel that if white people were attacked by Negroes—if the forces of law prove unable, or inadequate, or reluctant to protect those whites from those Negroes—then those white people should protect and defend themselves from those Negroes, using arms if necessary. And I feel that when the law fails to protect Negroes from whites' attack, then those Negroes should use arms, if necessary, to defend themselves."

"Malcolm X Advocates Armed Negroes!"

What was wrong with that? I'll tell you what was wrong. I was a black man talking about physical defense against the white man. The white man can lynch and burn and bomb and beat Negroes—that's all right: "Have patience" . . . "The customs are entrenched" . . . "Things are getting better."

Well, I believe it's a crime for anyone who is being brutalized to continue to accept that brutality without doing something to defend himself. If that's how "Christian" philosophy is interpreted, if that's what Gandhian philosophy teaches, well, then, I will call them criminal philosophies.

I tried in every speech I made to clarify my new position regarding white people—"I don't speak against the sincere, well-meaning, good white people. I have learned that there *are* some. I have learned that not all white people are racists. I am speaking against and my fight is against the white *racists*. I firmly believe that Negroes have the right to fight against these racists, by any means that are necessary."

But the white reporters kept wanting me linked with that word "violence." I doubt if I had one interview without having to deal with that accusation.

"I *am* for violence if non-violence means we continue postponing a solution to the American black man's problem—just to *avoid* violence. I don't go for non-violence if it also means a delayed solution. To me a delayed solution is a non-solution. Or I'll say it another way. If it must take violence to get the black man his human rights in this country, I'm *for* violence exactly as you know the Irish, the Poles, or Jews would be if they were flagrantly discriminated against. I am just as they would be in that case, and they would be for violence—no matter what the consequences, no matter who was hurt by the violence."

White society *hates* to hear anybody, especially a black man, talk about the crime the white man has perpetrated on the black man. I have always understood that's why I have been so frequently called "a revolutionist." It sounds as if *I* have done some crime! Well, it may be the American black man does need to become involved in a *real* revolution. The word for "revolution" in German is *Umwälzung.* What it means is a complete overturn—a complete change. The overthrow of King Farouk in Egypt and the succession of President Nasser is an example of a true revolution. It means the destroying of an old system, and its replacement with a new system. Another example is the Algerian revolution, led by Ben Bella; they threw out the French who had been there over 100 years. So how does anybody sound talking about the Negro in America waging some "revolution"? Yes, he is condemning a system—but he's not trying to overturn the system, or to destroy it. The Negro's so-called "revolt" is merely an asking to be *accepted* into the existing system! A *true* Negro revolt might entail, for instance, fighting for separate black states within this country—which several groups and individuals have advocated, long before Elijah Muhammad came along.

When the white man came into this country, he certainly wasn't demonstrating any "non-violence." In fact, the very man whose name symbolizes non-violence here today has stated:

"Our nation was born in genocide when it embraced the doctrine that the original American, the Indian, was an inferior race. Even before there were large numbers of Negroes on our shores, the scar of racial hatred had already disfigured colonial society. From the sixteenth century forward, blood flowed in battles over racial supremacy. We are perhaps the only nation which tried as a matter of national policy to wipe out its indigenous population. Moreover, we elevated that tragic experience into a noble crusade. Indeed, even today we have not permitted ourselves to reject or to feel remorse for this shameful episode. Our literature, our films, our drama, our folklore all exalt it. Our children are still taught to respect the violence which reduced a red-skinned people of an earlier culture into a few fragmented groups herded into impoverished reservations."

"Peaceful coexistence!" That's another one the white man has always been quick to cry. Fine! But what have been the deeds of the white man? During his entire advance through history, he has been waving the banner of Christianity . . . and carrying in his other hand the sword and the flintlock.

You can go right back to the very begining of Christianity. Catholicism, the genesis of Christianity as we know it to be presently constituted, with its hierarchy, was conceived in Africa—by those whom the Christian church calls "The Desert Fathers." The Christian church became infected with racism when it entered white Europe. The Christian church returned to Africa under the banner of the Cross—conquering, killing, exploiting, pillaging, raping, bullying, beating—and teaching white supremacy. This is how the white man thrust himself into the position of leadership of the world—through the use of naked physical power. And he was totally inadequate spiritually. Mankind's history has proved from one era to another that the true criterion of leadership is spiritual. Men are attracted by spirit. By power, men are *forced*. Love is engendered by spirit. By power, anxieties are created.

I am in agreement one hundred per cent with those racists who say that no government laws ever can *force* brotherhood. The only true world solution today is governments guided by true religion—of the spirit. Here in race-torn America, I am convinced that the Islam religion is desperately needed, particularly by the American black man. The black man needs to reflect that he has been America's most fervent Christian—and where has it gotten him? In fact, in the white man's hands, in the white man's interpretation . . . where has Christianity brought this *world*?

It has brought the non-white two-thirds of the human population to rebellion. Two-thirds of the human population today is telling the one-third minority white man, "Get out!" And the white man is leaving. And as he leaves, we see the non-white people returning in a rush to their original religions, which had been labeled "pagan" by the conquering white man. Only one religion—Islam—had the power to stand and fight the white man's Christianity for a *thousand years!* Only Islam could keep white Christianity at bay.

The Africans are returning to Islam and other indigenous religions. The Asians are returning to being Hindus, Buddhists and Muslims.

As the Christian Crusade once went East, now the Islamic Crusade is going West. With the East—Asia—closed to Christianity, with Africa rapidly being converted to Islam, with Europe rapidly becoming un-Christian, generally today it is accepted that the "Christian" civilization of America—which is propping up the white race around the world—is Christianity's remaining strongest bastion.

Well, if *this* is so—if the so-called "Christianity" now being practiced in America displays the best that world Christianity has left to offer—no one in his right mind should need any much greater proof that very close at hand is the *end* of Christianity.

Are you aware that some Protestant theologians, in their writings, are using the phrase "post-Christian era"—and they mean *now*?

And what is the greatest single reason for this Christian church's failure? It is its failure to combat racism. It is the old "You sow, you reap" story. The Christian church sowed racism—blasphemously; now it reaps racism.

Sunday mornings in this year of grace 1965, imagine the "Christian" conscience" of congregations guarded by deacons barring the door to black would-be worshipers, telling them "You can't enter *this* House of God!"

Tell me, if you can, a sadder irony than that St. Augustine, Florida —a city named for the black African saint who saved Catholicism from heresy—was recently the scene of bloody race riots.

I believe that God now is giving the world's so-called "Christian" white society its last opportunity to repent and atone for the crimes of exploiting and enslaving the world's non-white peoples. It is exactly as when God gave Pharaoh a chance to repent. But Pharaoh persisted in his refusal to give justice to those whom he oppressed. And, we know, God finally destroyed Pharaoh.

Is white America really sorry for her crimes against the black people? Does white America have the capacity to repent—and to atone? Does the capacity to repent, to atone, exist in a majority, in one-half, in even one-third of American white society?

Many black men, the victims—in fact most black men—would like to be able to forgive, to forget, the crimes.

But most American white people seem not to have it in them to make any serious atonement—to do justice to the black man.

Indeed, how *can* white society atone for enslaving, for raping, for unmanning, for otherwise brutalizing *millions* of human beings, for centuries? What atonement would the God of Justice demand for the robbery of the black people's labor, their lives, their true identities, their culture, their history—and even their human dignity?

A desegregated cup of coffee, a theater, public toilets—the whole range of hypocritical "integration"—these are not atonement.

After a while in America, I returned abroad—and this time, I spent eighteen weeks in the Middle East and Africa.

The world leaders with whom I had private audiences this time included President Gamal Abdel Nasser, of Egypt; President Julius K. Nyerere, of Tanzania; President Nnamoi Azikiwe, of Nigeria; Osagyefo Dr. Kwame Nkrumah, of Ghana; President Sekou Touré, of Guinea; President Jomo Kenyatta, of Kenya; and Prime Minister Dr. Milton Obote, of Uganda.

I also met with religious leaders—African, Arab, Asian, Muslim, and non-Muslim. And in all of these countries, I talked with Afro-Americans and whites of many professions and backgrounds.

An American white ambassador in one African country was Africa's most respected American ambassador: I'm glad to say that this was told to me by one ranking African leader. We talked for an entire afternoon. Based on what I had heard of him, I had to believe him when he told me that as long as he was on the African continent, he never thought in terms of race, that he dealt with human beings, never noticing their color. He said he was more aware of language differences than of color differences. He said that only when he returned to America would he become aware of color differences.

I told him, "What you are telling me is that it isn't the American white *man* who is a racist, but it's the American political, economic, and social *atmosphere* that automatically nourishes a racist psychology in the white man." He agreed.

We both agreed that American society makes it next to impossible for humans to meet in America and not be conscious of their color differences. And we both agreed that if racism could be removed, America could offer a society where rich and poor could truly live like human beings.

That discussion with the ambassador gave me a new insight—one which I like: that the white man is *not* inherently evil, but America's racist society influences him to act evilly. The society has produced and nourishes a psychology which brings out the lowest, most base part of human beings.

I had a totally different kind of talk with another white man I met in Africa—who, to me, personified exactly what the ambassador and I had discussed. Throughout my trip, I was of course aware that I was under constant surveillance. The agent was a particularly obvious and obnoxious one; I am not sure for what agency, as he never identified it, or I would say it. Anyway, this one finally got under my skin when I found I couldn't seem to eat a meal in the hotel without seeing him somewhere around watching me. You would have thought I was John Dillinger or somebody.

I just got up from my breakfast one morning and walked over to where he was and I told him I knew he was following me, and if he wanted to know anything, why didn't he ask me. He started to give me one of those too-lofty-to-descend-to-you attitudes. I told him then right to his face he was a fool, that he didn't know me, or what I stood for, so that made him one of those people who let somebody else do their thinking; and that no matter what job a man had, at least he ought to be able to think for himself. That stung him; he let me have it.

I was, to hear him tell it, anti-American, un-American, seditious, subversive, and probably Communist. I told him that what he said only proved how little he understood about me. I told him that the only thing the F.B.I., the C.I.A., or anybody else could ever find me guilty of, was being open-minded. I said I was seeking for the truth, and I was trying to weigh—objectively—everything on its own merit. I said what I was against was strait-jacketed thinking, and strait-jacketed societies. I said I respected every man's right to believe whatever his intelligence tells him is intellectually sound, and I expect everyone else to respect my right to believe likewise.

This super-sleuth then got off on my "Black Muslim" religious beliefs. I asked him hadn't his headquarters bothered to brief him—that my attitudes and beliefs were changed? I told him that the Islam I believed in now was the Islam which was taught in Mecca—that there was no God but Allah, and that Muhammad ibn Abdullah who lived in the Holy City of Mecca fourteen hundred years ago was the Last Messenger of Allah.

Almost from the first I had been guessing about something; and I took a chance—and I really shook up that "super-sleuth." From the consistent subjectivity in just about every thing he asked and said, I had deduced something, and I told him, "You know, I think you're a Jew with an Anglicized name." His involuntary expression told me I'd hit the button. He asked me how I knew. I told him I'd had so much experience with how Jews would attack me that I usually could identify them. I told him all I held against the Jew was that so many Jews actually were hypocrites in their claim to be friends of the American black man, and it burned me up to be so often called "anti-Semitic" when I spoke things I knew to be the absolute truth about Jews. I told him that, yes, I gave the Jew credit for being among all other whites the most active, and the most vocal, financier, "leader" and "liberal" in the Negro civil rights movement. But I said at the same time I knew that the Jew played these roles for a very careful strategic reason: the more prejudice in America could be focused upon the Negro, then the more the white Gentiles' prejudice would keep diverted off the Jew. I said that to me, one proof that all the civil rights posturing of so many Jews wasn't sincere was that so often in the North the quickest segregationists were Jews themselves. Look at practically everything the black man is trying to "integrate" into for instance; if Jews are not the actual owners, or are not in controlling positions, then they have major stockholdings or they are otherwise in powerful leverage positions—and do they really sincerely exert these influences? No!

And an even clearer proof for me of how Jews truly regard Negroes, I said, was what invariably happened wherever a Negro moved into any white residential neighborhood that was thickly Jewish. Who would always lead the whites' exodus? The Jews! Generally in these situations, some whites stay put—you just notice who they are: they're Irish Catholics, they're Italians; they're rarely ever any Jews. And, ironically, the Jews themselves often still have trouble being "accepted."

Saying this, I know I'll hear "anti-Semitic" from every direction again. Oh, yes! But truth is truth.

Politics dominated the American scene while I was traveling abroad this time. In Cairo and again in Accra, the American press wire services reached me with trans-Atlantic calls, asking whom did I favor, Johnson —or Goldwater?

I said I felt that as far as the American black man was concerned they were both just about the same. I felt that it was for the black man only a question of Johnson, the fox, or Goldwater, the wolf.

"Conservatism" in America's politics means "Let's keep the niggers in their place." And "liberalism" means "Let's keep the *knee*-grows in their place—but tell them we'll treat them a little better; let's fool them more, with more promises." With these choices, I felt that the American black man only needed to choose which one to be eaten by, the "liberal" fox or the "conservative" wolf—because both of them would eat him.

I didn't go for Goldwater any more than for Johnson—except that in a wolf's den, I'd always know exactly where I stood; I'd watch the dangerous wolf closer than I would the smooth, sly fox. The wolf's very growling would keep me alert and fighting him to survive, whereas I *might* be lulled and fooled by the tricky fox. I'll give you an illustration of the fox. When the assassination in Dallas made Johnson President, who was the first person he called for? It was for his best friend, "Dicky"—Richard Russell of Georgia. Civil rights was "a moral issue," Johnson was declaring to everybody—while his best friend was the Southern racist who *led* the civil rights opposition. How would some sheriff sound, declaring himself so against bank robbery—and Jesse James his best friend?

Goldwater as a man, I respected for speaking out his true convictions —something rarely done in politics today. He wasn't whispering to racists and smiling at integrationists. I felt Goldwater wouldn't have risked his unpopular stand without conviction. He flatly told black men he wasn't for them—and there is this to consider: always, the black people have advanced further when they have seen they had to rise up against a system that they clearly saw was outright against them. Under the steady lullabys sung by foxy liberals, the Northern Negro became a beggar. But the Southern Negro, facing the honestly snarling white man, rose up to battle that white man for his freedom—long before it happened in the North.

Anyway, I didn't feel that Goldwater was any better for black men than Johnson, or vice-versa. I wasn't in the United States at election time, but if I had been, I wouldn't have put myself in the position of voting for either candidate for the Presidency, or of recommending to any black man to do so. It has turned out that it's Johnson in the White House—and black votes were a major factor in his winning as decisively as he wanted to. If it had been Goldwater, all I am saying is that the black people would at least have known they were dealing with an honestly growling wolf, rather than a fox who could have them half-digested before they even knew what was happening.

I kept having all kinds of troubles trying to develop the kind of Black Nationalist organization I wanted to build for the American Negro. Why Black Nationalism? Well, in the competitive American society, how can there ever be any white-black solidarity before there is first some black solidarity? If you will remember, in my childhood I had been exposed to the Black Nationalist teachings of Marcus Garvey —which, in fact, I had been told had led to my father's murder. Even when I was a follower of Elijah Muhammad, I had been strongly aware of how the Black Nationalist political, economic and social philosophies had the ability to instill within black men the racial dignity, the incentive, and the confidence that the black race needs today to get up off its knees, and to get on its feet, and get rid of its scars, and to take a stand for itself.

One of the major troubles that I was having in building the organization that I wanted—an all-black organization whose ultimate objective was to help create a society in which there could exist honest white-black brotherhood—was that my earlier public image, my old so-called "Black Muslim" image, kept blocking me. I was trying to gradually reshape that image. I was trying to turn a corner, into a new regard by the public, especially Negroes; I was no less angry than I had been, but at the same time the true brotherhood I had seen in the Holy World had influenced me to recognize that anger can blind human vision.

Every free moment I could find, I did a lot of talking to key people whom I knew around Harlem, and I made a lot of speeches, saying: "True Islam taught me that it takes *all* of the religious, political, economic, psychological, and racial ingredients, or characteristics, to make the Human Family and the Human Society complete.

"Since I learned the *truth* in Mecca, my dearest friends have come to include *all* kinds—some Christians, Jews, Buddhists, Hindus, agnostics, and even atheists! I have friends who are called capitalists, Socialists, and Communists! Some of my friends are moderates, conservatives, extremists—some are even Uncle Toms! My friends today are black, brown, red, yellow, and *white!*"

I said to Harlem street audiences that only when mankind would submit to the One God who created all—only then would mankind even approach the "peace" of which so much *talk* could be heard . . . but toward which so little *action* was seen.

I said that on the American racial level, we had to approach the black man's struggle against the white man's racism as a human problem, that we had to forget hypocritical politics and propaganda. I said that both races, as human beings, had the obligation, the responsibility, of helping to correct America's human problem. The well-meaning white people, I said, had to combat, actively and directly, the racism in other white people. And the black people had to build within themselves much greater awareness that along with equal rights there had to be the bearing of equal responsibilities.

I knew, better than most Negroes, how many white people truly wanted to see American racial problems solved. I knew that many whites were as frustrated as Negroes. I'll bet I got fifty letters some days from white people. The white people in meeting audiences would throng around me, asking me, after I had addressed them somewhere, "What *can* a sincere white person do?"

When I say that here now, it makes me think about that little co-ed I told you about, the one who flew from her New England college down to New York and came up to me in the Nation of Islam's restaurant in Harlem, and I told her that there was "nothing" she could do. I regret that I told her that. I wish that now I knew her name, or where I could telephone her, or write to her, and tell her what I tell white people now when they present themselves as being sincere, and ask me, one way or another, the same thing that she asked.

The first thing I tell them is that at least where my own particular Black Nationalist organization, the Organization of Afro-American Unity, is concerned, they can't *join* us. I have these very deep feelings that white people who want to join black organizations are really just taking the escapist way to salve their consciences. By visibly hovering near us, they are "proving" that they are "with us." But the hard truth is this *isn't* helping to solve America's racist problem. The Negroes aren't the racists. Where the really sincere white people have got to do their "proving" of themselves is not among the black *victims*, but out on the battle lines of where America's racism really *is*—and that's in their own home communities; America's racism is among their own fellow whites. That's where the sincere whites who really mean to accomplish something have got to work.

Aside from that, I mean nothing against any sincere whites when I say that as members of black organizations, generally whites' very presence subtly renders the black organization automatically less effective. Even the best white members will slow down the Negroes' discovery of what they need to do, and particularly of what they can do —for themselves, working by themselves, among their own kind, in their own communities.

I sure don't want to hurt anybody's feelings, but in fact I'll even go so far as to say that I never really trust the kind of white people who are always so anxious to hang around Negroes, or to hang around in Negro communities. I don't trust the kind of whites who love having Negroes always hanging around them. I don't know—this feeling may be a throwback to the years when I was hustling in Harlem and all of those red-faced, drunk whites in the afterhours clubs were always grabbing hold of some Negroes and talking about "I just want you to know you're just as good as I am—"And then they got back in their taxicabs and black limousines and went back downtown to the places where they lived and worked, where no blacks except servants had better get caught. But, anyway, I know that every time that whites join a black organization, you watch, pretty soon the blacks will be leaning on the whites to support it, and before you know it a black may be up front with a title, but the whites, because of their money, are the real controllers.

I tell sincere white people, "Work in conjunction with us—each of us working among our own kind." Let sincere white individuals find all other white people they can who feel as they do—and let them form their own all-white groups, to work trying to convert other white people who are thinking and acting so racist. Let sincere whites go and teach non-violence to white people!

We will completely respect our white co-workers. They will deserve every credit. We will give them every credit. We will meanwhile be working among our own kind, in our own black communities—showing and teaching black men in ways that only other black men can—that the black man has got to help himself. Working separately, the sincere white people and sincere black people actually will be working together.

In our mutual sincerity we might be able to show a road to the salvation of America's very soul. It can only be salvaged if human rights and dignity, in full, are extended to black men. Only such real, meaningful actions as those which are sincerely motivated from a deep sense of humanism and moral responsibility can get at the basic causes that produce the racial explosions in America today. Otherwise, the racial explosions are only going to grow worse. Certainly nothing is ever going to be solved by throwing upon me and other so-called black "extremists" and "demagogues" the blame for the racism that is in America.

Sometimes, I have dared to dream to myself that one day, history may even say that my voice—which disturbed the white man's smugness, and his arrogance, and his complacency—that my voice helped to save America from a grave, possibly even a fatal catastrophe.

The goal has always been the same, with the approaches to it as different as mine and Dr. Martin Luther King's non-violent marching, that dramatizes the brutality and the evil of the white man against defenseless blacks. And in the racial climate of this country today, it is anybody's guess which of the "extremes" in approach to the black man's problems might *personally* meet a fatal catastrophe first—"non-violent" Dr. King, or so-called "violent" me.

Anything I do today, I regard as urgent. No man is given but so much time to accomplish whatever is his life's work. My life in particular never has stayed fixed in one position for very long. You have seen how throughout my life, I have often known unexpected drastic changes.

I am only facing the facts when I know that any moment of any day, or any night, could bring me death. This is particularly true since the last trip that I made abroad. I have seen the nature of things that are happening, and I have heard things from sources which are reliable.

To speculate about dying doesn't disturb me as it might some people. I never have felt that I would live to become an old man. Even before I was a Muslim—when I was a hustler in the ghetto jungle, and then a criminal in prison, it always stayed on my mind that I would die a violent death. In fact, it runs in my family. My father and most of his brothers died by violence—my father because of what he believed in. To come right down to it, if I take the kind of things in which I believe, then add to that the kind of temperament that I have, plus the one hundred per cent dedication I have to whatever I believe in—these are ingredients which make it just about impossible for me to die of old age.

I have given to this book so much of whatever time I have because I feel, and I hope, that if I honestly and fully tell my life's account, read objectively it might prove to be a testimony of some social value.

I think that an objective reader may see how in the society to which I was exposed as a black youth here in America, for me to wind up in a prison was really just about inevitable. It happens to so many thousands of black youth.

I think that an objective reader may see how when I heard "The white man is the devil," when I played back what had been my own experiences, it was inevitable that I would respond positively; then the next twelve years of my life were devoted and dedicated to propagating that phrase among the black people.

I think, I hope, that the objective reader, in following my life—the life of only one ghetto-created Negro—may gain a better picture and understanding than he has previously had of the black ghettoes which are shaping the lives and the thinking of almost all of the 22 million Negroes who live in America.

Thicker each year in these ghettoes is the kind of teen-ager that I was —with the wrong kinds of heroes, and the wrong kinds of influences. I am not saying that all of them become the kind of parasite that I was. Fortunately, by far most do not. But still, the small fraction who do add up to an annual total of more and more costly, dangerous youthful criminals. The F.B.I. not long ago released a report of a shocking rise in crime each successive year since the end of World War II—ten to twelve per cent each year. The report did not say so in so many words, but I am saying that the majority of that crime increase is annually spawned in the black ghettoes which the American racist society permits to exist. In the 1964 "long, hot summer" riots in major cities across the United States, the socially disinherited black ghetto youth were always at the forefront.

In this year, 1965, I am certain that more—and worse—riots are going to erupt, in yet more cities, in spite of the conscience-salving Civil Rights Bill. The reason is that the *cause* of these riots, the racist malignancy in America, has been too long unattended.

I believe that it would be almost impossible to find anywhere in America a black man who has lived further down in the mud of human society than I have; or a black man who has been any more ignorant than I have been; or a black man who has suffered more anguish during his life than I have. But it is only after the deepest darkness that the greatest joy can come; it is only after slavery and prison that the sweetest appreciation of freedom can come.

For the freedom of my 22 million black brothers and sisters here in America, I do believe that I have fought the best that I knew how, and the best that I could, with the shortcomings that I have had. I know that my shortcomings are many.

My greatest lack has been, I believe, that I don't have the kind of academic education I wish I had been able to get—to have been a lawyer, perhaps. I do believe that I might have made a good lawyer. I have always loved verbal battle, and challenge. You can believe me that if I had the time right now, I would not be one bit ashamed to go back into any New York City public school and start where I left off at the ninth grade, and go on through a degree. Because I don't begin to be academically equipped for so many of the interests that I have. For instance, I love languages. I wish I were an accomplished linguist. I don't know anything more frustrating than to be around people talking something you can't understand. Especially when they are people who look just like you. In Africa, I heard original mother tongues, such as Hausa, and Swahili, being spoken, and there I was standing like some little boy, waiting for someone to tell me what had been said; I never will forget how ignorant I felt.

Aside from the basic African dialects, I would try to learn Chinese, because it looks as if Chinese will be the most powerful political language of the future. And already I have begun studying Arabic, which I think is going to be the most powerful spiritual language of the future.

I would just like to *study*. I mean ranging study, because I have a wide-open mind. I'm interested in almost any subject you can mention. I know this is the reason I have come to really like, as individuals, some of the hosts of radio or television panel programs I have been on, and to respect their minds—because even if they have been almost steadily in disagreement with me on the race issue, they still have kept their minds open and objective about the truths of things happening in this world. Irv Kupcinet in Chicago, and Barry Farber, Barry Gray and Mike Wallace in New York—people like them. They also let me see that they respected my mind—in a way I know they never realized. The way I knew was that often they would invite my opinion on subjects off the race issue. Sometimes, after the programs, we would sit around and talk about all kinds of things, current events and other things, for an hour or more. You see, most whites, even when they credit a Negro with some intelligence, will still feel that all he can talk about is the race issue; most whites never feel that Negroes can contribute anything to other areas of thought, and ideas. You just notice how rarely you will ever hear whites asking any Negroes what they think about the problem of world health, or the space race to land men on the moon.

Every morning when I wake up, now, I regard it as having another borrowed day. In any city, wherever I go, making speeches, holding meetings of my organization, or attending to other business, black men are watching every move I make, awaiting their chance to kill me. I have said publicly many times that I know that they have their orders. Anyone who chooses not to believe what I am saying doesn't know the Muslims in the Nation of Islam.

But I am also blessed with faithful followers who are, I believe, as dedicated to me as I once was to Mr. Elijah Muhammad. Those who would hunt a man need to remember that a jungle also contains those who hunt the hunters.

I know, too, that I could suddenly die at the hands of some white racists. Or I could die at the hands of some Negro hired by the white man. Or it could be some brainwashed Negro acting on his own idea that by eliminating me he would be helping out the white man, because I talk about the white man the way I do.

Anyway, now, each day I live as if I am already dead, and I tell you what I would like for you to do. When I *am* dead—I say it that way because from the things I *know*, I do not expect to live long enough to read this book in its finished form—I want you to just watch and see if I'm not right in what I say: that the white man, in his press, is going to identify me with "hate."

He will make use of me dead, as he has made use of me alive, as a convenient symbol of "hatred"—and that will help him to escape facing the truth that all I have been doing is holding up a mirror to reflect, to show, the history of unspeakable crimes that his race has committed against my race.

You watch. I will be labeled as, at best, an "irresponsible" black man. I have always felt about this accusation that the black "leader" whom white men consider to be "responsible" is invariably the black "leader" who never gets any results. You only get action as a black man if you are regarded by the white man as "irresponsible." In fact, this much I had learned when I was just a little boy. And since I have been some kind of a "leader" of black people here in the racist society of America, I have been more reassured each time the white man resisted me, or attacked me harder—because each time made me more certain that I was on the right track in the American black man's best interests. The racist white man's opposition automatically made me know that I did offer the black man something worthwhile.

Yes, I have cherished my "demagogue" role. I know that societies often have killed the people who have helped to change those societies. And if I can die having brought any light, having exposed any meaningful truth that will help to destroy the racist cancer that is malignant in the body of America—then, all of the credit is due to Allah. Only the mistakes have been mine.

QUESTIONS

1. What is Malcolm's attitude toward violence and nonviolence?

2. When Malcolm was a follower of Elijah Muhammad, prophet of the Muslims in America, he accepted the belief that all whites were "devils," the enemies of the black man. Having left the movement, and having traveled throughout Africa, he came to believe that "the white man is *not* inherently evil." How, then, does he account for racism in America?

3. Summarize Malcolm's views of the role of the Christian church in helping to foster and institutionalize racism throughout the world. Does this conclusion seem justified to you?

4. How does Malcolm answer the charges that he is "anti-Semitic"?

5. What is Malcolm's position in this concluding chapter of the autobiography toward the meaning of and need for black nationalism? What advice does he give those whites who say they want to support the black man's struggle? Do you agree with his conclusions? Why or why not?

6. Why do you think Malcolm X has become a black hero? Is there support for your answer in this chapter?

On Becoming

Eldridge Cleaver

Folsom Prison
June 25, 1965

Nineteen fifty-four, when I was eighteen years old, is held to be a crucial turning point in the history of the Afro-American—for the U.S.A. as a whole—the year segregation was outlawed by the U.S. Supreme Court. It was also a crucial year for me because on June 18, 1954, I began serving a sentence in state prison for possession of marijuana.

The Supreme Court decision was only one month old when I entered prison, and I do not believe that I had even the vaguest idea of its importance or historical significance. But later, the acrimonious controversy ignited by the end of the separate-but-equal doctrine was to have a profound effect on me. This controversy awakened me to my position in America and I began to form a concept of what it meant to be black in white America.

Of course I'd always known that I was black, but I'd never really stopped to take stock of what I was involved in. I met life as an individual and took my chances. Prior to 1954, we lived in an atmosphere of novocain. Negroes found it necessary, in order to maintain whatever sanity they could, to remain somewhat aloof and detached from "the problem." We accepted indignities and the mechanics of the apparatus of oppression without reacting by sitting-in or holding mass demonstrations. Nurtured by the fires of the controversy over segregation, I was soon aflame with indignation over my newly discovered social status, and inwardly I turned away from America with horror, disgust and outrage.

In Soledad state prison, I fell in with a group of young blacks who, like myself, were in vociferous rebellion against what we perceived as a continuation of slavery on a higher plane. We cursed everything American—including baseball and hot dogs. All respect we may have had for politicians, preachers, lawyers, governors, Presidents, senators, congress-men was utterly destroyed as we watched them temporizing and com-promising over right and wrong, over legality and illegality, over con-stitutionality and unconstitutionality. We knew that in the end what they were clashing over was us, what to do with the blacks, and whether or not to start treating us as human beings. I despised all of them.

The segregationists were condemned out of hand, without even listening to their lofty, finely woven arguments. The others I despised for wasting time in debates with the segregationists: why not just crush them, put them in prison—they were defying the law, weren't they? I defied the law and they put me in prison. So why not put those dirty mothers in prison too? I had gotten caught with a shopping bag full of marijuana, a shopping bag full of love—I was in love with the weed and I did not for one minute think that anything was wrong with getting high. I had been getting high for four or five years and was convinced, with the zeal of a crusader, that marijuana was superior to lush—yet the rulers of the land seemed all to be lushes. I could not see how they were more justified in drinking than I was in blowing the gage. I was a grasshopper, and it was natural that I felt myself to be unjustly imprisoned.

While all this was going on, our group was espousing atheism. Un-sophisticated and not based on any philosophical rationale, our atheism was pragmatic. I had come to believe that there is no God; if there is, men do not know anything about him. Therefore, all religions were phony—which made all preachers and priests, in our eyes, fakers, in-cluding the ones scurrying around the prison who, curiously, could put in a good word for you with the Almighty Creator of the universe but could not get anything down with the warden or parole board—they could usher you through the Pearly Gates *after you were dead*, but not through the prison gate *while you were still alive and kicking*. Besides, men of the cloth who work in prison have an ineradicable stigma attached to them in the eyes of convicts because they escort condemned men into the gas chamber. Such men of God are powerful arguments in favor of atheism. Our atheism was a source of enormous pride to me. Later on, I bolstered our arguments by reading Thomas Paine and his devastating critique of Christianity in particular and organized religion in general.

Through reading I was amazed to discover how confused people were. I had thought that, out there beyond the horizon of my own ignorance, unanimity existed, that even though I myself didn't know what was happening in the universe, other people certainly did. Yet here I was discovering that the whole U.S.A. was in a chaos of disagreement over segregation/integration. In these circumstances I decided that the only safe thing for me to do was go for myself. It became clear that it was possible for me to take the initiative: instead of simply *reacting* I could *act*. I could unilaterally—whether anyone agreed with me or not—repudiate all allegiances, morals, values—even while continuing to exist within this society. My mind would be free and no power in the universe could force me to accept something if I didn't want to. But I would take my own sweet time. That, too, was a part of my new freedom. I would accept nothing until it was proved that it was good—for me. I became an extreme iconoclast. Any affirmative assertion made by anyone around me became a target for tirades of criticism and denunciation.

This little game got good to me and I got good at it. I attacked all forms of piety, loyalty, and sentiment: marriage, love, God, patriotism, the Constitution, the founding fathers, law, concepts of right-wrong-good-evil, all forms of ritualized and conventional behavior. As I pranced about, club in hand, seeking new idols to smash, I encountered really for the first time in my life, with any seriousness, The Ogre, rising up before me in a mist. I discovered, with alarm, that The Ogre possessed a tremendous and dreadful power over me, and I didn't understand this power or why I was at its mercy. I tried to repudiate The Ogre, root it out of my heart as I had done God, Constitution, principles, morals, and values—but The Ogre had its claws buried in the core of my being and refused to let go. I fought frantically to be free, but The Ogre only mocked me and sank its claws deeper into my soul. I knew then that I had found an important key, that if I conquered The Ogre and broke its power over me I would be free. But I also knew that it was a race against time and that if I did not win I would certainly be broken and destroyed. I, a black man, confronted The Ogre—the white woman.

In prison, those things withheld from and denied to the prisoner become precisely what he wants most of all, of course. Because we were locked up in our cells before darkness fell, I used to lie awake at night racked by painful craving to take a leisurely stroll under the stars, or to go to the beach, to drive a car on a freeway, to grow a beard, or to make love to a woman.

Since I was not married conjugal visits would not have solved my problem. I therefore denounced the idea of conjugal visits as inherently unfair; single prisoners needed and deserved *action* just as married prisoners did. I advocated establishing a system under Civil Service whereby salaried women would minister to the needs of those prisoners who maintained a record of good behavior. If a married prisoner preferred his own wife, that would be his right. Since California was not about to inaugurate either conjugal visits or the Civil Service, one could advocate either with equal enthusiasm and with the same result: nothing.

This may appear ridiculous to some people. But it was very real to me and as urgent as the need to breathe, because I was in my bull stage and lack of access to females was absolutely a form of torture. I suffered. My mistress at the time of my arrest, the beautiful and lonely wife of a serviceman stationed overseas, died unexpectedly three weeks after I entered prison; and the rigid, dehumanized rules governing correspondence between prisoners and free people prevented me from corresponding with other young ladies I knew. It left me without any contact with females except those in my family.

In the process of enduring my confinement, I decided to get myself a pin-up girl to paste on the wall of my cell. I would fall in love with her and lavish my affections upon her. She, a symbolic representative of the forbidden tribe of women, would sustain me until I was free. Out of the center of *Esquire,* I married a voluptuous bride. Our marriage went along swell for a time: no quarrels, no complaints. And then, one evening when I came in from school, I was shocked and enraged to find that the guard had entered my cell, ripped my sugar from the wall, torn her into little pieces, and left the pieces floating in the commode: it was like seeing a dead body floating in a lake. Giving her a proper burial, I flushed the commode. As the saying goes, I sent her to Long Beach. But I was genuinely beside myself with anger: almost every cell, excepting those of the homosexuals, had a pin-up girl on the wall and the guards didn't bother them. Why, I asked the guard the next day, had he singled me out for special treatment?

"Don't you know we have a rule against pasting up pictures on the walls?" he asked me.

"Later for the rules," I said. "You know as well as I do that that rule is not enforced."

"Tell you what," he said, smiling at me (the smile put me on my guard), "I'll compromise with you: get yourself a colored girl for a pinup—no white women—and I'll let it stay up. Is that a deal?"

I was more embarrassed than shocked. He was laughing in my face. I called him two or three dirty names and walked away. I can still recall his big moon-face, grinning at me over yellow teeth. The disturbing part about the whole incident was that a terrible feeling of guilt came over me as I realized that I had chosen the picture of the white girl over the available pictures of black girls. I tried to rationalize it away, but I was fascinated by the truth involved. Why hadn't I thought about it in this light before? So I took hold of the question and began to inquire into my feelings. Was it true, did I really prefer white girls over black? The conclusion was clear and inescapable: I did. I decided to check out my friends on this point and it was easy to determine, from listening to their general conversation, that the white woman occupied a peculiarly prominent place in all of our frames of reference. With what I have learned since then, this all seems terribly elementary now. But at the time, it was a tremendously intriguing adventure of discovery.

One afternoon, when a large group of Negroes was on the prison yard shooting the breeze, I grabbed the floor and posed the question: which did they prefer, white women or black? Some said Japanese women were their favorite, others said Chinese, some said European women, others said Mexican women—they all stated a preference, and they generally freely admitted their dislike for black women.

"I don't want nothing black but a Cadillac," said one.

"If money was black I wouldn't want none of it," put in another.

A short little stud, who was a very good lightweight boxer with a little man's complex that made him love to box heavyweights, jumped to his feet. He had a yellowish complexion and we called him Butterfly.

"All you niggers are sick!" Butterfly spat out. "I don't like no stinking white woman. My grandma is a white woman and I don't even like her!"

But it just so happened that Butterfly's crime partner was in the crowd, and after Butterfly had his say, his crime partner said, "Aw, sit on down and quit that lying, lil o' chump. What about that gray girl in San Jose who had your nose wide open? Did you like her, or were you just running after her with your tongue hanging out of your head because you hated her?"

Partly because he was embarrassed and partly because his crime partner was a heavyweight, Butterfly flew into him. And before we could separate them and disperse, so the guard would not know who had been fighting, Butterfly bloodied his crime partner's nose. Butterfly got away but, because of the blood, his crime partner got caught. I ate dinner with Butterfly that evening and questioned him sharply about his attitude toward white women. And after an initial evasiveness he admitted that the white woman bugged him too. "It's a sickness," he said. "All our lives we've had the white woman dangled before our eyes like a carrot on a stick before a donkey: look but don't touch." (In 1958, after I had gone out on parole and was returned to San Quentin as a parole violater with a new charge, Butterfly was still there. He had become a Black Muslim and was chiefly responsible for teaching me the Black Muslim philosophy. Upon his release from San Quentin, Butterfly joined the Los Angeles Mosque, advanced rapidly through the ranks, and is now a full-fledged minister of one of Elijah Muhammad's mosques in another city. He successfully completed his parole, got married—to a very black girl—and is doing fine.)

From our discussion, which began that evening and has never yet ended, we went on to notice how thoroughly, as a matter of course, a black growing up in America is indoctrinated with the white race's standard of beauty. Not that the whites made a conscious, calculated effort to do this, we thought, but since they constituted the majority the whites brainwashed the blacks by the very processes the whites employed to indoctrinate themselves with their own group standards. It intensified my frustrations to know that I was indoctrinated to see the white woman as more beautiful and desirable than my own black woman. It drove me into books seeking light on the subject. In Richard Wright's *Native Son*, I found Bigger Thomas and a keen insight into the problem.

My interest in this area persisted undiminished and then, in 1955, an event took place in Mississippi which turned me inside out: Emmett Till, a young Negro down from Chicago on a visit, was murdered, allegedly for flirting with a white woman. He had been shot, his head crushed from repeated blows with a blunt instrument, and his badly decomposed body was recovered from the river with a heavy weight on it. I was, of course, angry over the whole bit, but one day I saw in a magazine a picture of the white woman with whom Emmett Till was said to have flirted. While looking at the picture, I felt that little tension in the center of my chest I experience when a woman appeals to me. I was disgusted and angry with myself. Here was a woman who had caused the death of a black, possibly because, when he looked at her, he also felt the same tensions of lust and desire in his chest—and probably for the same general reasons that I felt them. It was all unacceptable to me. I looked at the picture again and again, and in spite of everything and against my will and the hate I felt for the woman and all that she represented, she appealed to me. I flew into a rage at myself, at America, at white women, at the history that had placed those tensions of lust and desire in my chest.

Two days later, I had a "nervous breakdown." For several days I ranted and raved against the white race, against white women in particular, against white America in general. When I came to myself, I was locked in a padded cell with not even the vaguest memory of how I got there. All I could recall was an eternity of pacing back and forth in the cell, preaching to the unhearing walls.

I had several sessions with a psychiatrist. His conclusion was that I hated my mother. How he arrived at this conclusion I'll never know, because he knew nothing about my mother; and when he'd ask me questions I would answer him with absurd lies. What revolted me about him was that he had heard me denouncing the whites, yet each time he interviewed me he deliberately guided the conversation back to my family life, to my childhood. That in itself was all right, but he deliberately blocked all my attempts to bring out the racial question, and he made it clear that he was not interested in my attitude toward whites. This was a Pandora's box he did not care to open. After I ceased my diatribes against the whites, I was let out of the hospital, back into the general inmate population just as if nothing had happened. I continued to brood over these events and over the dynamics of race relations in America.

During this period I was concentrating my reading in the field of economics. Having previously dabbled in the theories and writings of Rousseau, Thomas Paine, and Voltaire, I had added a little polish to my iconoclastic stance, without, however, bothering too much to understand their affirmative positions. In economics, because everybody seemed to find it necessary to attack and condemn Karl Marx in their writings, I sought out his books, and although he kept me with a headache, I took him for my authority. I was not prepared to understand him, but I was able to see in him a thoroughgoing critique and condemnation of capitalism. It was like taking medicine for me to find that, indeed, American capitalism deserved all the hatred and contempt that I felt for it in my heart. This had a positive, stabilizing effect upon me —to an extent because I was not about to become stable—and it diverted me from my previous preoccupation: morbid broodings on the black man and the white woman. Pursuing my readings into the history of socialism, I read, with very little understanding, some of the passionate, exhortatory writings of Lenin; and I fell in love with Bakunin and Nechayev's *Catechism of the Revolutionist*—the principles of which, along with some of Machiavelli's advice, I sought to incorporate into my own behavior. I took the *Catechism* for my bible and, standing on a one-man platform that had nothing to do with the reconstruction of society, I began consciously incorporating these principles into my daily life, to employ tactics of ruthlessness in my dealings with everyone with whom I came into contact. And I began to look at white America through these new eyes.

Somehow I arrived at the conclusion that, as a matter of principle, it was of paramount importance for me to have an antagonistic, ruthless attitude toward white women. The term *outlaw* appealed to me and at the time my parole date was drawing near, I considered myself to be mentally free—I was an "outlaw." I had stepped outside of the white man's law, which I repudiated with scorn and self-satisfaction. I became a law unto myself—my own legislature, my own supreme court, my own executive. At the moment I walked out of the prison gate, my feelings toward white women in general could be summed up in the following lines:

TO A WHITE GIRL

I love you
Because you're white,
Not because you're charming
Or bright.
Your whiteness
Is a silky thread
Snaking through my thoughts
In redhot patterns
Of lust and desire.

I hate you
Because you're white.
Your white meat
Is nightmare food.
White is
The skin of Evil.
You're my Moby Dick,
White Witch,

Symbol of the rope and hanging tree,
Of the burning cross.

Loving you thus
And hating you so,
My heart is torn in two.
Crucified.

I became a rapist. To refine my technique and *modus operandi*, I started out by practicing on black girls in the ghetto—in the black ghetto where dark and vicious deeds appear not as aberrations or deviations from the norm, but as part of the sufficiency of the Evil of a day—and when I considered myself smooth enough, I crossed the tracks and sought out white prey. I did this consciously, deliberately, willfully, methodically—though looking back I see that I was in a frantic, wild, and completely abandoned frame of mind.

Rape was an insurrectionary act. It delighted me that I was defying and trampling upon the white man's law, upon his system of values, and that I was defiling his women—and this point, I believe, was the most satisfying to me because I was very resentful over the historical fact of how the white man has used the black woman. I felt I was getting revenge. From the site of the act of rape, consternation spreads outwardly in concentric circles. I wanted to send waves of consternation throughout the white race. Recently, I came upon a quotation from one of LeRoi Jones' poems, taken from his book *The Dead Lecturer*:

> A cult of death need of the simple striking arm under the street lamp. The cutters from under their rented earth. Come up, black dada nihilismus. Rape the white girls. Rape their fathers. Cut the mothers' throats.

I have lived those lines and I know that if I had not been apprehended I would have slit some white throats. There are, of course, many young blacks out there right now who are slitting white throats and raping the white girl. They are not doing this because they read LeRoi Jones' poetry, as some of his critics seem to believe. Rather, LeRoi is expressing the funky facts of life.

After I returned to prison, I took a long look at myself and, for the first time in my life, admitted that I was wrong, that I had gone astray —astray not so much from the white man's law as from being human, civilized—for I could not approve the act of rape. Even though I had some insight into my own motivations, I did not feel justified. I lost my self-respect. My pride as a man dissolved and my whole fragile moral structure seemed to collapse, completely shattered.

That is why I started to write. To save myself.

I realized that no one could save me but myself. The prison authori-

ties were both uninterested and unable to help me. I had to seek out
the truth and unravel the snarled web of my motivations. I had to find
out who I am and what I want to be, what type of man I should be,
and what I could do to become the best of which I was capable. I
understood that what had happened to me had also happened to countless other blacks and it would happen to many, many more.

I learned that I had been taking the easy way out, running away from
problems. I also learned that it is easier to do evil than it is to do good.
And I have been terribly impressed by the youth of America, black and
white. I am proud of them because they have reaffirmed my faith in
humanity. I have come to feel what must be love for the young people
of America and I want to be part of the good and greatness that they
want for all people. From my prison cell, I have watched America
slowly coming awake. It is not fully awake yet, but there is soul in the
air and everywhere I see beauty. I have watched the sit-ins, the freedom
raids, the Mississippi Blood Summers, demonstrations all over the country, the FSM movement, the teach-ins, and the mounting protest over
Lyndon Strangelove's foreign policy—all of this, the thousands of little
details, show me it is time to straighten up and fly right. That is why
I decided to concentrate on my writings and efforts in this area. We
are a very sick country—I, perhaps, am sicker than most. But I accept
that. I told you in the beginning that I am extremist by nature—so it
is only right that I should be extremely sick.

I was very familiar with the Eldridge who came to prison, but that
Eldridge no longer exists. And the one I am now is in some ways a
stranger to me. You may find this difficult to understand but it is very
easy for one in prison to lose his sense of self. And if he has been under-
going all kinds of extreme, involved, and unregulated changes, then he
ends up not knowing who he is. Take the point of being attractive to
women. You can easily see how a man can lose his arrogance or certainty
on that point while in prison! When he's in the free world, he gets
constant feedback on how he looks from the number of female heads
he turns when he walks down the street. In prison he gets only hate-
stares and sour frowns. Years and years of bitter looks. Individuality is
not nourished in prison, neither by the officials nor by the convicts. It
is a deep hole out of which to climb.

What must be done, I believe, is that all these problems—particularly
the sickness between the white woman and the black man—must be
brought out into the open, dealt with and resolved. I know that the
black man's sick attitude toward the white woman is a revolutionary
sickness: it keeps him perpetually out of harmony with the system that
is oppressing him. Many whites flatter themselves with the idea that the
Negro male's lust and desire for the white dream girl is purely an esthetic
attraction, but nothing could be farther from the truth. His motivation
is often of such a bloody, hateful, bitter, and malignant nature that
whites would really be hard pressed to find it flattering. I have discussed

these points with prisoners who were convicted of rape, and their motivations are very plain. But they are very reluctant to discuss these things with white men who, by and large, make up the prison staffs. I believe that in the experience of these men lies the knowledge and wisdom that must be utilized to help other youngsters who are heading in the same direction. I think all of us, the entire nation, will be better off if we bring it all out front. A lot of people's feelings will be hurt, but that is the price that must be paid.

It may be that I can harm myself by speaking frankly and directly, but I do not care about that at all. Of course I want to get out of prison, badly, but I shall get out some day. I am more concerned with what I am going to be after I get out. I know that by following the course which I have charted I will find my salvation. If I had followed the path laid down for me by the officials, I'd undoubtedly have long since been out of prison—but I'd be less of a man. I'd be weaker and less certain of where I want to go, what I want to do, and how to go about it.

The price of hating other human beings is loving oneself less.

QUESTIONS

1. During the early period of his imprisonment, Cleaver says, he decided that "the only safe thing to do was to go for myself. . . . My mind would be free and no power in the universe could force me to accept something I didn't want to." What led him to this decision?

2. Who was "The Ogre" that Cleaver discovered? In what sense did this discovery repudiate his decision and ability to be free?

3. Who were Lenin, Bakunin, Mechayev, and Machiavelli? What have they in common that so impressed Cleaver?

4. How did Cleaver elevate the act of rape to "a principle" so that it came to mean for him "an insurrectionary act"?

5. When Cleaver returned from parole to prison, his thinking underwent a profound change. He says, "I took a long look at myself and . . . . My pride as a man dissolved." Why, and how, had his perception of himself and his world changed? What did he turn to in order to save himself?

6. What is Cleaver's explanation of the "Negro male's lust and desire for the white dream girl" from the white point of view? from the black point of view? Why, in the end, does he feel these explanations are useful and important? Do you agree with him?

part 5

Critical Essays

A *survey of contemporary Afro-American literary criticism would show a progression from the rather parochial and over-commendatory studies by early twentieth-century critics like Benjamin Brawley, whose work was not wholly without merit, to the more complex and scholarly criticism of Sterling A. Brown and J. Saunders Redding. Whereas early critics were frequently at pains to establish the fact that some blacks did possess artistic genius and had produced writing of importance, present-day critics assume that these facts are self-evident and therefore address themselves to less obvious matters.*

The function of the Afro-American writer and the socio-aesthetic problems facing him as a result of the racial situation are, clearly, major concerns of the essayists represented in the following pages. Locke, in "Negro Youth Speaks," calls attention to the social aims and values of New Negro writing. Clarke, in "The Origin and Growth of Afro-American Literature," makes the point that the work of black authors is not to be assessed as literature alone, but must be seen in relation to the struggles of the Negro people. Jones expresses a similar, if more insurgent, view in "The Revolutionary Theater."

The portrayal of the Afro-American by black and white authors is a further concern of Negro critics and is the focus for Brown's penetrating analysis. Brown and Redding are equally sensitive to writing as art, and if their criticism contributes to the student's knowledge of the achievements and problems of Afro-American authors, it also suggests aesthetic standards applicable to American literature in general.

Negro Youth Speaks

Alain Locke

The younger generation comes, bringing its gifts. They are the first fruits of the Negro Renaissance. Youth speaks, and the voice of the New Negro is heard. What stirs inarticulately in the masses is already vocal upon the lips of the talented few, and the future listens, however the present may shut its ears. Here we have Negro youth, with arresting visions and vibrant prophecies; forecasting in the mirror of art what we must see and recognize in the streets of reality tomorrow, foretelling in new notes and accents the maturing speech of full racial utterance.

Primarily, of course, it is youth that speaks in the voice of Negro youth, but the overtones are distinctive; Negro youth speaks out of an unique experience and with a particular representativeness. All classes of a people under social pressure are permeated with a common experience; they are emotionally welded as others cannot be. With them, even ordinary living has epic depth and lyric intensity, and this, their material handicap, is their spiritual advantage. So, in a day when art has run to classes, cliques and coteries, and life lacks more and more a vital common background, the Negro artist, out of the depths of his group and personal experience, has to his hand almost the conditions of a classical art.

Negro genius to-day relies upon the race-gift as a vast spiritual endowment from which our best developments have come and must come. Racial expression as a conscious motive, it is true, is fading out of our latest art, but just as surely the age of truer, finer group expression is coming in—for race expression does not need to be deliberate to be vital. Indeed at its best it never is. This was the case with our instinctive and quite matchless folk-art, and begins to be the same again as we approach cultural maturity in a phase of art that promises now to be fully representative. The interval between has been an awkward age, where from the anxious desire and attempt to be representative much

---

that was really unrepresentative has come; we have lately had an art that was stiltedly self-conscious, and racially rhetorical rather than racially expressive. Our poets have now stopped speaking for the Negro —they speak as Negroes. Where formerly they spoke to others and tried to interpret, they now speak to their own and try to express. They have stopped posing, being nearer the attainment of poise.

The younger generation has thus achieved an objective attitude toward life. Race for them is but an idiom of experience, a sort of added enriching adventure and discipline, giving subtler overtones to life, making it more beautiful and interesting, even if more poignantly so. So experienced, it affords a deepening rather than a narrowing of social vision. The artistic problem of the Young Negro has not been so much that of acquiring the outer mastery of form and technique as that of achieving an inner mastery of mood and spirit. That accomplished, there has come the happy release from self-consciousness, rhetoric, bombast, and the hampering habit of setting artistic values with primary regard for moral effect—all those pathetic over-compensations of a group inferiority complex which our social dilemmas inflicted upon several unhappy generations. Our poets no longer have the hard choice between an over-assertive and an appealing attitude. By the same effort they have shaken themselves free from the minstrel tradition and the fowling-nets of dialect, and through acquiring ease and simplicity in serious expression, have carried the folk-gift to the altitudes of art. There they seek and find art's intrinsic values and satisfactions—and if America were deaf, they would still sing.

But America listens—perhaps in curiosity at first; later, we may be sure, in understanding. But—a moment of patience. The generation now in the artistic vanguard inherits the fine and dearly bought achievement of another generation of creative workmen who have been pioneers and path-breakers in the cultural development and recognition of the Negro in the arts. Though still in their prime, as veterans of a hard struggle, they must have the praise and gratitude that is due them. We have had, in fiction, Chestnutt and Burghardt Du Bois; in drama, Du Bois again and Angelina Grimke; in poetry Dunbar, James Weldon Johnson, Fenton and Charles Bertram Johnson, Everett Hawkins, Lucien Watkins, Cotter, Jameson; and in another file of poets, Miss Grimke, Anne Spencer, and Georgia Douglas Johnson; in criticism and *belles lettres*, Braithwaite and Dr. Du Bois; in painting, Tanner and Scott; in sculpture, Meta Warrick and May Jackson; in acting, Gilpin and Robeson; in music, Burleigh. Nor must the fine collaboration of white American artists be omitted; the work of Ridgeley Torrence and Eugene O'Neill in drama, of Stribling, and Shands and Clement Wood in fiction, all of which has helped in the bringing of the materials of Negro life out of the shambles of conventional polemics, cheap romance and journalism into the domain of pure and unbiassed art. Then, rich in this legacy, but richer still, I think, in their own endowment of talent, comes the youngest generation of our Afro-American culture: in music Diton, Dett, Grant Still, and Roland Hayes; in fiction, Jessie Fauset, Walter White, Claude McKay (a forthcoming book);[1] in drama, Willis Richardson; in the field of the short story, Jean Toomer, Eric Walrond, Rudolph Fisher; and finally a vivid galaxy of young Negro poets, McKay, Jean Toomer, Langston Hughes and Countee Cullen.

These constitute a new generation not because of years only, but because of a new aesthetic and a new philosophy of life. They have all swung above the horizon in the last three years, and we can say without disparagement of the past that in that short space of time they have gained collectively from publishers, editors, critics and the general public more recognition than has ever before come to Negro creative artists in an entire working lifetime. First novels of unquestioned distinction, first acceptances by premier journals whose pages are the ambition of veteran craftsmen, international acclaim, the conquest for us of new provinces of art, the development for the first time among us of literary coteries and channels for the contact of creative minds, and most important of all, a spiritual quickening and racial leavening such as no generation has yet felt and known. It has been their achievement also to bring the artistic advance of the Negro sharply into stepping alignment with contemporary artistic thought, mood and style. They are thoroughly modern, some of them ultra-modern, and Negro thoughts now wear the uniform of the age.

Through their work, these younger artists have declared for a lusty vigorous realism; the same that is molding contemporary American letters, but their achievement of it, as it has been doubly difficult, is doubly significant. The elder generation of Negro writers expressed itself in cautious moralism and guarded idealizations; the trammels of Puritanism were on its mind because the repressions of prejudice were heavy on its heart. They felt art must fight social battles and compensate social wrongs; "Be representative": put the better foot foremost, was the underlying mood. Just as with the Irish Renaissance, there were the riots and controversies over Synge's folk plays and other frank realisms of the younger school, so we are having and will have turbulent discussion and dissatisfaction with the stories, plays and poems of the younger Negro group. But writers like Rudolph Fisher, Zora Hurston, Jean Toomer, Eric Walrond, Willis Richardson, and Langston Hughes take their material objectively with detached artistic vision; they have no thought of their racy folk types as typical of anything but themselves or of their being taken or mistaken as racially representative. Contrast Ellen Glasgow's *Barren Ground* with Thomas Nelson Page, or Waldo Frank's *Holiday* with anything of Mr. Cable's, and you will get the true clue for this contrast between the younger and the elder generations of

---

[1] [*Home to Harlem* (New York: Harper & Brothers, 1928).]

Negro literature; Realism in "crossing the Potomac" had also to cross the color line. Indeed it was the other way round; the pioneer writing of the fiction of the New South was the realistic fiction of Negro life. Fortunately just at the time the younger generation was precipitating out, *Batouala* came to attention through the award of the Prix Goncourt to René Maran, its author, in 1923. Though *Batouala* is not of the American Negro either in substance or authorship, the influence of its daring realism and Latin frankness was educative and emancipating. And so not merely for modernity of style, but for vital originality of substance, the young Negro writers dig deep into the racy peasant undersoil of the race life. Jean Toomer writes:

> Georgia opened me. And it may well be said that I received my initial impulse to an individual art from my experience there. For no other section of the country has so stirred me. There one finds soil, soil in the sense the Russians know it,—the soil every art and literature that is to live must be imbedded in.

The newer motive, then, in being racial is to be so purely for the sake of art. Nowhere is this more apparent, or more justified than in the increasing tendency to evolve from the racial substance something technically distinctive, something that as an idiom of style may become a contribution to the general resources of art. In flavor of language, flow of phrase, accent of rhythm in prose, verse and music, color and tone of imagery, idiom and timbre of emotion and symbolism, it is the ambition and promise of Negro artists to make a distinctive contribution. Much of this is already discernible. The interesting experiment of Weldon Johnson in *Creation: A Negro Sermon,* to transpose the dialect motive and carry it through in the idioms of imagery rather than the broken phonetics of speech, is a case in point. In music such transfusions of racial idioms with the modernistic styles of expression has already taken place; in the other arts it is just as possible and likely. Thus under the sophistications of modern style may be detected in almost all our artists a fresh distinctive note that the majority of them admit as the instinctive gift of the folk-spirit. Toomer gives a musical folk-lilt and a glamorous sensuous ecstasy to the style of the American prose modernists. McKay adds Aesop and peasant irony to the social novel and folk clarity and naïveté to lyric thought. Fisher adds the terseness and emotional raciness of Uncle Remus to the art of Maupassant and O. Henry. Walrond has a tropical color and almost volcanic gush that are unique even after more than a generation of exotic word painting by master artists. Langston Hughes has a distinctive fervency of color and rhythm, and a Biblical simplicity of speech that is colloquial in derivation, but full of artistry. Roland Hayes carries the rhapsodic gush and depth of folk-song to the old masters. Countee Cullen blends the simple with the sophisticated so originally as almost to put the vineyards themselves into his crystal goblets.

There is in all the marriage of a fresh emotional endowment with the finest niceties of art. Here for the enrichment of American and modern art, among our contemporaries, in a people who still have the ancient key, are some of the things we thought culture had forever lost. Art cannot disdain the gift of a natural irony, of a transfiguring imagination, of rhapsodic Biblical speech, of dynamic musical swing, of cosmic emotion such as only the gifted pagans knew, of a return to nature, not by way of the forced and worn formula of Romanticism, but through the closeness of an imagination that has never broken kinship with nature. Art must accept such gifts, and revaluate the giver.

Not all the new art is in the field of pure art values. There is poetry of sturdy social protest, and fiction of calm, dispassionate social analysis. But reason and realism have cured us of sentimentality: instead of the wail and appeal, there is challenge and indictment. Satire is just beneath the surface of our latest prose, and tonic irony has come into our poetic wells. These are good medicines for the common mind, for us they are necessary antidotes against social poison. Their influence means that at least for us the worst symptoms of the social distemper are passing. And so the social promise of our recent art is as great as the artistic. It has brought with it, first of all, that wholesome, welcome virtue of finding beauty in oneself; the younger generation can no longer be twitted as "cultural nondescripts" or accused of "being out of love with their own nativity." They have instinctive love and pride of race, and, spiritually compensating for the present lacks of America, ardent respect and love for Africa, the motherland. Gradually, too, under some spiritualizing reaction, the brands and wounds of social persecution are becoming the proud stigmata of spiritual immunity and moral victory. Already enough progress has been made in this direction so that it is no longer true that the Negro mind is too engulfed in its own social dilemmas for control of the necessary perspective of art, or too depressed to attain the full horizons of self and social criticism. Indeed, by the evidence and promise of the cultured few, we are at last spiritually free, and offer through art an emancipating vision to America. But it is a presumption to speak further for those who in the selections of their work in the succeeding sections speak so adequately for themselves.

QUESTIONS

1. What distinction does Locke draw between racial expression as a conscious motive and as a group expression?

2. Locke feels that the Afro-American writer could offer "something technically distinctive, something that as an idiom of style may become a contribution to the general resources of art." What examples does he cite in support of this idea?

3. Locke concludes this essay, published in 1925, by maintaining that the black writer and the black man are "at last spiritually free." This freedom, Locke asserts, will be useful in offering "through art an emancipating vision to America." What does he think this emancipating vision will be? How accurate do you think his prediction has been?

A Century of Negro Portraiture in American Literature

Sterling A. Brown

I

Over a century ago, in November, 1863, Harriet Beecher Stowe wrote that she was going to Washington to satisfy herself that "the Emancipation Proclamation was a reality and a substance not to fizzle out. . . ." She meant to talk to "Father Abraham himself." When she was ushered into his study, her frailty startled President Lincoln. As his big knotted hand took her small one, he quizzed: "So this is the little lady who made this big war." Pressed by her eagerness, Lincoln assured Harriet Beecher Stowe that he was determined to issue the Emancipation Proclamation on New Year's Day.

In spite of Lincoln's gallant exaggeration, his estimate of the impact of *Uncle Tom's Cabin* showed his old canniness. His secretary of state, not so given to overstatement, said that "without *Uncle Tom's Cabin* there would have been no Abraham Lincoln"; and here William Seward also spoke cannily. For the novel had been an instantaneous success here and abroad. Many of Father Abraham's hundred thousand strong had read it a decade earlier in their forming years; many carried it in their knapsacks, and it had dramatized for both North and South the American moral dilemmas and something of the humanity involved in the controversy over slavery.

Herman Melville had expressed antislavery opinions even earlier in *Mardi*. The approach, however, was oblique, and the antislavery sections were only a small part of a murky allegory, which was to be largely unread in contrast to Mrs. Stowe's popular success. Still, *Mardi* is pertinent here for Melville's clear indictment of slavery, his dread and prophecy of the inevitable clash of the irreconcilable viewpoints about slavery and the Negro. Describing the Capitol of Vivenza (his name for the United States) Melville singled out the creed "All Men are born Free and Equal," noting that an addition, in minute hieroglyphics, read: "all except the tribe of Hamo." On the flag being hoisted over the Capitol, rèd stripes corresponded to marks on the back of the slave who was doing the hoisting. Strangers visiting the South of Vivenza discovered that the slaves were men. For this a haughty spokesman denounced them as "firebrands come to light the flame of revolt." This grim prophet, a fictionalized Calhoun properly named Nullo, swore that the first blow struck for the slaves would "dissolve the Union of Vivenza's vales." Like his allegorical visitors, Melville was troubled over what seemed an irrepressible conflict between North and South and, dreading war, concluded that only Time "must befriend these thralls." In spite of his doubts about the best course, he was nevertheless certain that slavery was "a blot, foul as the crater pool of hell."

These two significant novelists of a century ago indicate how influential the treatment of Negro life and character has been in American history and literature. From the outset of our national life "Negro character," if such a loose term may be used at the beginning of this essay, has intrigued American authors. Their portraits have evinced varying degrees of sympathy and understanding, skill and power. Their motives have been manifold. Their success has not been marked.

Before the Civil War creative literature dealing with Negro life was abundant, though not distinguished. Minor efforts at real characterization—some perceptive, some vague, some tentative guesses about half-strangers—occur in Cooper, Poe, William Gilmore Simms, and the southern humorists. By and large, however, the Negro in the literature of this period was a mere pawn in the growing debate over slavery. With the overwhelming success of *Uncle Tom's Cabin* in 1852 the battle of the books was joined, and torrents of proslavery replies rushed from the presses. These were ungainly books, crude sentimentalizings and melodramatizings of the proslavery argument of Dew and Harper, of Calhoun and Fitzhugh. Slaves chanted paeans to the Arcadian existence of the old South; others walked the woods as embodiments of the various Bible Defenses of Slavery—one of them, for instance, pulling a much thumbed copy of the Sacred Book out of his overalls to confound a Yankee abolitionist who was haunting this Eden. The wisest slaves rejected freedom; the maladjusted and the half-wits ran away to the North where they either died in snow drifts (they needed master to tell them to come in out of the snow) or else they saw the light, and stole away, back to the Southland and slavery (a kind of Underground Railroad in reverse). One novel, *Life at the South, or Uncle Tom's Cabin As It Is*[1] closes with another Tom, disillusioned with the North,

---

[1] To illustrate some of the absurdities cited and the repetition that really amounted to plagiarism, compare this novel with one that preceded it by twenty years. In *The Yemassee* (1832), by William Gilmore Simms, a heroic slave, the properly named Hector, is offered his freedom:

"I d--n to h---, maussa if I gwine to be free!" roared the adhesive black, in a tone of unrestrainable determination . . . "Tis onpossible, maussa, and dere's

heading back South. "And if the reader shall chance to travel the high road, as it winds up the valley of the Shenandoah, above Winchester, he will find no slave more contented than Uncle Tom." A tall, tall order. Carry me back to old Virginny.

They would have to carry him back to get him there, was what a Negro like Frederick Douglass thought; and this opinion was shared by such other stout-hearted fugitives as Martin Delany, David Ruggles, Sojourner Truth, Harriet Tubman, and William Wells Brown. These and many other Negroes fought in the antislavery crusade; several used stirring autobiographies, pamphlets, journalism and oratory in the battle. Creative literature, however, was the exception with them; an embattled people used literature as a weapon, as propaganda; not as exploration, but as exposé of injustice. There were a few short stories and novels, and hortatory poetry. The truth of Negro life and character, however, is in such an autobiography as Douglass's *My Bondage and My Freedom* more than in the fiction and poetry of the time.

Also engaged in this crusade were white abolitionist poets—Bryant, Longfellow, Whittier—and novelists like Harriet Beecher Stowe. Their hearts were better than their circumstantial material; they, as Lowell said of Mrs. Stowe, "instinctively went right to the organic elements of human nature, whether under a white skin or black"; they knew the right thing—that men should be free. But they lacked realistic knowledge of Negro life and experience, and for this lack sentimental idealism could not compensate. Before the Civil War, therefore, the characterization of the Negro was far from the complexity that we now know was there; it was oversimplified—the contented slave, and his corollary, the wretched freedman; the comic minstrel on the one hand, and the persecuted victim, the noble savage, the submissive Christian, the tragic octoroon on the other.[2]

---

no use for to talk about it. Enty I know wha' kind of ting freedom is wid black man? Ha! you make Hector free, he turn wuss than poor buckra, he tief out of de shop—he git drunk and lie in de ditch—den if sick come, he roll, he toss in de wet grass of de stable. You come in de morning, Hector dead . . ."

Twenty years later, in 1852, in *Life at the South, or Uncle Tom's Cabin As It Is*, the author, W. L. G. Smith, has a character also named Hector, who is also offered his freedom. And he also says:

"I damn to hell, massa, if I gwine to be free, roared the adhesive black in a tone of unrestrainable determination . . ." etc. *ad literatim et ad nauseum*.

[2] "I swear their nature is beyond my comprehension. A strange people!—merry 'mid their misery—laughing through their tears, like the sun shining through the rain. Yet what simple philosophers they! They tread life's path as if 'twere strewn with roses devoid of thorns, and make the most of life with natures of sunshine and song."

"Natures of sunshine and song." Most readers of this passage would take it to refer to the American Negro. Instead it is about the Irish, spoken by an English officer

II

If, before Appomatox, *Uncle Tom's Cabin* was undoubtedly the champion in the battle of the books, for a long time afterwards the proslavery defense was victorious. The plantation tradition, glorifying slavery as a benevolent guardianship, crystallized. Negro and white characters were neatly packaged. Inevitable were old marse, the essence of chivalry; young missy, 100 percent southern womanhood, the essence of charm; and young marse, chip off the old block, the essence of dash and courage; all essences. Negro characters were grooved also: the mammy, proud of her quality whitefolks, the wise upbringer of their children (there is little mention of her own); her male counterpart, also worshipful of his whitefolks, devoted to their glory and service; and the clown, the razor-toting, watermelon-eating singer and dancer, with a penchant for big words he could neither understand nor pronounce, whom the thriving black-face minstrel shows made one of America's favorite theatrical personages.

Among the authors who established the plantation tradition, Thomas Nelson Page and Joel Chandler Harris were most persuasive. These and their fellows were children when the Civil War broke out; they had known Negro children as playmates; they remembered their grandfathers and fathers and uncles with ancestral pride; they saw the old South through the haze of retrospect; they invested the Lost Cause with the glamor of the defeated and the departed. They combined the chuckling of humorous, philosophical slaves with the pathos of ill-starred aristocrats. Frequenters of the Negro quarters, rapt listeners to old Negro yarn spinners in their absorptive years, blessed with sharp eyes and ears and retentive memories, these authors were able to convey the plausible, surface realism of local color. The dialect, often meticulously rendered, rang true; if the words were right, the thoughts behind them had to be right. A Negro folkline, "You can read my letters, but you sho' cain't read my mind," should have caused them and their readers some doubt —but for all of their claim that they knew the Negro, *that* was *one* line, and *one* aspect of his character that they did not know.

---

in a play dealing with one of the most tragic periods in the history of the persecution of the Irish. (From Sterling A. Brown, *The Negro in American Fiction* [Washington, D.C.: 1931], p. 1.)

Stereotyping is a thrice-told tale. The treatment of the Jewish character in English, European, and American literature, is certainly another instance. Years ago, a perceptive commentator on our popular art, Isaac Goldberg, pointed to the startling fact that the three most popular butts of comedy on our vaudeville stage were the Irishman, the Negro, and the Jew, the three most persecuted minorities at that moment of American History.

So Page has his inveterate old uncles reminiscing on the good old days before the war, to a white stranger who asks just the right question and then stands back while the torrent leaps: a stranger who never for a moment suspects guile or irony or forgetfulness or inaccuracy. "Dem was good ole times, Marster, de bes' Sam ever see," is one refrain that is repeated. These old uncles are more ventriloquist's dummies than people, but to the readers of the eighties, they were appealing and persuasive. A vouched-for legend tells us that Thomas Wentworth Higginson, the abolitionist friend of John Brown, the man who was wounded in a fight in Boston to keep a fugitive slave from being returned to the South, the colonel of a Negro regiment in the Civil War, this man, the legend goes, who had fought so strenuously for the Negro, was discovered thirty years after the war in his study, in tears from reading *In Ole Virginia* by Thomas Page.[3]

Joel Chandler Harris was readier to show some harshness in the ante-bellum South, but his picture remains one of mutual affection and kindness. A surly, intractable Blue Dave is rehabilitated when he finds another master as good as his first one, who had died; Free Joe, who has no one to look after him, a misfit among the happier slaves, dies disconsolate, and ineffectual, and free. Harris contributed minor masterpieces in his Br'er Rabbit Tales; these are his garnerings of rich yield, and without his perceptiveness some of the world's best folk literature might have perished. But despite his disclaimer, Harris *did* doctor the tales he picked up in the slave quarters; they are not genuinely folk—of the folk, by the folk, to the folk, for the folk—but they are told by an old uncle to entertain a little white boy. The framework in which they are told is the plantation tradition. When Harris used Uncle Remus as a kind of columnist for the *Atlanta Constitution*, as he often did, Uncle Remus is closer kin to Henry Grady and the New South than to Remus's African forebears. Still in his inimitable speech he deplores education of Negroes as the "ruination of this country . . . a barrel stave [he says] can fling mo' sense into [his] people in one minute than all de schoolhouses betwixt dis and de State er Midgigan." There are two Uncle Remuses. The inferior one was a dialect-talking version of a Georgia politician, and for all of his pithiness he is more cracker-box philosopher than sage of the quarters.

But Page and Harris, and a horde of followers were popular in the leading Northern magazines and converted much of the North, which was ready to forget the late grueling contest. They presented a glowing picture of the kindlier aspects of slavery. Their cardinal principles were mutual affection between the races; and the peculiar endowment of each race to occupy its role: one race the born master, one race the born slave. The road to reunion was opening; tension was relaxing; the

---

[3] Paul H. Buck, *The Road to Reunion* (1865–1900) (Boston: 1937), p. 235.

troubled past could be forgotten, the wrongs could be covered over, perhaps they had not been so bad, perhaps they could go away. So the Plantation Tradition became fixed.

During the Reconstruction, other stereotypes were added to those of the contented slave, the comic minstrel, and the wretched freedman.[4] These were the brute Negro and the tragic mulatto. Page contrasted the old issue Negro, loyal and contented (in Page's version) with the new issue, who were disloyal, ungrateful, and discontented, ruined by emancipation. These new Negroes were shown as insulting swaggerers. They were often in Federal uniforms, or they engaged in politics. The docile mastiffs had become mad dogs; the carriers of the rabies were carpetbaggers, scalawags, Union troops, and Yankee schoolmarms. A sort of Ku Klux Klan fiction emerged; insolent Negroes, often rapists, were shown in atrocity stories, and the knightly Klan rode, white sheeted, to restore southern civilization and to protect southern womanhood.[5] As a colleague, E. Franklin Frazier, used to quip: "The closer a Negro got to the ballot box, the more he looked like a rapist."

The tragic mulatto stereotype stemmed from the antislavery crusade, whose authors used it, partly to show miscegenation as an evil of slavery, partly as an attempt to win readers' sympathies by presenting central characters who were physically very like the readers. Antislavery authors, Harriet Beecher Stowe included, held to a crude kind of racism. Their near-white characters are the intransigent, the resentful, the mentally alert—for biological, not social, reasons. In the proslavery argument, the mixed blood characters are victims of a divided inheritance[6] and proof of the disastrous results of amalgamation. Most of the villains in reconstruction fiction are mixed bloods, "inheriting the vices of both races and the virtues of neither." The mulatto, or quadroon, or octoroon heroine has been a favorite for a long time; in books by white authors

---

[4] The effect, of course, was not confined to the last century. In the first doctoral dissertation written on this subject, the critic pontificates that in one twenty-six line sketch by Joel Chandler Harris about Br'er Fox and Br'er Mud Turtle (I quote): "the whole range of the Negro character is revealed thoroughly." John Herbert Nelson, *The Negro Character in American Literature* (Lawrence, Kansas: The Department of Journalism Press, 1926), p. 118.

[5] Two of the most widely known Hollywood motion pictures have made great use of the formulas of the plantation tradition and especially of the brute Negro. These are D. W. Griffith's *The Birth of a Nation* (based upon the melodramatic novels of Thomas Dixon, *The Clansman* and *The Leopard Spots*), and Margaret Mitchell's *Gone With the Wind*, in which the glamor of Scarlett O'Hara and Rhett Butler should not blind us to the trite stereotyping of character and social background.

[6] What might be called the fractional theory of personality gets its *reductio ad absurdum* in Roark Bradford's *This Side of Jordan* (1929).

"The blade of a razor flashed . . . Her Negro Blood sent it unerringly between

the whole desire of her life is to find a white lover; then balked by the dictates of her society, she sinks to a tragic end. In our century, Negro authors have turned the story around; now after restless searching, she finds peace only after returning to her own people. In both cases, however, the mulatto man or woman is presented as a lost, unhappy, woebegone abstraction.

The fiction of George Washington Cable pays great attention to the free people of color of old Louisiana, whose rigid caste restrictions brought tragedy to quadroon and octoroon heroines. But Cable did not limit his sympathy for the victims of slavery to this unfortunate caste; his picture of old Louisiana was colorful but crowded with authoritative antiquarian detail. Whether educated free man of color, or illiterate field hand, or captured African Prince Bras-Coupé, who killed rather than serve as slave, Cable gave shrewd, knowing interpretations of Negro character. The first genuine southern liberal, Cable knew too much about slavery to idealize the old regime, and he was sensitively aware of the dark shadows of the past on the South of his day. The best local colorist of Louisiana, he found his social sympathies too broad for his native section, and he spent his last years in self-imposed exile.

One of Cable's services to American literature lies in his re-enforcing of Mark Twain's growing liberality concerning Negroes. *Huckleberry Finn* is more telling an indictment of slavery than patently antislavery novels are. The callousness of a small God-fearing town toward Negroes, the conditioning of a small boy, so that the word "abolitionist" is the worst insult he can imagine; the topsy-turvyness of Huck's self-condemnation when he decides that he will help Jim escape only because he

---

two ribs. Her Indian blood sent it back for an unnecessary second and third slash."

It might be hazarded that her Eskimo blood kept her from being chilled with horror.

Fannie Hurst's *Imitation of Life* contains another gem. Of the fair-skinned heroine, Peola, we get this analysis from her mother:

"It may be mixed up wid plenty of white blood . . . but thin out chicken gravy wid water an' it remains [sic!] chicken gravy, only not so good. . . ."

She prays for her octoroon daughter:

"Lord git de white horses drove out of her blood. Kill de curse—shame de curse her light-colored pap lef' for his baby. . . . Chase de wild white horses tramplin' on my chile's happiness. . . . It's de white horses dat's wild, a-swimmin in de blood of mah chile."

It is submitted that with all those horses running wild in Peola's aorta, she could hardly be a stable character. From this novel, of which Hollywood has made two increasingly saccharine versions, oral tradition among Negroes has taken the name of Peola for a fair skinned girl; not in respect, however, but in burlesque.

hasn't been brought up right and is in the devil's grip; the characterization of Jim, superstitious but shrewd, kindly, self-sacrificial, but determined to be free, not contented in slavery—all of these are vividly
rendered. A single passage of dialogue and the pretensions of the plantation tradition are shredded away. Consider this scene: Jim is on the
raft; Huck sets off in the canoe, ostensibly to learn the name of the town
they are passing but really to betray Jim to the slavehunters.

> "Putty soon I'll be a-shout'n for joy, an I'll say its all on account
> o'Huck I's a free man; en I couldn't ever been free if it hadn't ben
> for Huck; Huck done it . . . Dah you goes, de ole true Huck, de
> on'y white gen'lman dat ever kep' his promise to ole Jim."

This tobacco-chewing, pipe-smoking, barefooted one-gallused Missouri
kid, this truant from learning, the delinquent son of the town drunk—
now on his way to betray his buddy—becomes "the only white gentleman that ever kept his promise to old Jim." Twain's irony does not
leave the old tradition of noblesse oblige much to stand on.

Negro writers at the turn of the century also deepened the portraiture.
According to William Dean Howells, Paul Laurence Dunbar was the
"first American Negro to feel the Negro life aesthetically and express it
lyrically." Influenced almost inevitably by the powerful plantation tradition, most of his poems about slavery echo Irwin Russell, Page and Joel
Chandler Harris, but his poems about the Negro life of his own day
are affectionate, sympathetic, and winning. Characters that had been
treated as clownish were now revealed as more richly human. Dunbar
was of the school of James Whitcomb Riley—of the happy hearthside
and pastoral contentment. He was a gentle person, and even if publishing conditions had permitted it, he probably would not have chosen
the prevalent harshness to write about. In a few short stories and poems
in standard English he showed bitterness, but this is typically oblique
as in "We Wear the Mask," a poem containing a true metaphor but
more plaintive than revealing.

Dunbar's contemporary, Charles Waddell Chesnutt, was concerned
with the harsher—and more typical aspects—of life in the South, and
with the problems of the color line. His volume of folk tales (*The
Conjure Woman*, 1899) seems to resemble the tales of Page and Harris,
but on close reading Chesnutt is quite different. His tales are told by
a shrewd, self-serving Uncle, whose characterizations of both Negroes
and whites is salty—and no nonsense about the good old days. Chesnutt
based one of his strongest novels, *The Marrow of Tradition* (1901), on
the riot in Wilmington, North Carolina. This novel and *The Colonel's
Dream* (1905) show a grasp of social reality, and a powerful ability to
dramatize his material.

The novels of Albion Tourgee, who served as an officer in the Union
Army and remained in North Carolina as a "carpetbagger," are informed and powerful, and with the fiction of Chesnutt, are necessary

correctives to the Ku Klux Klan fiction of the post-war South. A *Fool's Errand* (1879) and *Bricks Without Straw* (1880) are melodramatic —fighting fire with fire—but they come closer to the complex realities of the time and anticipate the fiction of the twentieth century more than those of any other writer save Chesnutt.

III

At the turn of the century W. E. B. Dubois started his distinguished career with *The Souls of Black Folk*, which is still one of the best interpretations of Negro life and aspirations. On the creative side, Dubois continued to write poems, short stories, novels, autobiographies and essays, but none of these excel this pioneering work which was marked by impassioned polemics against compromise, incisive irony at hypocrisy, sensitive brooding over the dilemmas of democracy, and affirmation of race pride and solidarity.

A key essay by Dubois, called "The Sorrow Songs," was one of the earliest and best interpretations of the spirituals. Dubois' awareness of the dignity and beauty of Negro folk music was broadened and deepened by James Weldon Johnson. In addition to editing two comprehensive volumes of spirituals with his brother, J. Rosamond Johnson, he commented upon Negro musical shows, ragtime, and the beginnings of jazz from the vantage point of a participant in their history. His novel, *Autobiography of an Ex-Colored Man* (1912), was the first to deal with Negro life on several levels, from the folk to the sophisticated. It is rather more a chart of Negro life than a novel, but it contains informed analysis and valid interpretation. Johnson's Preface to the *Book of American Negro Poetry* (1922) boldly advanced the claims of the Negro's creativeness. Johnson's own earlier poems, collected in *Fifty Years and Other Poems* (1917), looked backward in genre pieces of the school of Dunbar, and looked at the present and towards the future in hortatory and lyrical verse. In the commemorative title poem, Johnson insisted on the Negro's belonging to America, on his services, and on his potential. As with Dubois, creative literature for Johnson was the other arm to propagandistic work for the NAACP.

Johnson's hope for more adequate and accurate presentation of Negro life was not long in coming. The time—the post-war decade, with its revolt against squeamishness, repression, and Babbittry—was favorable. The lost generation seemed to find itself in Harlem or the Caribbean or Africa; youth rekindled the flame in Harlem where a magazine blazed forth for one issue with the name "Fire!" Carl Van Doren felt that the decided need of American literature for "color, music, gusto, the free expression of gay or desperate moods" could best be filled by the exploration of Negro life and character. Exploitation, however, rather than exploration, was as often as not the result. Eugene O'Neill's *The Emperor Jones* (1920) ushered in the decade: the play was theatrically effective, with a Negro of some aggressiveness and truculence, until then a rarity on the stage, at the tragic center instead of in comic relief, but it relied overly on tomtoms and atavism. So did O'Neill's generally unconvincing *All God's Chillun Got Wings*, which caused a tremendous imbroglio on Broadway, for all of its essential conformism to racial myths.

The technical facility of Vachel Lindsay's *The Congo* (1914) made it too popular; its repetend:

> Then I saw the Congo, creeping through the black
> Cutting through the jungle with a golden track

seemed to be the marching song of the white writers on safari to the newly discovered Harlem and other *terras incognitas*. Even as humane an author as Waldo Frank in *Holiday* defined white and Negro "consciousness" too schematically and too expeditiously. Sherwood Anderson's *Dark Laughter* used "the Negro way of life of levee loungers" to beat such whipping boys and girls as American neuroticism and acquisitiveness. John W. Vandercook brought back from Haiti and Surinam inspiring romances of heroism and noble savagery but, not content with these, he lectured the American Negro for having degenerated from his distinguished forebears in the Surinam bush. In *Tom-Tom* (1926), Vandercook related how the spectacle of a quadroon-octoroon chorus and "several wealthy well-educated mulatto families" in the choice seats—upon his one visit to a Harlem theatre—awoke him to "the supreme tragedy of the Negro." The chorus and the audience clarified race differences for him. "We [the whites]," he states, "are optical —intellectual. They are auricular—emotional." W. B. Seabrooks' books on Haiti exploited the orgiastic and voodooistic. The French novelist Paul Morand wrote a group of stories called *Magie Noire* (1928), in which atavism was luridly and absurdly expressed; in one story, for instance, a Negro intellectual attending a Pan-African convention in Brussels visits a Negro Museum and immediately runs berserk. Ronald Firbank's Mayfair burlesque, *Prancing Nigger* (1924) was exactly titled. Perhaps the epitome of the trend was Carl Van Vechten's *Nigger Heaven* (1925), in which Harlem, the heaven, was flamboyant and erotic.

The craft and viewpoint of Carl Van Vechten and his fellows influenced Negro writers, and the frequent interracial parties compounded the interest. Only a few of the Harlem indigènes withstood the blandishments of the aesthetes and the hedonists: the best of those who wrote about Harlem were Rudolph Fisher, an insouciant O. Henry of Baghdad-on-the-Hudson, and Claude McKay, an unvarnished realist. But even these accented the instinctual, hedonistic, and peculiar.

The Harlemites that emerged from the pages of novels by both white and Negro authors in this period were exotic primitives, whose dances —the Charleston, the "black bottom," the "snake hips," the "walking the dog"—were tribal rituals; whose music with wa-wa trumpets and trombones and drum batteries doubled for tom-toms; whose chorus girls with bunches of bananas girdling their shapely middles nurtured tourists' delusions of the "Congo creeping through the black." *Joie de vivre* was a racial monopoly: rhythm and gaiety were on one side— the darker—of the racial line. "That's why darkies were born" sang a Negro jazz musician who should have known better. "The whites have only money, privilege, power; Negroes have cornered the joy" was the theme of a Negro novelist, who did know better.

The amorality and irresponsibility of the youthful rebels was reproved by such genteel critics as Benjamin Brawley. The burgeoning jazz met with disfavor among the Negro middle-class, who wished to conform to socially-approved standards. The leaders of the NAACP felt that the characterization of Harlem sweet-backs and hot mammas did injustice to their propaganda and purposes. After chiding younger Negro authors, Dubois turned in *Dark Princess* (1928) to what he considered the proper study of writers: the rising tide of color. Though idealized and contrived, this novel handled Pan-Africanism and the emergence of Asia and Africa with prescience. Walter White's *Fire in the Flint* (1925, an anti-lynching novel) and *Flight* (1926, an anti-passing-for-white novel), were also idealized and tractarian, though informed and somewhat new in material. To Jessie Fauset and Nella Larsen, delineators of Negro middle-class life, proving a point meant more than presenting people. Properly resentful of the nonsense about inherent racial traits; irked by the theories of "race differences," such novelists blinked at the realities of differences (social and cultural) between the races. Occasionally, in their novels about passing Negroes, especially Jessie Fauset's *Comedy: American Style* (1933), the intraracial color snobbishness and the latent self-hatred of anti-Negro Negroes could be glimpsed, but these glimpses were rare, and the usual picture was bland, at once self-pitying and self-congratulatory.

Such novelists, according to Wallace Thurman's *Infants of the Spring* (1932), write only to "apprise white humanity of the better classes among Negro humanity." A sharp-eyed, nay-saying young Negro, Thurman also lampooned the phoney primitivism of his confrères. One of the best satires of the pretense and sham rife at this time came from E. Simms Campbell, whose talent for cartooning extended to pen as well as to brush and palette. He remembered:

> intellectual parties where Negroes who were in the theatre were looked upon as social plums and the dumbest and most illiterate were fawned over by Park Avenue . . . [and where] the intellectual stink could have been cut with a knife—a dull knife.[7]

---

[7] "Blues," in *Jazzmen*, ed. by F. Ramsey, Jr. and C. E. Smith (New York: 1939), pp. 103–04.

The poets of the period spoke more deeply than the novelists. Claude McKay's *Harlem Shadows* (1922) was original and authentic in its controlled craftsmanship and in its revelation of a personality: an independent, angry radical—now excoriating America for its injustices, now rousing race solidarity, now setting nostalgic vignettes of his native Jamaica against the tragic but fascinating Harlem. Less militant, but as deeply engaged by "race," Countee Cullen also brought disciplined technique to the revelation of a subtle, sophisticated consciousness, as in "Heritage," "The Shroud of Color," and various cutting epigrams. Langston Hughes was less conventional in technique than these two poets, and less subjective, taking the Negro folk—particularly the urban masses—for his subject. For over three decades, in more than a dozen books, Hughes has told their story, interpreted their lives, and made use of their language, lore, and song to point up his own commentary on America.

Among others, Waring Cuney, Frank Horne, and three women poets —Georgia Douglass Johnson, Angelina Grimke, and Ann Spencer— wrote truthfully about themselves, and thereby widened and deepened the self-portraiture of Negroes. One of the finest books of poems of the twenties was James Weldon Johnson's *God's Trombones* (1927), in which he recreated the eloquence of the old Negro preacher. This work not only marked a development from apologistic rhetoric and sentimentalized genre poetry, but also in its respect for the intrinsic dignity of folk-stuff showed younger writers the way to go, much as Yeats and Synge had previously shown young Irish writers.

Two striking books of this movement were Jean Toomer's *Cane* (1923) and Eric Walrond's *Tropic Death* (1926). These authors were alike in being masters of their craft and, unfortunately, in falling silent after the publication of one book each. Toomer is a poet in the few lyrics in *Cane,* and even more so in his evocative prose. No imaginative work since *The Souls of Black Folk* had so deeply explored Negro life in the deep South, in border cities, in the North, among the folk, the urban masses, the bourgeoisie, the intellectuals; and none had revealed it so beautifully. Walrond's *Tropic Death* is a brilliantly impressionistic, obliquely, subtly communicated series of portraits of the author's native West Indies.

In 1925 Du Bose Heyward wrote a poetic novel about a crippled beggar named Porgy of Catfish Row, Charleston, S. C. Through the success of the novel, its dramatization by the Theatre Guild, its several versions in moving pictures, and the folk opera (by Du Bose and his wife Dorothy Heyward, and George and Ira Gershwin), Porgy is the most widely known Negro character (nationally and internationally) since Uncle Tom. Heyward, a white South Carolinian, was a sensitive and sympathetic observer of Negroes, especially on the waterfront. His poem "Jazzbo Brown" and his second novel *Mamba's Daughters* (1925) were fresh and honest. Julia Peterkin, another South Carolinian, was also a careful and absorptive observer of life on the plantations in such books as *Green Thursday* (1924) and *Scarlet Sister Mary* (1928). Both Heyward and Mrs. Peterkin veered toward the exotic primitive, however; a fellow South Carolinian, E. C. L. Adams, gave a fuller picture of the workaday life of Negroes, with none of the harshness minimized in two books of dialogues: *Congaree Sketches* (1927) and *Nigger to Nigger* (1928). These books, with their vividness of folk-speech, the irony, starkness and knowingness of the talkers, added a new dimension to the treatment of the Negro folk. No white folklorist (not even Harris) no Negro folklorist (not even Chesnutt) knew so much and rendered it so well as this white country doctor in the Congaree River section of South Carolina. Howard Odum and Guy Johnson at the University of North Carolina studied Negro folk songs for clues to understanding Negro life; as by-products, Odum produced three novels about a synthesized roustabout, Left Wing Gordon, who attains a certain convincingness and complexity; and Johnson wrote the first and best study of the steel driver John Henry, who is now in the pantheon of American folk heroes.

John Henry was debunked and belittled in Roark Bradford's *John Henry* (1932), from which a bad musical was made. Bradford was born on a plantation worked by Negroes, had a Negro nurse, and several Negroes as boyhood friends. He had watched them (in his words) "at work in the fields, in the levee camps, and on the river . . . at home, in church, at their picnics and their funerals." A gifted mimic, like Harris, he was able to reproduce the folk vocabulary and syntax, and books like *Ol' Man Adam An' His Chillun* (1928) and *King David and the Philistine Boys* (1930) are burlesque masterpieces. Dividing Negroes into three types, "the nigger, the colored person, and the Negro—upper case N." Bradford takes his stand by the first type, and though delighted to be in his company, sees him solely as primitive and uproariously funny.[8] Bradford could hardly have respected John Henry who was a steel-driving *man*.

Since Bradford also did not respect the folk-Negro's religion, it is strange that his travesties of the Bible in *Ol' Man Adam An' His Chillun* served as a springboard for Marc Connelly's play *The Green Pastures*. Connelly, however, though not so soaked in local color as Bradford, was wise enough to know that there was more than farce to the folk, was humane enough to see the true values of material that Bradford underestimated, and was a canny stage artificer. He made full use of the understanding and advice of Richard Harrison and his fine troupe of Negro actors, and finally was inspired to set the play in a framework of spirituals sung authentically by the Hall Johnson choir. A miracle in two senses of the word, *The Green Pastures*, according to Kenneth Burke, exploited the "child symbol":

---

[8] *Ol' Man Adam An' His Chillun* (New York: 1928), p. x.

The Negroes of "The Green Pastures" with their heavenly clam-
bakes, mildly disconsolate "Lawd," the incongruous Africanization
of the Biblical legends, can carry one into a region of gentleness
that is in contrast with the harsh demands of our day, caressing.

In contrast to this play, Burke set Hall Johnson's *Run, Little Chillun!*,
a play written from within about a Negro religious cult, which "brings
out an aspect of the Negro-symbol with which our theatre-going public is not theatrically at home: the power side of the Negro." [9] Burke
was not surprised at the sluggishness of the general public's interest, but
he deplored it. In the three decades since, *The Green Pastures* has been
revived as a play and movie and has been much anthologized, but the
text of *Run, Little Chillun!* is unavailable.

IV

Even while Burke was so writing, however, stress was being
shifted from quaint philosophers of the quarters in the good old days
to the oppressed victims or the aroused laborers in the troublesome,
workaday present. Recognition that the Negro was crucial in labor's
march to democracy and that the Negro *belongs*, or must belong, here
and now, supplanted delusions of his "'special endowment," special behavior and special niche in American life. It was important for writers,
both Negro and white, to recognize these truths, though today they
may seem truisms. The thirties had this healthy influence in thought
about *the* Negro: unfortunately, however, enforcement of economic and
political creeds interfered (as did antislavery convictions earlier) with
complex and convincing characterization. A new type of Negro did
emerge in the forceful plays of Paul Green, whose dramaturgy, combined with Richard Wright's fervor and understanding, produced *Native Son*, one of America's few distinguished tragedies dealing with
racial materials.

In the depression various brands of radicalism, whether derived from
Socialism, Communism, Garveyism, the IWW or just grass-roots dis-
sidence, found Negro life and character to be unworked mines. The
old firehouse, Scott Nearing, after writing the grim *Black America*
(1929), piled the woes of that exposé on the head of a Negro family
in *Freeborn* (1932), the first revolutionary novel of Negro life. For all
of its veracity the momentum of the novel was lessened by the fact that
it was "unpublishable by any commercial concern." A journalistic radical, John Spivak exposed the chain gang system in *Georgia Nigger*
(1932), but here as in so many "proletarian" novels characterization

---

[9] "Negro's Pattern of Life," *Saturday Review of Literature*, X (July 29, 1933), pp.
10–14.

was strangled by radical theory, with the last twist given by melodramatic clichés. The best "proletarian" works on Negro life were Grace Lumpkin's novel A *Sign for Cain* (1935) and Paul Peters' and George Sklar's drama *Stevedore* (1934). Both set at the center of the stage a self-respecting, virile, quiet but strong hero, slowly but surely awakened, capable of the greatest trust, willing and ready to die for the causes of race advance and economic brotherhood. From the nobility of an Uncle Tom we now get the nobility of the working-class hero. We also get repetitions of the despicable hat-in-hand tattling Negro, the strong matriarch, and the supposed clown, whose mask is irony; and on the white side, the brutal sheriff, the wishy-washy liberal and (counterpart to the Negro hero) the courageous organizer. One of the stock incidents in these works is the consummation of the triumphant march, hand in hand, and rank by rank, of the white and black workers of the world. After thirty years such a march still occurs far less in life than it did in the novels and plays of the thirties.

That there were such people and such events in America goes without saying, but that the actuality of Negro experience and its literary representation do not always coincide should also at this point go without saying. The Negro author most influenced by neo-Marxist literary canons was Richard Wright. After, and even during, his brief visitation with the Communist Party, Wright was uncomfortable with the working-class hero, however, and was more at home artistically portraying lower-class victims and arraigning American injustices: mob violence in the South, ghetto deprivations and frustrations in the North. From "Big Boy" to Bigger Thomas, Wright presented in such dynamic books as *Uncle Tom's Children*, *Native Son* and *Black Boy* the searing effects of poverty and prejudice on sensitive Negro youths. Wright's indignation was enormous and his power to communicate the violence and shock was great. Carrying a personal anger too deep for him to master through art, he sought Europe for a resting place. There he became increasingly the interpreter of the American Negro to the European intellectuals, and also, increasingly, he lost touch with the realities of the racial situation in the states. The native son died before he could return home; had he returned he would have found himself not so lost, so alienated, so outside. His own insight, dedication and craft have helped bring about this changed situation.

At a crucial point in his career, Wright was aided by the John Reed Clubs (leftist writing groups) and the Federal Writers' Project. A child of the New Deal (more accurately a stepchild), the Federal Writers' Project gave employment to Negro authors as diverse as Claude McKay and Frank Yerby; Ted Poston and Willard Motley; Arna Bontemps and Roi Ottley; Zora Neale Hurston and Henry Lee Moon. One achievement of the Writers' Project, through its city, county, state and regional guides, was the sponsorship of local history and lore, both current and historic. Negro writers benefited from these interests. Far

more revelatory than the Harlem fad were Zora Neal Hurston's re-
warding novels of her native Florida: *Jonah's Gourd Vine* (1934) and
Their Eyes Were Watching God (1937), and best of all, *Mules and
Men* (1935), in which Miss Hurston, a trained anthropologist, becomes the first Negro to join the many authors who have ploughed the
fertile fields of Negro folk life. From a horde of narratives by living
ex-slaves, the folklorist B. A. Botkin assembled the indispensable *Lay
My Burden Down* (1945), a folk history of slavery of surprising worth;
and Roscoe E. Lewis collected a mass of material and fashioned it
into *The Negro in Virginia*, the pioneer in a series, doomed by the
short life of the project, that would have dealt regionally with Negro
life. Sufficient material was salvaged from the excellent notes on Negroes in New York to supply Roi Ottley's bright, informative narratives,
New World A-Coming (1943) and *Black Odyssey* (1948). Arna Bontemps in his first-rate novel of a Negro insurrection, *Black Thunder*
(1936), turned away from the hedonistic fiction that he exploited in
God Sends Sunday (1931), to a more important interest in the history
of the American Negro—a subject that has busied him fruitfully ever
since.

The population of William Faulkner's Yoknapatawpha County contains many Negroes, and they are certainly not the least interesting persons to William Faulkner's readers, or to himself. Faulkner's depth in
characterizing Negroes increased with the years; whereas in an earlier
novel, *Soldier's Pay*, he accepted the myths of *his* own tribal past, soon
he steadily began to see Negroes whole, and with *Go Down, Moses* he
defied several of his region's set beliefs concerning the Negro. In his
last years, Faulkner was rejected by his fellow Oxonians as too liberal,
and accepted (gingerly) by Negro intellectuals as not liberal enough.
His essential liberalism on race can be questioned (his correspondence
to his "new Southern" spokesman Gavin Stevens, a lawyer who grows
in good will to the Negro, but also and better in good understanding,
needs study). There is no questioning, however, that in ploughing
deeply into the soil of his single county, Faulkner was wise, prescient,
and rewarded. What seems at first glance the familiar stereotyping becomes, on true reading, complex and revelatory, e.g., Dilsey is far more
than the old mammy; Joe Christmas more than the tragic mulatto;
Nancy Manigault more than the depraved "wench." But Faulkner also
presents new people, unnoticed before but here candidly portrayed: the
admirable Lucius Beauchamps, Sam Fathers, and the Centaur in Brass.
When spouting the Southern liberal's ambivalent credo (cf. Gavin
Stevens' long-windedness in *Intruder in the Dust*) Faulkner is unconvincing or wrong, but when he stands back and lets his Negro character
speak out and act out, Faulkner is right, and often superb.

Faulkner's éclat has dimmed the achievement of several other Southern novelists, who, in dealing with the Negro, often did what Faulkner
could not or would not do. One example is Erskine Caldwell, a genuine

liberal, who in such stories as "The People Vs. Abe Latham, Colored," "Kneel to the Rising Sun," and "Candy Man Beechum," and in a novel, *Trouble in July*, has snapshots and photographs that are fresh and authentic. Other examples are Hamilton Basso, especially in his *Courthouse Square* (1936), and William March in *Come In at the Door*. Both deal with areas of Negro experience untouched by Faulkner, as does, to cite a current example Harper Lee's *To Kill a Mockingbird*. A historical novelist, T. S. Stribling has written a trilogy of a Southern family—both branches, Negro and white—in *The Forge* (1931), *The Store* (1933), and *Unfinished Cathedral* (1934). This masterpiece of re-creating the past is most unfairly neglected today.

Another underestimated novel on race relations is *Strange Fruit* (1944), by Lillian Smith. Here, like Faulkner, Miss Smith explores the conventionally stereotyped liaison between Negro woman and white man. Miss Smith's psychological probing results in much that is clarifying and revealing. The ambivalence of the white youth is dramatized in *Strange Fruit*; it is analyzed and substantiated in *Killers of the Dream* (1949). This book also is neglected by the "southern critical establishment," though were some of its members to read it they might learn about themselves. *Strange Fruit* was made into a play and created a stir. At the same time, *Deep Are the Roots* by Arnaud D'Usseau and James Gow handled an interracial liaison on a higher level than had been usual. Other dramas getting to grips with the reality of Negro experience were *Jeb*, and a Negro adaptation of a play on Polish life, *Anna Lucasta* by Philip Yordan. The griefs of a Polish family were easily transposed to a Negro family.

The Negro intellectual—as intellectual, not merely victim or malcontent—is missing from American fiction. Even college life has been scanted as a subject. An underestimated book, Bucklin Moon's *Without Magnolias* (1949) is a well-done, serious presentation of a Southern Negro college. It includes sharp *aperçus* and insights, surprising at first when one realizes that the author was a white man, but not surprising when one recalls that George Washington Cable, Mark Twain, Albion Tourgee and Lillian Smith also wore their color lightly.

Moon's book on Negro academics is broader and more firmly based than J. Saunders Redding's novel on college life, *Stranger and Alone* (1950). More revealing autobiographically than fictionally, *Stranger and Alone* lacks the power and insight that mark *No Day of Triumph*, Redding's distinguished work of reportage, whose gallery of people—Southern, Northern, Negro, white—and whose searching commentary deserve to be better known. Redding's *On Being Negro in America* has the ambitious reach of books so titled; it grasps both truths and truisms. Although Redding terms it his valedictory to "race," it is no such thing, of course, nor could it be. Instead it signaled the beginning of a career as a sort of Negro roving ambassador, depriving us of one of the sharpest and best informed observers of the American scene. Carl Rowan's career is similar: after keen and persuasive reportage on the Negro in America in *South of Freedom* and *Go Down to Sorrow,* he then traveled and reported on India, Pakistan and Southeast Asia in *The Pitiful and the Proud.*

While as Director of the United States Information Agency Rowan presented America's cause to the world in Washington, D. C., Chester Himes raged at America's ways in Paris. As rebellious as Richard Wright but even more nihilistic and despairing, Himes has most fully presented the misanthropic, frustrated, furious young Negro, insulted and injured, uprooted and lost in the novels, *If He Hollers* (1945), *Lonely Crusade* (1947), and the largely autobiographical *Third Generation* (1954), a searing attack on the Negro bourgeoisie. No one can stay long near Himes's characters and feel at all easy with such "racialistic" abstractions as humility, forgivingness, cheerfulness and contentment.

Another expatriate, Julian Mayfield, wrote three significant novels before departing for the greener fields of Ghana. These were *The Hit, The Long Night* (1958) and *The Grand Parade* (1960). The first two, with Ann Petry's *The Street* (1946), are authentic slices of Harlem life, refuting the repeated lie of Harlem the playground. Many young Negro novelists have found that one novel in everyman's life and have written it in sociological and naturalistic terms, generally in urban settings, under the influence of Dreiser, Farrell, and especially Wright and Himes. William Gardner Smith's *The Last of the Conquerors* centers around the life of Negroes in the armed forces occupying Germany, and the outlook is new and sharp. John O. Killens, in what might be considered a "proletarian novel" showed a man's upbringing in *Youngblood,* a powerful but more hopeful book than any by Wright or Himes. Killens's *And Then We Heard the Thunder* (1962) is so far the best treatment of the Negro soldier in fiction. It is an angry book but rich in sardonic humor and a wide gallery of interesting, diversified people. Similarly sardonic and powerful though less successful as a novel is Hari Rhodes's *A Chosen Few* which deals with Negroes in the Marine Corps. The same qualities of rage, violence, and honesty mark the novels of John Williams, whose novels *Sissie* (1963) and *The Angry Ones,* and the anthology *The Angry Black* (1962), mark a newcomer of promise and strength.

Of fiction dealing with Negro life during the last two decades, Ralph Ellison's *Invisible Man* has invited most critical attention. This picaresque novel, something of a black *Candide,* stirred so much interest and belief in its variety and authenticity of characters, both Negro and white, that the old stereotypes were shaken. Carrying his naive hero from boyhood in Oklahoma to manhood in Harlem, Ellison gives a wonderful series of vignettes, rich in farce, comedy, irony, satire, melodrama, tragedy and grotesquerie, all set solidly in Negro experience. Like Voltaire's *Candide,* Ellison's hero ends up by cultivating his garden in an underground hole in Gotham. Though he is defeated, his creator is triumphant, and one of his triumphs is that it will be hard for cardboard heroes and villains to occupy the fictional stage any longer.

Because of Ellison's silence since *Invisible Man*, broken intermittently, of course, by his perceptive essays, James Baldwin is today the best known Negro writer, and partly because of the paper-back revolution is probably the best known American Negro writer in history. *Go Tell It On the Mountain* is a winning novel, rich in emotion and understanding, leaning heavily upon Baldwin's autobiography, as almost all of his work does, including his latest, the widely discussed *Another Country*. Baldwin's essays, especially *The Fire Next Time*, mark him as the most powerful and prophetic voice of the young militants in SNCC and CORE. There is such a bond between him and the youngsters that one hopes he has at last come home again. Gifted as a novelist and essayist, he has written two startling plays: *Blues for Mr. Charlie*, a play written in the wake of Birmingham, exacerbated and ferocious, but to at least one critic less lasting than *Amen Corner*, which the gifted Frank Silvera has staged on both coasts.

When *Amen Corner* had its premiere several years ago at Howard University it seemed to some that here was the finest grasp of Negro life and character yet encountered on a stage. Lorraine Hansberry's *Raisin in the Sun* belongs in its fine company, for presentation of people, people who happen to be Negroes, people of a different category from Porgy and Scarlet Sister Mary and Lulu Belle and Uncle Tom and The Octoroon. And Ossie Davis's hilarious *Purlie Victorious* also has people in it, of a different section, hemisphere, world, universe from Amos an' Andy, Stepin Fetchit and Uncle Remus. Incidentally, the humor of Dick Gregory, Jackie Mabley and Godfrey Cambridge belongs with this type of genuine Negro humor, as remote from the usual radio, movie farce as Charlie Chaplin is from the Katzenjammer Kids.

The plays of LeRoi Jones have also caused a stir. In spite of the considerable talents of this young poet-playwright, the unadulterated hatred of his plays seems factitious, not real. That white Greenwich Village audiences are titillated by *The Toilet*, the *Dutchman* and *The Slave* is certain, but this says more about them than about Negro life in America. A wave of masochism swings in; cries of *peccavi, peccavimus* fill the air; but this does not mean that the cause is art or insight or revelation.

A healthier kind of writing, less desperate, less frenetic, but as concerned with injustice is the developing literature of the freedom movement. Times of gestation, conception, birth and early nurturing of a revolution are not necessarily times that produce creative literature. The types of writing for these activists are tracts, pamphlets, advertisements, slogans, squibs, lampoons, parodies, burlesques. Closest to fiction and drama are the autobiographical narratives, fragments recollected in whatever tranquillity is permitted by jail sentences or returns to campuses and jobs. There are signs of such autobiographical renderings from such activists as Michael Thelwell, Len Holt, Claude Brown, Bill Mahoney, and Charles Cobb, to name only the few freedom fighters whom the author knows best. A good anthology has just been issued by *Freedomways* which is called *Mississippi: Opening the Closed Society*. This issue is earnest that the novels and poems and plays will come. As long as these young people hold fiercely to their hope, and to their conviction, singingly proclaimed, that "We Shall Overcome," the good writing will someday come. We can wait. These young people are in a worthy tradition: that of David Walker, David Ruggles, Frederick Douglass, Harriet Tubman, Sojourner Truth, William Nell, Martin Delany, Henry Highland Garnet, Samuel Ringgold Ward and William Wells Brown, that driving wedge of Negro propagandists who functioned so ably a century ago.

V

But this, it seems, is where I came in. The images of Negroes in fiction and drama have increased in number, and their manifold identities have been further recognized. More readers and writers seem aware of the humanist's concern "that the discovery and explanation of the individual . . . in space and time shall not be reduced to a point where his particular character is lost"; where he becomes:

> indistinguishable from any other person who possesses the same race, milieu and moment. . . . Even when we turn . . . to the study of communities and states, cultures and civilizations, we are equally anxious to make every possible distinction, to recognize every qualitative difference. In the humanist's quest, similarities, whether between individual human beings or between cultural patterns, are useful only insofar as they lead to the discovery of differences; these resemblances are never absolute, they are merely means to discourse, and they have a way of disappearing just as soon as one turns from the larger group to examine the individuals in whom a fleeting resemblance has been caught.[10]

Stereotyping is on the way out. Besides the enormous, comprehensive literature on races and cultures, readers, theatregoers, creative writers and critics have developed a sophistication boding ill for the allegorical, the simplistic, the superficial characterization of the past. The dangers and unreality of schematic, too well-made plotting; the weakness of

---

[10] Harcourt Brown, "Science and the Human Comedy: Voltaire," in *Science and the Modern Mind*, ed. by G. Holton (Boston: 1958), p. 20.

flat and one-sided characters in distinction to round and complex characters; the pronounced effect of setting on character so that setting itself becomes a character; the ineffectuality of thesis-ridden novels; all of these have grown clearer. Readers and writers learn that deductive, expository and direct delineation is patently inferior to inductive, indirect delineation; that readers welcome discovery instead of indoctrination; that showing, in fiction, is better than telling. So the expounding, grouping, consigning, assuming, relegating phases of stereotyping disappear.

Fiction and drama have led in the destruction or at least the displacement of the stereotypes. The social revolution at home and the emergent nations abroad have had repercussions in the cultural world.[11] A willingness—nay, an eagerness—to learn the truth is coupled with a willingness to grant dignity to others. Even Hollywood has made a belated start toward pictures of genuine Negro life. It is television, however, that has rushed in where movies and even Broadway long feared to tread.

Nevertheless, stereotyping is not altogether out. The hipster generation, Norman Mailer pontificates, was attracted to what *the Negro* had to offer (italics mine, but let Mailer take over):

> In such places as Greenwich Village, a *ménage-à-trois* was completed—the bohemian and the juvenile delinquent came face-to-face with the Negro, and the hipster was a fact in American life— And in this wedding of the white and black it was the Negro who brought the cultural dowry. Any Negro who wishes to live must live with danger from his first day, and no experience can be casual to him, no Negro can saunter down a street with any real certainty that violence will not visit him on his walk. The cameos of security for the average white: mother and the home, job and the family, are

---

[11] As one instance: nearly forty years ago, when a Negro husband was to be seen kissing his white wife's hand in O'Neill's *All God's Chillun Got Wings*, a mob was threatened in New York City. Today both on and off Broadway interracial liaisons are common in plays, e.g.: *The Owl and the Pussy Cat*, *No Strings*, *The Slave*. Odets's *Golden Boy* was wrenched from a play about an Italian pugilist violinist to one about a Negro pugilist-song-and-dance-man whose sweetheart is a white woman.

Concerning television: one single Negro viewer, glowing when he sees his people in unfamiliar roles still wearies of the word "dignity" in its millionth application and wishes (1) that the Negro lawyer might lose at least one case (Perry Mason did); (2) that Negroes might be arrested for some crimes that they did commit; (3) that some Negroes not so unfailingly noble and sacrificial might also be shown; and (4) that Negroes might be allowed to use language not so stilted—that like other characters, they might be permitted one slave expression, one split verb, one modifier that dangles, and God save us one—just one dialectical trope. Nevertheless if one has to choose between the ennoblement and Aunt Jemima, this reviewer will have to endure the ennoblement.

not even a mockery to millions of Negroes; they are impossible. The Negro has the simplest of alternatives: live a life of constant humility or ever-threatening danger. In such a pass where paranoia is as vital to survival as blood, the Negro had stayed alive and begun to grow by following the need of his body where he could. Knowing in the cells of his existence that life was war, nothing but war, the Negro (all exceptions admitted) could rarely afford the sophisticated inhibitions of civilization, and so he kept for his survival the art of the primitive, he lived in the enormous present, he subsisted for his Saturday night kicks, relinquishing the pleasures of the mind for the more obligatory pleasures of the body, and in his music he gave voice to the character and quality of his existence, to his rage and the infinite variations of joy, lust, languor, growl, cramp, pinch, scream and despair of his orgasm.[12]

To which, astounded, one Negro at least can only say, slipping into a consonant Freudian argot: "Poppycock." This is a Greenwich Village refurbishing of old stereotypes.[13] The *ménage-à-trois* of which Mailer speaks derives from this earlier trio (1) the Abolitionist insistence on the utter debasement of slavery, (2) the Marxist theory of the class struggle transferred to race, and (3) the glorification of the exotic primitive rife in the miscalled Jazz Age. If Mailer seeks the real *ménage-à-trois* that birthed this monstrosity let him seek out Harriet Beecher Stowe, Earl Browder, and Carl Van Vechten, with James Ford dropping in. What an unholy triangle that turned out to be!

Concerning stereotyping even Robert Penn Warren has his quandaries; uncertain as to who speaks today for the Negro, he admits to a bewildering diversity among the subjects of his long search. This is a promising sign, for Warren once was sure about the Negro, using a buzzard to speak for him the prognostication: "Nigger, your breed ain't metaphysical." Today while discussing a Negro metaphysical novelist, Warren praises Ralph Ellison for theorizing about "the basic unity of experience . . ." and also about "the rich variety" of Negroes and their experience in American life. He quotes Ellison approvingly:

> For even as his life toughens the Negro, even as it brutalizes him, sensitizes him, dulls him, goads him to anger, moves him to irony, sometimes fracturing and sometimes affirming his hopes . . . it *conditions* him to deal with *his* life, and no mere abstraction in somebody's head.[14]

---

[12] *Advertisements for Myself* (New York: 1959), p. 306.

[13] The quadroon, octoroon hedonists who throng the fiction of the Beats are merely the granddaughters of the tragic mulattoes of the old stereotype. Kerouac's *Subterraneans* has a close cousin to the Tawny Messalina of Seventh Avenue in Van Vechten's *Nigger Heaven*. She has been here before.

[14] *Who Speaks for the Negro* (New York: 1965), p. 351.

Warren finds Ellison refreshing for reinspecting the "standard formula-
tions," the "mere stereotypes" of the Revolution. Well, the sun do
move.

But the writer feels no need to default to Warren, even though
Warren is currently the authority on the Civil War and Segregation
and, in some quarters, of the Civil Rights Revolution. For this is where
I came in. Over thirty years ago I wrote:

> One manifest truth, however, is this: the sincere, sensitive artist,
> willing to go beneath the clichés of popular belief to get at an under-
> lying reality, will be wary of confining a race's entire character to a
> half-dozen narrow grooves. He will hardly have the temerity to say
> that his necessarily limited observation of a few Negroes in a re-
> stricted environment can be taken as the last word about some
> mythical *the* Negro. He will hesitate to do this, even though he had
> a Negro mammy, or spent a night in Harlem, or has been a Negro
> all his life. The writer submits that such an artist is the only one
> worth listening to, although the rest are legion.[15]

In the intervening years there have been many writers worth listening
to, though not so many as hoped for, who saw Negro life steadily and
whole. Nevertheless, clichés and stereotypes linger, and even burgeon.
The conclusion, in these much later years, still holds. It is here that I
take my stand.

QUESTIONS

1. This essay, written in 1966, summarizes over a century of
change in the depiction of blacks by both white and black American
writers. In general, how does Brown characterize the changing stereotypes of the "contented slave," the "plantation tradition," the "brute
Negro," the "tragic mulatto," and the "exotic primitive"?

2. Brown feels that the black poets of the twenties spoke more
deeply and truthfully than the novelists of that period. What new
qualities did poets such as Claude McKay, Langston Hughes, Countee
Cullen, and James Weldon Johnson bring to their writing?

3. In the thirties, Brown states, there was a shift in the literary
image of the blacks. What was the change, and what were some of the
forces he cites that brought it about?

4. Brown suggests that advances in portraying blacks were,
ironically, "strangled" at least twice by white "radical theory." What

---

[15] "Negro Character as Seen by White Authors," *Journal of Negro Education*, II,
2 (April, 1933), p. 203.

evidence does he find for this in the early abolitionist writing and in the later "proletarian" novels?

5. Both Joel Chandler Harris and E. C. L. Adams were white writers who used Negro folk material in their writings about blacks. What is Brown's evaluation of their treatment of this material?

6. What important contributions were made by "expatriate writers" such as Chester Himes, Julian Mayfield, and John O. Killens?

7. In part V of his essay, Brown states that "stereotyping is on the way out." What reasons does he give to support this statement?

8. What changes in aesthetic values does Brown cite that affected both black and white literature?

American Negro Literature

J. Saunders Redding

There is this about literature by American Negroes—it has uncommon resilience. Three times within this century it has been done nearly to death: once by indifference, once by opposition, and once by the unbounded enthusiasm of its well-meaning friends.

By 1906, Charles W. Chesnutt, the best writer of prose fiction the race had produced, was silent; Paul Laurence Dunbar, the most popular poet, was dead. After these two, at least in the general opinion, there were no other Negro writers. Booker Washington had published *Up from Slavery*, but Washington was no writer—he was the orator and the organizer of the march to a questionable new Canaan. The poetic prose of Du Bois, throbbing in *The Souls of Black Folk*, had not yet found its audience. Polemicists like Monroe Trotter, Kelly, Miller and George Forbes were faint whispers in a lonesome wood. Indifference had stopped the ears of all but the most enlightened who, as often as not, were derisively labeled "nigger lovers."

But this indifference had threatened even before the turn of the century. Dunbar felt it, and the purest stream of his lyricism was made bitter and all but choked by it. Yearning for the recognition of his talent as it expressed itself in the pure English medium, he had to content himself with a kindly, but condescending praise of his dialect pieces. Time and again he voiced the sense of frustration brought on by the neglect of what he undoubtedly considered his best work. Writing dialect, he told James Weldon Johnson, was "the only way he could get them to listen to him." His literary friend and sponsor, William D. Howells, at that time probably the most influential critic in America, passing over Dunbar's verse in pure English with only a glance, urged him to write "of his own race in its own accents of our English."

During Dunbar's lifetime, his pieces in pure English appeared more or less on sufferance. The very format of the 1901 edition of *Lyrics of the Hearthside*, the book in which most of his non-dialect poetry was

FROM *The American Scholar*, Vol. 18, No. 2 (Spring 1949). Copyright © 1949 by the United Chapters of Phi Beta Kappa. Reprinted by permission of the publishers.

published, suggests this. No fancy binding on this book, no handsome paper, no charming, illustrative photographs. *Lyrics of the Hearthside* was the least publicized of all his books of poetry, and four lines from his "The Poet" may tell why.

> He sang of love when earth was young,
> And love itself was in his lays,
> But, ah, the world it turned to praise
> A jingle in a broken tongue.

Enough has been said about the false concepts, the stereotypes which were effective—and to some extent are still effective—in white America's thinking about the Negro for the point not to be labored here. History first, and then years of insidious labor to perpetuate what history had wrought, created these stereotypes. According to them, the Negro was a buffoon, a harmless child of nature, a dangerous despoiler (the concepts were contradictory), an irresponsible beast of devilish cunning —soulless, ambitionless and depraved. The Negro, in short, was a higher species of some creature that was not quite man.

What this has done to writing by American Negroes could easily be imagined, even without the documentation, which is abundant. No important critic of writing by American Negroes has failed to note the influence of the concept upon it. Sterling Brown, one of the more searching scholars in the field, gives it scathing comment in "The Negro Author and His Publisher." James Weldon Johnson touches upon it in his preface to the 1931 edition of his anthology, but he does so even more cogently in "The Negro Author's Dilemma." The introduction to Countee Cullen's *Caroling Dusk* is a wry lament over it. In *The New Negro*, Alain Locke expresses the well-founded opinion that the Negro "has been a stock figure perpetuated as an historical fiction partly in innocent sentimentalism, partly in deliberate reactionism."

There can be no question as to the power of the traditional concepts. The Negro writer reacted to them in one of two ways. Either he bowed down to them, writing such stories as would do them no violence; or he went to the opposite extreme and wrote for the purpose of invalidating, or at least denying, the tradition. Dunbar did the former. Excepting only a few, his short stories depict Negro characters as whimsical, simple, folksy, not-too-bright souls, all of whose social problems are little ones, and all of whose emotional cares can be solved by the intellectual or spiritual equivalent of a stick of red peppermint candy. It is of course significant that three of his four novels are not about Negroes at all; and the irony of depicting himself as a white youth in his spiritual autobiography, *The Uncalled,* needs no comment.

Charles Chesnutt's experience is also to the point. When his stories began appearing in the *Atlantic Monthly* in 1887, it was not generally known that their author was a Negro. Stories like "The Gray Wolf's

Ha'nt" and "The Goophered Grapevine" were so detached and objective that the author's race could not have been detected from a reading of them. The editor of the *Atlantic Monthly*, Walter H. Page, fearing that public acknowledgment of it would do the author's work harm, was reluctant to admit that Chesnutt was a Negro, and the fact of his race was kept a closely guarded secret for a decade.

It was this same fear that led to the rejection of Chesnutt's first novel, *The House behind the Cedars*, for "a literary work by an American of acknowledged color was a doubtful experiment . . . entirely apart from its intrinsic merit." The reception of Chesnutt's later books—those that came after 1900—was to prove that literary works by an "American of color" were more than doubtful experiments. *The Colonel's Dream* and *The Marrow of Tradition* did not pay the cost of the paper and the printing. They were honest probings at the heart of a devilish problem; they were, quite frankly, propaganda. But the thing that made the audience of the day indifferent to them was their attempt to override the concepts that were the props of the dialect tradition. Had Chesnutt not had a reputation as a writer of short stories (which are, anyway, his best work), it is likely that his novels would not have been published at all.

The poetry of Dunbar and the prose of Chesnutt proved that even with the arbitrary limitations imposed upon them by historical convention, Negro writers could rise to heights of artistic expression. They could even circumvent the convention, albeit self-consciously, and create credible white characters in a credible white milieu.

II

After about 1902, indifference began to crystallize into opposition to the culture-conscious, race-conscious Negro seeking honest answers to honest questions. It was opposition to the Negro's democratic ambitions which were just then beginning to burgeon. It was opposition to the Negro who was weary of his role of clown, scapegoat, doormat. And it was, of course, opposition to the Negro writer who was honest and sincere and anxious beyond the bounds of superimposed racial polity.

There is danger here of over-simplifying a long and complex story. Even with the advantage of hindsight, it is hard to tell what is cause and what effect. But let us have a look at some of the more revealing circumstances. In 1902 came Thomas Dixon's *The Leopard's Spots*, and three years later *The Clansman*. They were both tremendously popular. In 1906 there were race riots in Georgia and Texas, in 1908 in Illinois. . . . By this later year, too, practically all of the Southern states had disfranchised the Negro and made color caste legal. . . . The Negro's talent for monkeyshines had been exploited on the stage, and coon songs (some by James Weldon Johnson and his brother!) had attained wide popularity. Meantime, in 1904, Thomas Nelson Page had published the bible of reactionism, *The Negro, the Southerner's Problem*. And, probably most cogent fact of all, Booker Washington had reached the position of undisputed leader of American Negroes by advocating a racial policy strictly in line with the traditional concept.

There had been a time when the old concept of the Negro had served to ease his burden. He had been laughed at, tolerated, and genially despaired of as hopeless in a modern, dynamic society. White Americans had become used to a myth—had, indeed, convinced themselves that myth was reality. All the instruments of social betterment—schools, churches, lodges—adopted by colored people were the subjects of ribald jokes and derisive laughter. Even the fact that the speeches which Booker Washington was making up and down the country could have been made only by a really intelligent and educated man did not strike them as a contradiction of the concept. And anyway, there was this about Washington: he was at least half-white, and white blood in that proportion excused and accounted for many a thing, including being intelligent, lunching with President Theodore Roosevelt, and getting an honorary degree from Harvard.

Today any objective judgment of Booker Washington's basic notion must be that it was an extension of the old tradition framed in new terms. He preached a message of compromise, of humility, of patience. Under the impact of social change the concept was modified to include the stereotype of the Negro as satisfied peasant, a docile servitor under the stern but kindly eye of the white boss; a creature who had a place, knew it, and would keep it unless he got *bad* notions from somewhere. The merely laughable coon had become also the cheap laborer who could be righteously exploited for his own good and to the greater glory of God. By this addition to the concept, the Negro-white status quo— the condition of inferior-superior caste—could be maintained in the face of profound changes in the general society.

What this meant to the Negro artist and writer was that he must, if he wished an audience, adhere to the old forms and the acceptable patterns. It meant that he must work within the limitations of the concept, or ignore his racial kinship altogether and leave unsounded the profoundest depths of the peculiar experiences which were his by reason of his race. But fewer and fewer Negro writers were content with the limitations. The number of dialect pieces (the term includes the whole tradition) written after 1907 is very small indeed. Among Negro writers the tradition had lost its force and its validity. White writers like Julia Peterkin and Gilmore Millen, and, in a different way, Carl Van Vechten and DuBose Heyward, were to lend it a spurious strength down through the 1920's.

Negro writers of unmistakable talent chose the second course, and some of them won high critical praise for their work in non-racial themes.

Their leader was William Stanley Braithwaite. Save only a few essays written at the behest of his friend, W. E. B. Du Bois, nothing that came from his pen had anything about it to mark it as Negro. His leading essays in the Boston *Transcript*, his anthologies of magazine verse, and his own poetry, might just as well have been written by someone with no background in the provocative experience of being colored in America.

Though the other Negro poets of this genre (which was not entirely a genre) developed a kind of dilettanist virtuosity, none carried it to Braithwaite's amazing lengths of self-conscious contrivance. They were simpler and more conventional in their apostasy. Alice Dunbar, the widow of Paul, wrote sonnets of uncommon skill and beauty. Georgia Johnson and Anne Spenser were at home in the formal lyric, and James Weldon Johnson in "The White Witch" and "My City" set a very high standard for his fellow contributors to the *Century Magazine*.

But given the whole web of circumstance—empirical, historic, racial, psychological—these poets must have realized that they could not go on in this fashion. With a full tide of race-consciousness bearing in upon them individually and as a group, they could not go on forever denying their racehood. To try to do this at all was symptomatic of neurotic strain. They could not go on, and they did not. The hardiest of them turned to expression of another kind the moment the pressure was off.

The pressure was not off for another decade and a half. As a matter of fact, it mounted steadily. For all of Booker Washington's popularity and idelogical appeal among whites, who had set him up as *the* leader of the Negro race, and for all of his power, there was rebellion against him in the forward ranks of Negroes. Rebellion against Washington meant dissatisfaction with the social and economic goals which he had persuaded white Americans were the proper goals for the Negro race. The whites had not counted on this disaffection, and their reaction to it was wilful, blind opposition.

What had happened was that Booker Washington, with the help of the historic situation and the old concept, had so thoroughly captured the minds of those white people who were kindly disposed to Negroes that not another Negro had a chance to be heard. Negro schools needing help could get it from rich and powerful whites only through Booker Washington. Negro social thought wanting a sounding board could have it only with the sanction of the Principal of Tuskegee. Negro politicians were helpless without his endorsement. Negro seekers after jobs of any consequence in either public or private capacities begged recommendations from Booker Washington.

This despotic power—and there is scarcely another term for it—was stultifying to many intelligent Negroes, especially in the North. White editors, who would have published anything under the signature of Booker Washington, consistently rejected all but the most innocuous work of other Negroes. Publishers were not interested in the ideas of Negroes unless those ideas conformed to Washington's, or in creative work by and about Negroes unless they fell into the old pattern.

So intelligent, articulate Negroes grew insurgent, and the leader of this insurgence was W. E. B. Du Bois. Nor was his the only voice raised in protest. Charles Chesnutt spoke out, and so did John Hope and Kelly Miller. In 1900 the *Chicago Defender* had been founded, and in 1901 Monroe Trotter's *Boston Guardian*. Courageous as these polemical organs were, they had not yet grown into full effectiveness. Neither had Du Bois, but he was growing fast. By 1903 the Atlanta University Studies of the Negro were coming out regularly under his editorship. In that year he published *The Souls of Black Folk*, which contained the essay "Of Mr. Booker T. Washington and Others," sharply critical of the Tuskegee leader. Du Bois was in on the founding of the National Association for the Advancement of Colored People, and in 1910 he became editor of the new monthly, the *Crisis*.

From the very first the *Crisis* was much more than the official organ of the N.A.A.C.P. It was a platform for the expression of all sorts of ideas that ran counter to the notion of Negro inferiority. Excepting such liberal and nonpopular journals as the *Atlantic Monthly* and *World's Work* and the two or three Negro newspapers that had not been bought or throttled by the "Tuskegee Machine," the *Crisis* was the only voice the Negro had. The opposition to that voice was organized around the person and the philosophy of Booker Washington, and there were times when this opposition all but drowned out the voice.

Nevertheless protestation and revolt were becoming bit by bit more powerful reagents in the social chemistry that produced the New Negro. Year by year more Negroes were transformed—and a lot of them needed transforming. Once James Weldon Johnson himself had written "coon songs" and been content to carol with sweet humility "Lift Every Voice and Sing." When Johnson wrote it in 1900, it had the approval of Booker Washington and became the "Negro National Anthem." Then followed Johnson's period of apostasy and such jejune pieces as "The Glory of the Day Was in Her Face," among others. But in 1912, when he was already forty-one, he wrote the novel *The Autobiography of an Ex-Colored Man*, and in 1917 he cried out bitterly that Negroes must cease speaking "servile words" and must "stand erect and without fear."

III

Other factors than simple protest contributed to the generation of the New Negro. In the first place, the notions regarding the Old Negro were based on pure myth. The changes occurring at the onset of war in Europe sloughed off some of the emotional and intellectual accretions, and the Negro stood partially revealed for what he was—a fellow whose opportunities had been narrowed by historical fallacies, "a creature of moral debate," but a man pretty much as other men. The war, which made him an inter-sectional migrant, proved that he, too, sought more economic opportunities, the protection of laws even-handedly administered, the enlargement of democracy. He, too, was a seeker for the realities in the American dream.

But when in 1917 the Negro was called upon to protect that dream with his blood, he revealed himself more fully. He asked questions and demanded answers. Whose democracy? he wanted to know; and why, and wherefore? There followed the promises, which were certainly sincerely meant in the stress of the times. Then came the fighting and dying—and, finally, came a thing called Peace. But in 1919 and after, there were the race riots in the nation's capital, in Chicago, in Chester, Pennsylvania, and in East St. Louis.

By this time the New Negro movement was already stirring massively along many fronts. In the 1920's Negroes cracked through the prejudices that had largely confined them to supernumerary roles on Broadway. *Shuffle Along* was praised as "a sparkling, all-Negro musical of unusual zest and talent." Charles Gilpin's portrayal of the Emperor Jones was the dramatic triumph of 1921. The Garvey Movement, fast getting out of bounds, swept the country like a wildfire. James Weldon Johnson published an anthology of Negro verse. The monumental historical studies of the Negro were begun by Carter Woodson. *The Gift of Black Folk, Color, Fire In the Flint, Weary Blues, God's Trombones, Walls of Jericho*, and *Home to Harlem* had all been published, read, discussed, praised or damned by 1928.

Fortunately some of the talents that produced these works were genuine. Had this not been so, the New Negro movement in art and literature would surely have come to nothing. The best of Johnson, Hughes, Cullen, McKay, Fisher and Du Bois would have lived without the movement, but the movement without them would have gone the way of mah-jongg. Their work considerably furthered the interest of white writers and critics in Negro material and Negro art expression. Whatever else Eugene O'Neill, Paul Rosenfeld and DuBose Heyward did, they gave validity to the new concept of the Negro as material for serious artistic treatment.

Writing by Negroes beginning with this period and continuing into the early thirties had two distinct aspects. The first of these was extremely arty, self-conscious and experimental. Jean Toomer's *Cane* and the "racial-rhythm" and jazz-rhythm poetry of Hughes represent it most notably, while the magazines *Harlem* and *Fire*, which published a quantity of nonsense by writers unheard of since, were its special organs. But the times were themselves arty and experimental. That Negro writers could afford to be touched by these influences was a good sign. It was healthy for them to be blown upon by the winds of literary freedom—even of license—that blew upon e.e. cummings, Dos Passos and Hemingway. If their self-conscious experimentation proved nothing lasting, it at least worked no harm.

One searches in vain for a phrase to characterize the exact impulses behind the second aspect, which is the one best remembered. It ·was chock-full of many contradictory things. It showed itself naïve and sophisticated, hysterical and placid, frivolous and sober, free and enslaved. It is simple enough to attribute this contrariety to the effects of the war; but the atavistic release of certain aberrant tendencies in writing by Negroes in this period cannot be matched in all the rest of contemporary writing. The period produced the poignant beauty of Johnson's *God's Trombones* and the depressing futility of Thurman's *The Blacker the Berry*. Within a span of five years McKay wrote the wholesome *Banjo* and the pointlessly filthy *Banana Bottom*. The Hughes who wrote "I've Known Rivers" and "Mother to Son" could also find creative satisfaction in the bizarre "The Cat and the Saxophone."

The mass mind of white America fastened upon the exotic and the atavistic elements and fashioned them into a fad, the commercialized products of which were manufactured in Harlem. That that Harlem itself was largely synthetic did not seem to matter. It was "nigger heaven." There, the advertised belief was, Dullness was dethroned: Gaiety was king! The rebels from Sauk Center and Winesburg, Main Street and Park Avenue, sought carnival in Harlem. "Life," the burden of the dithyrambics ran, "had surge and sweep there, and blood-pounding savagery."

Commercialism was the bane of the Negro renaissance of the twenties. Jazz music became no longer the uninhibited expression of unlearned music-makers, but a highly sophisticated pattern of musical sounds. The "Charleston" and the "Black Bottom" went down to Broadway and Park Avenue. Losing much of its folk value, the blues became the "torch song" eloquently sung by Ruth Etting and Helen Morgan. Negro material passed into the less sincere hands of white artists, and Negro writers themselves, from a high pitch of creation, fell relatively and pathetically silent.

IV

When Richard Wright's *Uncle Tom's Children* was published in 1938, only the least aware did not realize that a powerful new pen was employing itself in stern and terrible material; when *Native Son* appeared in 1940, even the least aware realized it. The first book is a clinical study of human minds under the stress of violence; the second is a clinical study of the social being under the cumulative effects of organized repression. The two books complement each other. The theme of both is prejudice, conceptual prejudgment—the effects of this upon the human personality. For Wright deals only incidentally—and for dramatic purposes, and because of the authenticity of empiricism —with *Negro* and *white*. "Bigger Thomas was not black all the time," Wright wrote in "How Bigger Was Born." "He was white, too, and there were literally millions of him, *everywhere*. . . . Certain modern experiences were creating types of personalities whose existence ignored racial and national lines. . . ."

Some critics have said that the wide appeal of Wright's work (it has been translated into a dozen languages) is due to the sensationalism in it, but one can have serious doubts that the sensationalism comes off well in translation. What does come off well is the concept of the primary evil of prejudice. This all peoples would understand, and a delineation of its effects, particular though it be, interests them in the same way and for the same reason that love interests them. *Black Boy*, which does not prove the point, does not deny it either. Even here it may be argued that Wright delineates and skewers home the point that "to live habitually as a superior among inferiors . . . is a temptation and a hubris, inevitably deteriorating."

So Wright is a new kind of writer in the ranks of Negroes. He has extricated himself from the dilemma of writing exclusively for a Negro audience and limiting himself to a glorified and race-proud picture of Negro life, and of writing exclusively for a white audience and being trapped in the old stereotypes and fixed opinions that are bulwarks against honest creation. Negro writers traditionally have been impaled upon one or the other horn of this dilemma, sometimes in spite of their efforts to avoid it. Langston Hughes was sincere when he declared, back in the twenties, that Negro writers cared nothing for the pleasure or displeasure of either a white or a colored audience—he was sincere, but mistaken.

A writer writes for an audience. Until recently Negro writers have not believed that the white audience and the colored audience were essentially alike, because, in fact, they have not been essentially alike. They have been kept apart by a wide socio-cultural gulf, by differences of concept, by cultivated fears, ignorance, race- and caste-consciousness. Now that gulf is closing, and Negro writers are finding it easier to appeal to the two audiences without being either false to the one or subservient to the other. Thus Margaret Walker, writing for the two audiences now becoming one, can carry away an important poetry prize with her book *For My People*. No longer fearing the ancient interdiction, Chester Himes in *If He Hollers Let Him Go* and *Lonely Crusade* writes of the sexual attraction a white woman feels for a Negro man. In *Knock On Any Door* Willard Motley can concern himself almost entirely with white characters. On the purely romantic and escapist side, Frank Yerby's *The Foxes of Harrow* sells over a million copies, and

The Vixens and *The Golden Hawk* over a half-million each. Anthologists no longer think it risky to collect, edit and issue the works of Negro writers.

Facing up to the tremendous challenge of appealing to two audiences, Negro writers are extricating themselves from what has sometimes seemed a terrifying dilemma. Working honestly in the material they know best, they are creating for themselves a new freedom. Though what is happening seems very like a miracle, it has been a long, long time preparing. Writing by American Negroes has never before been in such a splendid state of health, nor had so bright and shining a future before it.

QUESTIONS

1. Redding, writing in 1949, concludes his essay by stating that black writers were finding it easier to appeal to both black and white audiences than ever before. According to his historical study of black literature, how had the black writer formerly reacted to and confronted the problem of his relationship to his audience?

2. What is Redding's evaluation of the role Booker T. Washington played in the evolution of black literature?

3. In his discussion of the New Negro movement, Redding suggests that in the nineteen-twenties and thirties black writing had two distinct aspects or trends: the "extremely arty, self-conscious and experimental," and an aspect best characterized as "exotic" and "atavistic." How does he explain and evaluate these trends?

4. What does Redding mean when he states that the "rebels from Sauk Center and Winesburg, Main Street and Park Avenue, sought carnival in Harlem"?

5. Why, according to Redding, was the era of "unbounded enthusiasm" and "commercialism" also the "bane of the Negro Renaissance in the twenties"?

6. In part IV of his essay, Redding discusses the influence and importance of Richard Wright. He says Wright was "a new kind of writer in the ranks of Negroes." How was Wright's approach different from that of black writers before him?

The Origin and Growth of Afro-American Literature

John Henrik Clarke

Africans were great story tellers long before their first appearance in Jamestown, Virginia, in 1619. The rich and colorful history, art and folklore of West Africa, the ancestral home of most Afro-Americans, present evidence of this, and more.

Contrary to a misconception which still prevails, the Africans were familiar with literature and art for many years before their contact with the Western world. Before the breaking up of the social structure of the West African states of Ghana, Melle (Mali) and Songhay, and the internal strife and chaos that made the slave trade possible, the forefathers of the Africans who eventually became slaves in the United States lived in a society where university life was fairly common and scholars were beheld with reverence.

There were in this ancestry rulers who expanded their kingdoms into empires, great and magnificent armies whose physical dimensions dwarfed entire nations into submission, generals who advanced the technique of military science, scholars whose vision of life showed foresight and wisdom, and priests who told of gods that were strong and kind. To understand fully any aspect of Afro-American life, one must realize that the black American is not without a cultural past, though he was many generations removed from it before his achievements in American literature and art commanded any appreciable attention.

I have been referring to the African Origin of Afro-American Literature and history. This preface is essential to every meaningful discussion of the role of the Afro-American in every major aspect of American life, past and present. Before getting into the main body of this talk I want to make it clear that the Black Race did not come to the United States culturally empty-handed.

I will elaborate very briefly on my statement to the effect that "the forefathers of the Africans who eventually became slaves in the United States once lived in a society where university life was fairly common and scholars were beheld with reverence."

During the period in West African history—from the early part of the fourteenth century to the time of the Moorish invasion in 1591, the City of Timbuktu, with the University of Sankore in the Songhay Empire, was the intellectual center of Africa. Black scholars were enjoying a renaissance that was known and respected throughout most of Africa and in parts of Europe. At this period in African history, the University of Sankore, at Timbuktu, was the educational capital of the Western Sudan. In his book *Timbuktu the Mysterious*, Felix DuBois gives us the following description of this period:

"The scholars of Timbuktu yielded in nothing, to the saints in their sojourns in the foreign universities of Fez, Tunis and Cairo. They astounded the most learned men of Islam by their erudition. That these Negroes were on a level with the Arabian Savants is proved by the fact that they were installed as professors in Morocco and Egypt. In contrast to this, we find that the Arabs were not always equal to the requirements of Sankore."

I will speak of only one of the great black scholars referred to in the book by Felix DuBois.

Ahmed Baba was the last chancellor of the University of Sankore. He was one of the greatest African scholars of the late sixteenth century. His life is a brilliant example of the range and depth of West African intellectual activity before the colonial era. Ahmed Baba was the author of more than 40 books; nearly every one of these books had a different theme. He was in Timbuktu when it was invaded by the Moroccans in 1592, and he was one of the first citizens to protest this occupation of his beloved home town. Ahmed Baba, along with other scholars, was imprisoned and eventually exiled to Morocco. During his expatriation from Timbuktu, his collection of 1,600 books, one of the richest libraries of his day, was lost.

Now, West Africa entered a sad period of decline. During the Moorish occupation, wreck and ruin became the order of the day. When the Europeans arrived in this part of Africa and saw these conditions, they assumed that nothing of order and value had ever existed in these countries. This mistaken impression, too often repeated, has influenced the interpretation of African and Afro-American life in history for over 400 years.

Negroes played an important part in American life, history and culture long before 1619. Our relationship to this country is as old as the country itself.

Africans first came to the new world as explorers. They participated in the exploratory expeditions of Balboa, the discoverer of the Pacific, and Cortes, the conqueror of Mexico. An African explorer helped to open up New Mexico and Arizona and prepared the way for the settlement of the Southwest. Africans also accompanied French Jesuit missionaries on their early travels through North America.

In the United States, the art and literature of the Negro people has had an economic origin. Much that is original in black American folklore, or singular in "Negro spirituals" and blues, can be traced to the economic institution of slavery and its influence upon the Negro's soul.

After the initial poetical debut of Jupiter Hammon and Phillis Wheatley, the main literary expression of the Negro was the slave narrative. One of the earliest of these narratives came from the pen of Gustavas Vassa, an African from Nigeria. This was a time of great pamphleteering in the United States. The free Africans in the North, and those who had escaped from slavery in the South, made their mark upon this time and awakened the conscience of the nation. Their lack of formal educational attainments gave their narratives a strong and rough-hewed truth, more arresting than scholarship.

Gustavas Vassa established his reputation with an autobiography, first printed in England. Vassa, born in 1745, was kidnapped by slavers when he was 11 years old and taken to America. He was placed in service on a plantation in Virginia. Eventually, he was able to purchase his freedom. He left the United States, made his home in England and became active in the British anti-slavery movement. In 1790, he presented a petition to Parliament to abolish the slave trade. His autobiography, *The Interesting Narrative of the Life of Gustavas Vassa*, was an immediate success and had to be published in five editions.

At the time when slave ships were still transporting Africans to the New World, two 18th century Negroes were writing and publishing works of poetry. The first of these was Jupiter Hammon, a slave in Queens Village, Long Island. In 1760, Hammon published *An Evening Thought: Salvation by Christ, With Penitential Cries* . . . In all probability this was the first poem published by an American Negro. His most remarkable work, "An address to the Negroes of New York," was published in 1787. Jupiter Hammon died in 1800.

Phillis Wheatley (1753–1784), like Hammon, was influenced by the religious forces of Wesley-Whitefield revival. Unlike Hammon, however, she was a writer of unusual talent. Though born in Africa, she acquired in an incredibly short time both the literary culture and the religion of her New England masters. Her writings reflect little of her race and much of the age in which she lived. She was a New England poet of the third quarter of the 18th century, and her poems reflected the poetic conventions of the Boston Puritans with whom she lived. Her fame continued long after her death in 1784 and she became one of the best known poets of New England.

Another important body of literature came out of this period. It is the literature of petition, written by free black men in the North, who were free in name only. Some of the early petitioners for justice were Caribbean-Americans who saw their plight and the plight of the Afro-Americans as one and the same.

In 18th century America, two of the most outstanding fighters for liberty and justice were the West Indians—Prince Hall and John B. Russwurm. When Prince Hall came to the United States, the nation was in turmoil. The colonies were ablaze with indignation. Britain, with a series of revenue acts, had stoked the fires of colonial discontent. In Virginia, Patrick Henry was speaking of liberty or death. The cry, "No Taxation Without Representation," played on the nerve strings of the nation. Prince Hall, then a delicate-looking teenager, often walked through the turbulent streets of Boston, an observer unobserved.

A few months before these hectic scenes, he had arrived in the United States from his home in Barbados, where he was born about 1748, the son of an Englishman and a free African woman. He was, in theory, a free man, but he knew that neither in Boston nor in Barbados were persons of African descent free in fact. At once, he questioned the sincerity of the vocal white patriots of Boston. It never seemed to have occurred to them that the announced principles motivating their action was stronger argument in favor of destroying the system of slavery. The colonists held in servitude more than a half million human beings, some of them white; yet they engaged in the contradiction of going to war to support the theory that all men were created equal.

When Prince Hall arrived in Boston, that city was the center of the American slave trade. Most of the major leaders of revolutionary movement, in fact, were slaveholders or investors in slave-supported businesses. Hall, like many other Americans, wondered: what did these men mean by freedom?

The condition of the free black men, as Prince Hall found them, was not an enviable one. Emancipation brought neither freedom nor relief from the stigma of color. They were still included with slaves, indentured servants, and Indians in the slave codes. Discriminatory laws severely circumscribed their freedom of movement.

By 1765, Prince Hall saw little change in the condition of the blacks, and though a freeman, at least in theory, he saw his people debased as though they were slaves still in bondage. These things drove him to prepare himself for leadership among his people. So, through diligence and frugality, he became a property owner, thus establishing himself in the eyes of white people as well as the blacks.

But the ownership of property was not enough. He still had to endure sneers and insults. He went to school at night, and later became a Methodist preacher. His church became the forum for his people's grievances. Ten years after his arrival in Boston, he was the accepted leader of the black community.

In 1788, Hall petitioned the Massachusetts Legislature, protesting the kidnapping of free Negroes. This was a time when American patriots were engaged in a constitutional struggle for freedom. They had proclaimed the inherent rights of all mankind to life, liberty and the pursuit of happiness. Hall dared to remind them that the black men in the

United States were human beings and as such were entitled to freedom and respect for their human personality.

Prejudice made Hall the father of African secret societies in the United States. He is the father of what is now known as Negro Masonry. Hall first sought initiation into the white Masonic Lodge in Boston, but was turned down because of his color. He then applied to the Army Lodge of an Irish Regiment. His petition was favorably received. On March 6, 1775, Hall and fourteen other black Americans were initiated in Lodge Number 441. When, on March 17, the British were forced to evacuate Boston, the Army Lodge gave Prince Hall and his colleagues a license to meet and function as a Lodge. Thus, on July 3, 1776, African Lodge No. 1 came into being. This was the first Lodge in Masonry established in America for men of African descent.

The founding of the African Lodge was one of Prince Hall's greatest achievements. It afforded the Africans in the New England area a greater sense of security, and contributed to a new spirit of unity among them. Hall's interest did not end with the Lodge. He was deeply concerned with improving the lot of his people in other ways. He sought to have schools established for the children of the free Africans in Massachusetts. Of prime importance is the fact that Prince Hall worked to secure respect for the personality of his people and also played a significant role in the downfall of the Massachusetts slave trade. He helped to prepare the groundwork for the freedom fighters of the 19th and 20th centuries, whose continuing efforts have brought the black American closer to the goal of full citizenship.

The literature of petition was continued by men like David Walker whose *Appeal*, an indictment of slavery, was published in 1829. Dynamic ministers like Samuel Ringgold Ward and Henry Highland Garnet joined the ranks of the petitioners at the time a journalist literature was being born.

Frederick Douglass, the noblest of American black men of the 19th century, was the leader of the journalist group. He established the newspaper North Star and, later, the magazine Douglass Monthly. John B. Russwurm and Samuel Cornish founded the newspaper Freedom's Journal in 1827.

In 1829, a third poet, George Moses Horton, published his book, *The Hope of Liberty*. In his second volume, *Naked Genius* (1865), he expressed his anti-slavery convictions more clearly. George Moses Horton was the first slave poet to openly protest his status.

Throughout the early part of the 19th century, the slave narrative became a new form of American literary expression.

The best known of these slave narratives came from the pen of Frederick Douglass, the foremost Negro in the anti-slavery movement. His first book was *The Narrative of the Life of Frederick Douglass* (1845). Then years later, an improved and enlarged edition, *My Bondage and My Freedom*, was published. His third autobiography, *Life and Times of Frederick Douglass,* was published in 1881 and enlarged in 1892. Douglass fought for civil rights and against lynching and the Ku Klux Klan. No abuse of justice escaped his attention and his wrath.

It was not until 1887 that an Afro-American writer emerged who was fully a master of the short story as a literary form. This writer was Charles W. Chesnutt. Chesnutt, an Ohioan by birth, became a teacher in North Carolina while still in his middle teens. He studied the traditions and superstitions of the people that he taught and later made this material into the ingredient of his best short stories. In August 1887, his short story, "The Goophered Grapevine," appeared in the Atlantic Monthly. This was the beginning of a series of stories which were later brought together in his first book, *The Conjure Woman* (1899). "The Wife of His Youth" also appeared in the Atlantic (July 1898) and gave the title to his second volume, *The Wife of His Youth and Other Stories of the Color Line* (1899). Three more stories appeared later: "Baxter's Procrustes" in the Atlantic (June, 1904), and "The Doll" and "Mr. Taylor's Funeral" in The Crisis magazine (April, 1912 and April–May, 1915).

Chesnutt's novels did not measure up to the standards he had set with his short stories, though they were all competently written. In 1928, he was awarded the Spingarn Medal for his "pioneer work as a literary artist depicting the life and struggle of Americans of Negro descent."

Paul Laurence Dunbar, a contemporary of Charles W. Chesnutt, made his reputation as a poet before extending his talent to short stories. Both Dunbar and Chesnutt very often used the same subject matter in their stories. Chesnutt was by far the better writer, and his style and attitude differed radically from Dunbar's.

Dunbar's pleasant folk tales of tradition-bound plantation black folk were more acceptable to a large white reading audience with preconceived ideas of "Negro characteristics." In all fairness, it must be said that Dunbar did not cater to this audience in all of his stories. In such stories as "The Tragedy at Three Forks," "The Lynching of Jube Benson" and "The Ordeal of Mt. Hope," he showed a deep concern and understanding of the more serious and troublesome aspects of Afro-American life. Collections of his stories are: *Folks from Dixie* (1898), *The Strength of Gideon* (1900), *In Old Plantation Days* (1903), and *The Heart of Happy Hollow* (1904). Only one of his novels, *The Sport of the Gods* (1902) is mainly concerned with Afro-American characters.

Chesnutt and Dunbar, in their day, reached a larger general reading audience than any of the black writers who came before them. The period of the slave narratives had passed. Yet, the black writer was still an oddity and a stepchild in the eyes of most critics. This attitude continued in a lessening degree throughout one of the richest and most productive periods in Afro-American writing in the United States—the period called "the Negro Renaissance." The community of Harlem was the center and spiritual godfather and midwife for this renaissance. The cultural emancipation of the Afro-American that began before the first

World War was now in full force. The black writer discovered a new voice within himself and liked the sound of it. The white writers who had been interpreting our life with an air of authority and a preponderance of error looked at last to the black writer for their next cue. In short story collections like Jean Toomer's *Cane* (1923) and Langston Hughes' *The Ways of White Folks* (1934) heretofore untreated aspects of Afro-American life were presented in an interesting manner that was unreal to some readers because it was new and so contrary to the stereotypes they had grown accustomed to.

In her book *Mules and Men* (1935), Zora Neal Hurston presented a collection of folk tales and sketches that showed the close relationship between humor and tragedy in Afro-American life. In doing this, she also fulfilled the first requirement of all books—to entertain and guide the reader through an interesting experience that is worth the time and attention it takes to absorb it. In other stories like *The Gilded Six Bits*, *Drenched in Light* and *Spunk* another side of Miss Hurston's talent was shown.

In the midst of this renaissance, two strong voices from the West Indians were heard. Claude McKay in his books *Ginger-Town* (1932) and *Banana Bottom* (1933), wrote of life in his Jamaican homeland in a manner that debunked the travelogue exoticism usually attributed to Negro life in the Caribbean area. Before the publication of these books, Harlem and its inhabitants had already been the subject matter for a group of remarkable short stories by McKay and the inspiration for his book, *Home to Harlem*, still the most famous novel ever written about that community.

In 1926, Eric Walrond, a native of British Guiana, explored and presented another side of West Indian life in his book, *Tropic Death*, a near classic. In these 10 naturalistic stories, Eric Walrond concerns himself mostly with labor and living conditions in the Panama Canal Zone where a diversity of people and ways of life meet and clash, while each tries to survive at the expense of the other. Clear perception and strength of style enabled Mr. Walrond to balance form and content in such a manner that the message was never intruded upon the unfolding of the stories.

Rudolph Fisher, another bright star of the Harlem literary renaissance, was first a brilliant young doctor. The new and light touch he brought to his stories of Afro-American life did not mar the serious aspect that was always present. The message in his comic realism was more profound because he was skillful enough to weave it into the design of his stories without destroying any of their entertainment value. His stories "Blades of Steel," "The City of Refuge" and "The Promised Land" were published in the Atlantic Monthly. "High Yaller" appeared in The Crisis magazine during the hey-day of that publication, and was later reprinted in the O'Brien anthology, *Best Short Stories of 1934*. Unfortunately, he died before all of his bright promise was fulfilled.

The Harlem literary renaissance was studded with many names. Those already mentioned are only a few of the most outstanding. During the period of this literary flowering among black writers, Harlem became the Mecca, the stimulating Holy City, drawing pilgrims from all over the country and from some places abroad. Talented authors, playwrights, painters and sculptors came forth eagerly showing their wares.

Three men, W. E. B. Du Bois, James Weldon Johnson and Alain Locke, cast a guiding influence over this movement without becoming a part of the social climbing and pseudo-intellectual aspect of it. W. E. B. Du Bois, by continuously challenging the old concepts and misinterpretations of Afro-American life, gave enlightened new directions to a whole generation. As editor of The Crisis, he introduced many new black writers and extended his helpful and disciplining hand when it was needed. Following the death of Booker T. Washington and the decline of the Booker T. Washington school of thought, he became the spiritual father of the new black intelligentsia.

James Weldon Johnson moved from Florida to New York. His diversity of talent established his reputation long before the beginning of the "New Negro literary movement." Later, as a participant in and historian of the movement, he helped to appraise and preserve the best that came out of it. In his books, *Autobiography of an Ex-Colored Man* (1912), *The Book of American Negro Poetry* (1922), *Black Manhattan* (1930), and *Along This Way*, an autobiography (1933), James Weldon Johnson showed clearly that Negro writers have made a distinct contribution to the literature of the United States. His own creative talent made him one of the most able of these contributors.

Alain Locke is the writer who devoted the most time to the interpretation of the "New Negro literary movement" and to Afro-American literature in general. In 1925, he expanded the special Harlem issue of the magazine Survey Graphic (which he edited) into the anthology, *The New Negro*. This book is a milestone and a guide to Afro-American thought, literature and art in the middle twenties. The objective of the volume "to register the transformation of the inner and outer life of the Negro in America that had so significantly taken place in the last few preceding years," was ably achieved. For many years, Mr. Locke's annual appraisal of books by and about Negroes, published in Opportunity magazine, was an eagerly awaited literary event.

Early in the Harlem literary renaissance period, the black ghetto became an attraction for a varied assortment of white celebrities and just plain thrill-seeking white people lost from their moorings. Some were insipid rebels, defying the mores of their upbringing by associating with Negroes on a socially equal level. Some were too rich to work, not educated enough to teach, and not holy enough to preach. Others were searching for the mythological "noble savage"—the "exotic Negro."

These professional exotics were generally college educated Negroes who had become estranged from their families and the environment of their upbringing. They talked at length about the great books within them waiting to be written. Their white sponsors continued to subsidize them while they "developed their latent talent." Of course the "great books" of these camp followers never got written and, eventually, their white sponsors realized that they were never going to write—not even a good letter. Ironically, these sophisticates made a definite contribution to the period of the "New Negro literary renaissance." In socially inclined company, they proved that a black American could behave with as much attention to the details of social protocol as the best bred and richest white person in the country. They could balance a cocktail glass with expertness. Behind their pretense of being writers they were really actors —and rather good ones. They were generally better informed than their white sponsors and could easily participate in a discussion of the writings of Marcel Proust, in one minute, and the music of Ludwig Von Beethoven the next. As social parasites, they conducted themselves with a smoothness approaching an artistic accomplishment. Unknown to them, their conduct had done much to eliminate one of the major prevailing stereotypes of Afro-American life and manners.

Concurrently with the unfolding of this mildly funny comedy, the greatest productive period in Afro-American literature continued. The more serious and talented black writers were actually writing their books and getting them published.

Opportunity magazine, then edited by Charles Johnson, and The Crisis, edited by W. E. B. Du Bois, were the major outlets for the new black writers.

Opportunity short story contests provided a proving ground for a number of competent black writers. Among the prize winners were Cecil Blue, John F. Matheus, Eugene Gordon and Marita Bonner.

Writers like Walter White, Jessie Fauset, Wallace Thurman, Nella Larsen, George S. Schuyler, Sterling A. Brown and Arna Bontemps had already made their debut and were accepted into the circle of the matured.

The stock market collapse of 1929 marked the beginning of the depression and the end of the period known as "The Negro Renaissance." The "exotic Negro," professional and otherwise, became less exotic now that a hungry look was upon his face. The numerous white sponsors and well-wishers who had begun to flock to Harlem ten years before no longer had time or money to explore and marvel over Harlem life. Many Harlem residents lived and died in Harlem during this period without once hearing of the famous literary movement that had flourished and declined within their midst. It was not a mass movement. It was a fad, partly produced in Harlem and partly imposed on Harlem. Most of the writers associated with it would have written just as well at any other time.

In the intervening years between the end of "The Negro Renaissance" and the emergence of Richard Wright, black writers of genuine talent continued to produce books of good caliber. The lack of sponsorship and pampering had made them take serious stock of themselves and their intentions. The Crisis, organ of the National Association for the Advancement of Colored People, and Opportunity, organ of the National Urban League, continued to furnish a publishing outlet for new black writers. The general magazines published stories by black writers intermittently, seemingly on a quota basis.

During this period writers like Ralph Ellison, Henry B. Jones, Marian Minus, Ted Poston, Lawrence D. Reddick and Grace W. Thompkins published their first short stories.

In 1936 Richard Wright's first short story to receive any appreciable attention, "Big Boy Leaves Home," appeared in the anthology, *The New Caravan*. "The Ethics of Living Jim Crow: An Autobiographical Sketch" was published in *American Stuff*, anthology of the Federal Writers Project, the next year. In 1938, when his first book, *Uncle Tom's Children*, won a $500 prize contest conducted by Story Magazine, his talent received national attention. With the publication of his phenomenally successful novel, *Native Son*, in 1940, a new era in Afro-American literature had begun. Here, at last, was a black writer who undeniably wrote considerably better than many of his white contemporaries. As a short story craftsman, he was the most accomplished black writer since Charles W. Chesnutt.

After the emergence of Richard Wright, the period of indulgence for Negro writers was over. Hereafter, black writers had to stand or fall by the same standards and judgments used to evaluate the work of white writers. The era of the patronized and pampered black writer had at last come to an end. The closing of this era may, in the final analysis, be the greatest contribution Richard Wright made to the status of Negro writers and to Negro literature.

When the United States entered the second World War, the active Negro writers, like most other writers in the country, turned their talents to some activity in relation to the war.

The first short stories of Ann Petry began to appear in The Crisis. *The Negro Caravan*, the best anthology of Negro literature since Alain Locke edited *The New Negro* sixteen years before, had already appeared with much new material. Chester B. Himes, a dependable writer during the depression period, managed to turn out a number of remarkable short stories while working in shipyards and war industries in California. In 1944, he received a Rosenwald Fellowship to complete his first novel, *If He Hollers Let Him Go*. In 1945, Frank Yerby won an O. Henry Memorial Award for his excellent short story, "Health Card," which had been published in Harper's Magazine a year before.

A new crop of post-war black writers was emerging. In their stories they treated new aspects of Afro-American life or brought new insights to the old aspects. Principally, they were good story tellers, aside from any message they wanted to get across to their readers. The weepy sociological propaganda stories (so prevalent during the depression era) had had their day with the Negro writer and all others. There would still be protest stories, but the protest would now have to meet the standards of living literature.

Opportunity and The Crisis, once the proving ground for so many new black writers, were no longer performing that much needed service. The best of the new writers found acceptance in the general magazines. Among these are James Baldwin, Lloyd Brown, Arthur P. Davis, Owen Dodson, Lance Jeffers, John O. Killens, Robert H. Lucas, Albert Murray, George E. Norford, Carl R. Offord, John H. Robinson, Jr., John Caswell Smith, Jr. and Mary E. Vroman.

With the rise of nationalism and independent states in Africa, and the rapid change of the status of the Negro in the United States, the material used by black writers and their treatment of it did, of necessity, reflect a breaking away from the old mooring.

Among black writers the period of the 1940's was the period of Richard Wright. The period of the 1960's was the period of James Baldwin.

The now flourishing literary talent of James Baldwin had no easy birth, and he did not emerge overnight, as some of his new discoverers would have you believe. For years this talent was in incubation in the ghetto of Harlem, before he went to Europe a decade ago in an attempt to discover the United States and how he and his people relate to it. The book in which that discovery is portrayed, *The Fire Next Time*, is a continuation of his search for place and definition.

Baldwin, more than any other writer of our times, has succeeded in restoring the personal essay to its place as a form of creative literature. From his narrow vantage point of personal grievance, he has opened a "window on the world." He plays the role traditionally assigned to thinkers concerned with the improvement of human conditions—that of alarmist. He calls national attention to things in the society that need to be corrected and things that need to be celebrated.

When Richard Wright died in Paris in 1960, a new generation of black writers, partly influenced by him, was beginning to explore, as Ralph Ellison said, "the full range of American Negro humanity." In the short stories and novels of such writers as Frank London Brown, William Melvin Kelly, LeRoi Jones, Paule Marshall, Rosa Guy and Ernest J. Gaines, both a new dimension and a new direction in writing is seen. They have questioned and challenged all previous interpretations of Afro-American life. In doing this, they have created the basis for a new American literature.

The black writer and his people are now standing at the crossroads of history. This is the black writer's special vantage point, and this is what makes the task and the mission of the black writer distinctly different from that of the white writer. The black writer, concerned with creating a work of art in a segregated society, has a double task. First: he has to explain the society to himself and create his art while opposing that society. Second: he cannot be honest with himself or his people without lending his support, at least verbally, to the making of a new society that respects the dignity of men.

The black writer must realize that his people are now entering the last phase of a transitional period between slavery and freedom. It is time for the black writer to draw upon the universal values in his people's experience, just as Sean O'Casey and Sholem Aleichem drew upon the universal values in the experiences of the Irish and the Jews. In the next phase of Afro-American writing, a literature of celebration must be created—not a celebration of oppression, but a celebration of survival in spite of it.

QUESTIONS

1. In his survey of the cultural and scholarly life of the fore-fathers of the Africans who eventually became slaves in the United States, Clarke states that "one must realize that the black American is not without a cultural past." What evidence does he give to support his contention that the West African states were highly complex and developed? What caused the collapse of this civilization, and why, according to Clarke, did this collapse influence the interpretation of African and Afro-American life thereafter?

2. What are the differences between the literature of petition and the slave narrative?

3. What important role did Prince Hall play in the fight for freedom and in the abolitionist movement in Massachusetts?

4. In his discussion of the Harlem Literary Renaissance, Clarke says, "It was a fad, partly produced in Harlem and partly imposed on Harlem." What does he mean? What is his final appraisal of its value to the black literary movement?

5. Clarke pays particular attention to the work of W. E. B. Du Bois, James Weldon Johnson, and Alain Locke. What significant contribution did each of these men make to the development of Afro-American writing?

6. Clarke concludes his essay by stating that the "black writer and his people are now standing at the crossroads of history. This is the black writer's special vantage point, and this is what makes the task and mission of the black writer distinctly different from that of the white writer." What does Clarke see to be the "double task" of the black writer, and what does he suggest must be the "next phase of Afro-American writing"?

The Revolutionary Theater

LeRoi Jones

The Revolutionary Theater should force change; it should be change. (All their faces turned into the lights and you work on them black nigger magic, and cleanse them at having seen the ugliness. And if the beautiful see themselves, they will love themselves.) We are preaching virtue again, but by that to mean NOW, toward what seems the most constructive use of the world.

The Revolutionary Theater must EXPOSE! Show up the insides of these humans, look into black skulls. White men will cower before this theater because it hates them. Because they themselves have been trained to hate. The Revolutionary Theater must hate them for hating. For presuming with their technology to deny the supremacy of the Spirit. They will all die because of this.

The Revolutionary Theater must teach them their deaths. It must crack their faces open to the mad cries of the poor. It must teach them about silence and the truths lodged there. It must kill any God anyone names except Common Sense. The Revolutionary Theater should flush the fags and murders out of Lincoln's face.

It should stagger through our universe correcting, insulting, preaching, spitting craziness—but a craziness taught to us in our most rational moments. People must be taught to trust true scientists (knowers, diggers, oddballs) and that the holiness of life is the constant possibility of widening the consciousness. And they must be incited to strike back against *any* agency that attempts to prevent this widening.

The Revolutionary Theater must Accuse and Attack anything that can be accused and attacked. It must Accuse and Attack because it is a theater of Victims. It looks at the sky with the victims' eyes, and moves the victims to look at the strength in their minds and their bodies.

Clay in *Dutchman*, Ray in *The Toilet*, Walker in *The Slave*, are all victims. In the Western sense they could be heroes. But the Revolutionary Theater, even if it is Western, must be anti-Western. It must

FROM *Liberator*, Vol. 5, No. 7 (July 1965). Copyright © 1965 by *Liberator*. Reprinted by permission.

show horrible coming attractions of *The Crumbling of the West*. Even as Artaud designed *The Conquest of Mexico*, so we must design *The Conquest of White Eye*, and show the missionaries and wiggly Liberals dying under blasts of concrete. For sound effects, wild screams of joy, from all the peoples of the world.

The Revolutionary Theater must take dreams and give them a reality. It must isolate the ritual and historical cycles of reality. But it must be food for all those who need food, and daring propaganda for the beauty of the Human Mind. It is a political theater, a weapon to help in the slaughter of these dim-witted fatbellied white guys who somehow believe that the rest of the world is here for them to slobber on.

This should be a theater of World Spirit. Where the spirit can be shown to be the most competent force in the world. Force. Spirit. Feeling. The language will be anybody's, but tightened by the poet's backbone. And even the language must show what the facts are in this consciousness epic, what's happening. We will talk about the world; and the preciseness with which we are able to summon the world will be our art. Art is method. And art, "like any ashtray or senator," remains in the world. Wittgenstein said ethics and aesthetics are one. I believe this. So the Broadway theater is a theater of reaction whose ethics, like its aesthetics, reflect the spiritual values of this unholy society, which sends young crackers all over the world blowing off colored people's heads. (In some of these flippy Southern towns they even shoot up the immigrants' Favorite Son, be it Michael Schwerner or JFKennedy.)

The Revolutionary Theater is shaped by the world, and moves to reshape the world, using as its force the natural force and perpetual vibrations of the mind in the world. We are history and desire, what we are, and what any experience can make us.

It is a social theater, but all theater is social theater. But we will change the drawing rooms into places where real things can be said about a real world, or into smoky rooms where the destruction of Washington can be plotted. The Revolutionary Theater must function like an incendiary pencil planted in Curtis Lemay's cap. So that when the final curtain goes down brains are splattered over the seats and the floor, and bleeding nuns must wire SOS's to Belgians with gold teeth.

Our theater will show victims so that their brothers in the audience will be better able to understand that they are the brothers of victims, and that they themselves are victims if they are blood brothers. And what we show must cause the blood to rush, so that pre-revolutionary temperaments will be bathed in this blood, and it will cause their deepest souls to move, and they will find themselves tensed and clenched, even ready to die, at what the soul has been taught. We will scream and cry, murder, run through the streets in agony, if it means some soul will be moved, moved to actual life understanding of what the world is, and what it ought to be. We are preaching virtue and feeling, and a natural sense of the self in the world. All men live in the world, and the world ought to be a place for them to live.

What is called the imagination (from image, magi, magic, magician, etc.) is a practical vector from the soul. It stores all data, and can be called on to solve all our "problems." The imagination is the projection of ourselves past our sense of ourselves as "things." Imagination (Image) is all possibility, because from the image, the initial circumscribed energy, any use (idea) is possible. And so begins that image's use in the world. Possibility is what moves us.

The popular white man's theater like the popular white man's novel shows tired white lives, and the problems of eating white sugar, or else it herds bigcaboosed blondes onto huge stages in rhinestones and makes believe they are dancing or singing. WHITE BUSINESSMEN OF THE WORLD, DO YOU WANT TO SEE PEOPLE REALLY DANCING AND SINGING??? ALL OF YOU GO UP TO HARLEM AND GET YOURSELF KILLED. THERE WILL BE DANCING AND SINGING, THEN, FOR REAL!! (In *The Slave*, Walker Vessels, the black revolutionary, wears an armband, which is the insignia of the attacking army—a big red-lipped minstrel, grinning like crazy.)

The liberal white man's objection to the theater of the revolution (if he is "hip" enough) will be on aesthetic grounds. Most white Western artists do not need to be "political," since usually, whether they know it or not, they are in complete sympathy with the most repressive social forces in the world today. There are more junior birdmen fascists running around the West today disguised as Artists than there are disguised as fascists. (But then, that word, *Fascist*, and with it, *Fascism*, has been made obsolete by the words *America*, and *Americanism*.) The American Artist usually turns out to be just a super-Bourgeois, because, finally, all he has to show for his sojourn through the world is "better taste" than the Bourgeois—many times not even that.

Americans will hate the Revolutionary Theater because it will be out to destroy them and whatever they believe is real. American cops will try to close the theaters where such nakedness of the human spirit is paraded. American producers will say the revolutionary plays are filth, usually because they will treat human life as if it were actually happening. American directors will say that the white guys in the plays are too abstract and cowardly ("don't get me wrong . . . I mean aesthetically . . .") and they will be right.

The force we want is of twenty million spooks storming America with furious cries and unstoppable weapons. We want actual explosions and actual brutality: AN EPIC IS CRUMBLING and we must give it the space and hugeness of its actual demise. The Revolutionary Theater, which is now peopled with victims, will soon begin to be peopled with new kinds of heroes—not the weak Hamlets debating whether or not they are ready to die for what's on their minds, but men and women (and minds) digging out from under a thousand years of "high art" and weak-faced dalliance. We must make an art that will function so as to call down the actual wrath of world spirit. We are witch doctors and assassins, but we will open a place for the true scientists to expand our consciousness. This is a theater of assault. The play that will split the heavens for us will be called THE DESTRUCTION OF AMERICA. The heroes will be Crazy Horse, Denmark Vesey, Patrice Lumumba, and not history, not memory, not sad sentimental groping for a warmth in our despair; these will be new men, new heroes, and their enemies most of you who are reading this.

QUESTIONS

1. What does Jones mean when he says that the language of the theater of revolution will be "anybody's, but tightened by the poet's backbone"?

2. Jones says that he agrees with the philosopher Wittgenstein that "ethics and aesthetics are one." What does this statement imply in relation to the theater and Jones's attitude toward it?

3. Comment upon Jones's statement that "we are preaching virtue and feeling, and a natural sense of the self in the world. All men live in the world, and the world ought to be a place for them to live." Why does Jones believe this objective makes his theater "revolutionary"?

4. Does Jones expect the liberal white audience to be sympathetic to the theater of revolution? What does he expect their objections to be? Do you think he believes they will support it, be influenced by it, or ignore it?

5. If you were a beginning playwright (black or white), and you were deeply aroused—sympathetically or unsympathetically—by Jones's call for a theater of revolution, what kind of play or plays would you write to support your ideas? (Suggest topics and possible outlines of plot.)

Notes on the Authors

JAMES BALDWIN (1924–) Born in Harlem, Baldwin lived as an expatriate in Europe from 1948 to 1958. His reputation as an essayist was established by his *Notes of a Native Son* (1955) and, subsequently, by *Nobody Knows My Name* (1961) and *The Fire Next Time* (1963). His works of fiction include *Go Tell It on the Mountain* (1953), *Giovanni's Room* (1958), *Another Country* (1962), *Going to Meet the Man* (short stories, 1965), and *Tell Me How Long the Train's Been Gone* (1968). He has also written plays, the best known of which is *Blues for Mister Charlie* (1959).

GERALD WILLIAM BARRAX (1933–) Born in Attalla, Alabama, Barrax grew up in Pittsburgh, served in the Air Force, and received his B.A. from Duquesne University. His poems have appeared in such magazines as *Four Quartets, Spirit,* and *Poetry.*

ARNA BONTEMPS (1902–) Born in Alexandria, Louisiana, Bontemps lived in New York during the nineteen-twenties and has spent most of his professional life as a librarian. For many years he was associated with Fisk University, and he is currently Curator of the James Weldon Johnson Collection at Yale. Among his many books are *God Sends Sunday* (1931), *Black Thunder* (1935), and *Drums at Dusk* (1939). *Personals* (1963) is a collection of his poetry. In collaboration with Langston Hughes he wrote *The Poetry of the Negro* (1949) and *The Book of Negro Folklore* (1959).

GWENDOLYN BROOKS (1917–) Born in Topeka, Kansas, and raised in Chicago, Gwendolyn Brooks has been writing poetry since her childhood. Her volumes of poems include *A Street in Bronzeville* (1945), *Annie Allen* (1949), for which she received the Pulitzer Prize in 1950, *The Bean Eaters* (1960), *Selected Poems* (1963), *In the Mecca* (1968), and *Riot* (1969). Her novel, *Maud Martha,* appeared in 1953.

STERLING A. BROWN (1901–) Born in Washington, D.C., Brown studied at Williams College and at Harvard, and he has taught at

Howard University for a number of years. A volume of his poetry appeared under the title *Southern Road* (1932); his works of criticism include *Negro Poetry and Drama* (1937) and *The Negro in American Fiction* (1938). He was one of the editors of *The Negro Caravan* (1941).

JOHN HENRIK CLARKE (1915–   )   Born in Union Springs, Alabama, and raised in Columbus, Georgia, Clarke moved to New York in 1933. He is a critic, editor, and anthologist, as well as a writer of fiction and poetry. *Rebellion in Rhyme* (1948) is a collection of his poetry. He is currently an associate editor of *Freedomways*.

ELDRIDGE CLEAVER (1936–   )   Born in Wabbaseka, Arkansas, Cleaver is Minister of Information for the National Black Panther party and was the 1968 Presidential candidate of the Peace and Freedom party. He has been jailed on a number of charges, and he wrote his best-selling book, *Soul on Ice* (1968), while in prison. An anthology of his addresses to universities entitled *Eldridge Cleaver: Post-Prison Writings and Speeches* appeared in 1969.

LUCILLE CLIFTON (1936–   )   Born in Depew, New York, Lucille Clifton attended Howard University and Fredonia State Teachers College. Her poetry has appeared in such journals as the *Negro Digest* and *The Massachusetts Review*. Her first volume of poems, *Good Times*, appeared in 1969.

COUNTEE CULLEN (1903–46)   Born in Baltimore, Maryland, and raised in New York, Cullen graduated from New York University in 1925, the year in which his first book of poems, *Color*, was published. The following year he received his M.A. from Harvard. He wrote one novel, *One Way to Heaven* (1932), and edited *Caroling Dusk: An Anthology of Verse by Negro Poets* (1927). Later collections of his own verse include *The Ballad of the Brown Girl* (1928), *The Black Christ and Other Poems* (1929), and *The Medea and Some Poems* (1935). A selection of his best poems appeared a year after his death under the title *On These I Stand*.

MARGARET DANNER   Born in Pryorsburg, Kentucky, Margaret Danner has lived most of her life in the Chicago area. She has won many poetry awards, and in 1960 she became the first poet in residence at Wayne State University, Detroit. She founded Boone House, a poetry and art center for Negro artists; participated in the First World Festival of Negro Arts (Dakar, Senegal, 1966); and has published and recorded her poetry. Her works include *To Flower: Poems* (1963), *Impressions of African Art Forums* (1961), *Poem Counterpoem* (with Dudley Randall, 1966), and *The Iron Lace* (1968).

OWEN DODSON (1914–   )   Born in Brooklyn and educated at Bates College and Yale University, Dodson is Chairman of the Drama Department at Howard University. His works include a book of poems, *Powerful Long Ladder* (1946) and a novel, *Boy at the Window* (1951).

RALPH ELLISON (1914–   )   Born in Oklahoma City, Ellison studied at Tuskegee Institute and held numerous jobs before publishing *Invisible Man* in 1952. This novel, one of the most brilliant to appear in the past two decades, won the National Book Award. A number of his essays were reprinted in *Shadow and Act* (1964).

ROBERT HAYDEN (1913–   )   Born in Detroit, Michigan, Hayden graduated from Wayne State University and received his M.A. from the University of Michigan, where he is presently writer-in-residence. His poems have been collected in *Heart-Shape in the Dust* (1940), *Figure of Time* (1955), *A Ballad of Remembrance* (1962), *Selected Poems* (1966), and *Words in the Mourning Time* (1971). He is the editor of *Kaleidoscope: Poems by American Negro Poets* (1967).

LANGSTON HUGHES (1902–67)   Born in Joplin, Missouri, Hughes attended Columbia and Lincoln universities. He traveled widely and worked for some time as a seaman. Though he wrote in many genres, he is best known for his short stories and poetry. *Laughing to Keep from Crying* (1952) and *The Best of Simple* (1961) are representative collections of his short stories; among his thirteen books of poetry are *The Weary Blues* (1926), *Shakespeare in Harlem* (1942), *Montage of a Dream Deferred* (1951), *Selected Poems* (1965), and *The Panther and the Lash* (1967). He edited (with Arna Bontemps) *The Poetry of the Negro* (1949) and *The Book of Negro Folklore* (1959), and wrote an autobiography, *The Big Sea* (1940). *The Langston Hughes Reader* (1966) is a generous sampling of his work.

JAMES WELDON JOHNSON (1871–1938)   Born in Jacksonville, Florida, Johnson became the first black admitted to the Florida bar since Reconstruction. Thereafter, his career included song-writing in New York, terms as consul in two posts, and teaching at Fisk University. His books include the novel *The Autobiography of an Ex-Colored Man* (1912) and such collections of poems as *Fifty Years and Other Poems* (1917), *God's Trombones* (1927), and *Selected Poems* (1935).

LEROI JONES (1934–   )   Born in Newark, New Jersey, Jones attended Howard University, the New School for Social Research, and Columbia University. Though primarily a poet, he has written plays, among them *Dutchman* (1964) and *The Slave* (1965); essays, collected in *Home* (1966); and articles and books on jazz. He has also published a novel,

The System of Dante's Hell (1966), and a collection of sixteen short stories, *Tales* (1967). His volumes of poems include *Preface to a Twenty-Volume Suicide Note* (1961), *The Dead Lecturer* (1964), and *Black Art* (1966).

ALAIN LOCKE (1886–1954)   Born in Philadelphia, Locke was educated at Oxford, Berlin, and Harvard universities. Aesthetician, literary critic, and social scientist, he was for many years chairman of the Philosophy Department at Howard University. He edited *The New Negro* (1925), a collection of writing that brought the Negro Renaissance to the public's awareness.

MALCOLM X (1925–65)   Born in Omaha, Nebraska, Malcolm X was the seventh child of Reverend Earl Little, an organizer for Marcus Garvey's Universal Negro Improvement Association. He became interested in the Black Muslim movement while in prison. After his release, he joined the movement, founding Muslim temples throughout the country. He visited Mecca, made trips to Africa, and became an important leader in the movement. In 1964 he broke with Elijah Muhammed, prophet and leader of the Muslims in America, forming his own group, the Organization of Afro-American Unity, and his Islamic religious center, the Muslim Mosque. During a meeting in the Audubon Ballroom in Harlem, on February 21, 1965, he was assassinated.

HERBERT WOODWARD MARTIN (1933–   )   Born in Birmingham, Alabama, Martin received his B.A. from the University of Toledo. He has held scholarships and fellowships at Antioch College, the University of Colorado, and Middlebury College's Bread Loaf writer's project. His poems have appeared in various periodicals. Poet-in-residence at Acquinas College from 1969 to 1970, he is currently an Assistant Professor of English at the University of Dayton.

CLAUDE MCKAY (1890–1948)   Born in Jamaica, McKay emigrated to the United States in 1912. His books of poetry include *Songs of Jamaica* (1912), *Harlem Shadows* (1922), and *Selected Poems* (1953). Three of his novels are *Home to Harlem* (1928), *Banjo* (1929), and *Banana Bottom* (1935). *A Long Way from Home* (1937) is his autobiography.

JAMES ALAN MCPHERSON (1943–   )   Born in Savannah, Georgia, McPherson graduated from Harvard Law School in 1968 and has taught English at the University of Iowa. His first collection of short stories, *Hue and Cry,* was published in 1969.

DUDLEY RANDALL (1914–   )   Born in Washington, D.C., Randall has published short stories, book reviews, criticism, poetry, and translations. In 1965 he established the Broadside Press, issuing works by a number of black writers. His press published his *Poem Counterpoem* (with Margaret Danner) in 1966. His most recent collection is *Cities Burning* (1968).

J. SAUNDERS REDDING (1906–) Born in Wilmington, Delaware, Redding attended Lincoln University and Brown University, where he received a Ph.D. He is widely respected as an essayist, literary critic, and writer of fiction. His nonfiction works include *To Make a Poet Black* (1939) and *On Being Negro in America* (1951); his novel, *Stranger and Alone*, appeared in 1950 and his autobiography, *No Day of Triumph*, in 1942.

ISHMAEL REED (1938–) Born in Chattanooga, Tennessee, Reed attended the University of Buffalo. He has published two novels, *The Free-Lance Pallbearers* (1967), and *Yellow Back Radio Broke-Down* (1969). His poetry has been included in numerous anthologies.

LYNN SHORTER (1946–) Born in New York, Lynn Shorter's poems have appeared in the *Journal of Black Poetry*.

MELVIN B. TOLSON (1900–66) Born in Moberly, Missouri, Tolson was educated at Fisk and Lincoln universities and received an M.A. from Columbia University. He was commissioned Poet Laureate of Liberia in 1947 to write the verse drama *Libretto for the Republic of Liberia,* published in 1953. His other books of poems are *Rendezvous with America* (1944) and the highly praised *Harlem Gallery* (1965).

JEAN TOOMER (1894–1967) Born in Washington, D.C., Toomer studied at the University of Wisconsin and the City College of New York. His first book, *Cane* (1923), a collection of short stories, poems, and sketches, established his reputation soon after its publication, but he wrote little after that. *Essentials,* a collection of aphorisms, appeared in 1931.

ALICE WALKER (1944–) Born in Eatonton, Georgia, Alice Walker received her B.A. from Sarah Lawrence College. She worked in voter registration in Georgia and has lived in Uganda and the Soviet Union. She was writer-in-residence and teacher of black studies at Jackson State College from 1968 to 1969. She is presently writer-in-residence at Tougaloo College, Mississippi. Her book of poems *Once* appeared in 1968, and a novel, *The Third Life of Grange Copeland*, appeared in 1970.

MARGARET WALKER (1915–) Born in Birmingham, Alabama, Margaret Walker attended Northwestern University, and received her M.A. from Iowa State University in 1944. Her first book of poems, *For My*

People, appeared in 1942, in connection with her having won the Yale University Younger Poets competition. *Jubilee,* a novel, was published in 1966.

DOUGLAS TURNER WARD (1931–   )   Born in Burnside, Louisiana, Ward grew up in New Orleans. He came to New York City in 1946, where he worked for three years as a journalist. He then became an actor and appeared in such plays as *A Raisin in the Sun* and *One Flew Over the Cuckoo's Nest.* His first produced plays, *Happy Ending* and *Day of Absence,* together received the Vernon Rice Drama Award and the 1966 Obie Award. With Robert Hooks, Ward established the resident Negro Ensemble Company, a group that provides training for actors, directors, and technicians for a Negro-oriented theater.

RICHARD WRIGHT (1908–60)   Born on a plantation near Natchez, Mississippi, Wright spent his youth in Memphis and migrated to Chicago while still a young man. His early writing was done while he was associated with the Communist party of the thirties. His first book, a collection of short stories, was entitled *Uncle Tom's Children* (1938). His best-known work is *Native Son* (1940), an important novel of the Chicago ghetto. Wright spent his last fifteen years as an expatriate living in Paris. His other works include *Bright and Morning Star* (1941), *The Outsider* (1953), and *Eight Men* (1961). His autobiographical memoir, *Black Boy,* appeared in 1945.

Topics for Writing and Research

I. Medium Length Papers

FICTION

1. Compare two of the short stories that present conflicting racial ideas. How are these ideas dramatized? How are they resolved?
2. Discuss the use and effect of irony in two of the short stories.
3. If you are familiar with Dostoyevsky's *Notes from Underground* and Ralph Ellison's *Invisible Man,* compare and contrast their use of the underground motif with that of Richard Wright's "The Man Who Lived Underground."
4. Analyze James Baldwin's use of point-of-view in his story, "Sonny's Blues." Whose story is it, the narrator's or Sonny's? How does an awareness of point-of-view enhance an appreciation of Baldwin's achievement in this story?
5. Compare two stories in which the notion of "flight," either physical or psychological (or both), appears. How central to the story is it? Does the character in flight grow to a new understanding of himself and his life? How? What is the response of those around him to his situation?
6. Discuss one of the stories in which the sense of place—the location, setting, and atmosphere—is central to the plot and thematic concerns of the author. How does the author make this sense of place vivid? What details does he present? How are minor characters used to enhance this vividness?

POETRY

1. Compare the poetry of two of the earlier poets with the poetry of two of the young, contemporary poets in terms of themes and techniques.
2. Discuss the treatment of the African heritage of the black

man as it appears in a number of selected poems in this anthology.

3. Describe and discuss the poetry of protest.

4. Discuss the treatment of "black identity" in selected poems.

DRAMA

1. Discuss the use and effect of satire in Douglas Turner Ward's *Day of Absence*.

2. Compare Ward's treatment of the theme of black-white relations with that of another contemporary black dramatist.

AUTOBIOGRAPHY

1. Compare the sense of personal metamorphosis or change in two of the selections. What stimulated or brought about change in the writer?

2. Discuss the sociological or psychological observations and insights of Malcolm X and Eldridge Cleaver as revealed in the selections from their autobiographies.

3. Describe James Baldwin's achievement of a sense of maturity, a coming of age. How does his sense of himself relate to his past, his family relationships?

4. Contrast Malcolm X's legacy as hero and spokesman with that of Martin Luther King, Jr.

5. Which of these selections most vividly presents the experience of being black in a white, racist society? Discuss the presentation of this experience by the author you have selected.

CRITICAL ESSAYS

1. Discuss the contribution to the New Negro movement of selected figures. Be sure to provide examples and documentation from both the literature and criticism.

2. Discuss the attitudes of the critics toward the white and black middle class. How are these attitudes reflected in the literature you have read?

3. Explore the African and American heritage of the black man in the United States as presented in selected critical and literary materials.

4. Using both criticism and literature, discuss the importance of one of the following to black writing: folk materials, music, biblical materials, slavery.

5. Compare the treatment in the critical discussions of the problem of "identity," giving special consideration to the way

in which this problem affects the relationship of the writer to his materials and to his audience.

6. Study the treatment in these critical selections of Afro-American protest writing and discuss its evolution and aims. Use the literature as examples of theme and substance.

II. Longer Papers

1. Read fully one of the autobiographies presented partially in this anthology and write an evaluation of a major theme or topic developed in it.

2. Study the arguments of a leading spokesman of the "Separatist School" and the arguments of a spokesman of the "Integrationist School" and evaluate the strengths and weaknesses of each.

3. Read a representative collection of contemporary black dramas and discuss the plays in terms of the drama of the absurd, the revolutionary drama, and the protest drama. You should focus upon two or three writers and compare their work in relationship to these theories. Or you may, instead, examine several representative plays, explaining which type you prefer and why.

4. Study the poetry or the short stories of your favorite black writer and discuss in detail his techniques, imagery, themes, and place in the history of black writing.

5. Examine and discuss the founding, history, and contribution of one of the important black journals that has been instrumental in the development of black writing in America. You should make liberal references to critics and writers associated with that journal.

6. Prepare a scholarly paper that studies in some depth the history of the use of folk materials in black writing, making sure that you cite the works of significant writers as representative figures.

7. Gather the reviews written by white critics and black critics of some selected group of black drama and compare their comments and attitudes.

8. Prepare a course prospectus, complete with bibliography and criticism, of one significant black writer (any genre) for an honors program devoted to the study of a single writer.

Bibliography

JOURNALS

Amistad. New York: Random House. Biannual.

CLA Journal. Baltimore: College Language Association, Morgan State College. Quarterly.

The Crisis. New York: Crisis Publishing, official organ of the NAACP. Monthly.

Freedomways. New York: Freedomways Associates. Quarterly.

Journal of Black Poetry. San Francisco: 1308 Mesonic Avenue No. 4. Quarterly.

Journal of Negro Education. Washington, D.C.: Bureau of Educational Research, Howard University. Quarterly.

Journal of Negro History. Kentucky: Southern Historical Association, University of Kentucky. Quarterly.

Liberator. New York: Afro-American Research Institute. Monthly.

Negro Digest. Chicago: Johnson Publishing. Monthly.

Phylon. Atlanta: Atlanta University. Quarterly.

Rights and Reviews. New York: Harlem CORE. Bimonthly.

BIBLIOGRAPHICAL SOURCES

Bibliographical Survey: The Negro in Print, 3 vols. Washington, D.C.: The Negro Bibliographic and Research Center, 1965–68.

Miller, Elizabeth W. *The Negro in America: A Bibliography.* Cambridge, Mass.: Harvard University Press, 1966.

The Negro in the United States: A List of Significant Books, 9th rev. ed. New York: New York Public Library, 1965.

Porter, Dorothy B. *North American Negro Poets: A Bibliographic Check List of Their Writings (1760–1944).* Hattiesburg, Miss.: The Book Farm, 1945. Reprinted, New York: Burt Franklin, 1963.

Welsch, Erwin K. *The Negro in the United States: A Research Guide.* Bloomington: Indiana University Press, 1965.

LITERARY HISTORY AND CRITICISM

The American Negro Writer and His Roots. Selected Papers from the
First Conference of Negro Writers, March 1959. New York:
American Society of African Culture, 1959.

Bone, Robert A. *The Negro Novel in America,* rev. ed. New Haven:
Yale University Press, 1965.

Brown, Sterling A. *The Negro in American Fiction.* Washington, D.C.:
Associates in Negro Folk Education, 1937.

———. *Negro Poetry and Drama.* Washington, D.C.: Associates in
Negro Folk Education, 1937.

Butcher, Margaret Just. *The Negro in American Culture.* New York:
Alfred A. Knopf, 1956.

Ford, Nick Aaron. *The Contemporary Negro Novel.* Boston: Meador,
1936.

Gayle, Addison, Jr. *Black Expression: Essays by and about Black Americans in the Creative Arts.* New York: Weybright and Talley,
1969.

Gloster, Hugh Morris. *Negro Voices in American Fiction.* Chapel Hill:
University of North Carolina Press, 1948.

Hill, Herbert, ed. *Anger, and Beyond: The Negro Writer in the United
States.* New York: Harper & Row, 1966.

Loggins, Vernon. *The Negro Author: His Development in America to
1900.* New York: Kennikat Press, 1931.

Margolies, Edward. *Native Sons: A Critical Study of Twentieth-Century
Negro-American Authors.* Philadelphia: J. B. Lippincott, 1969.

Redding, J. Saunders. *To Make a Poet Black.* Chapel Hill: University
of North Carolina Press, 1939.

FOLKLORE

Addison Gayle's *Black Expression* and Elizabeth W. Miller's *The Negro
in America* may be consulted for an extensive bibliography of
folk materials.

A	1
B	2
C	3
D	4
E	5
F	6
G	7
H	8
I	9
J	0